The New Leader's 100-Day Action Plan

How to Take Charge, Build Your Team, and Get Immediate Results

THIRD EDITION

GEORGE B. BRADT

JAYME A. CHECK

JORGE E. PEDRAZA

WILEY

John Wiley & Sons, Inc.

Published by John Wiley & Sons, Inc., Hoboken, New Jersey.
Published simultaneously in Canada.

For general information on our other products and services or for technical support, please contact our Customer Care Department within the United States at (800) 762-2974, outside the United States at (317) 572-3993 or fax (317) 572-4002.

Wiley also publishes its books in a variety of electronic formats. Some content that appears in print may not be available in electronic books. For more information about Wiley products, visit our web site at www.wiley.com.

Library of Congress Cataloging-in-Publication Data:

Bradt, George B.
  The new leader's 100-day action plan : how to take charge, build your team, and get immediate results / George B. Bradt, Jayme A. Check, Jorge E. Pedraza.—3rd ed.
    p. cm.
  Includes bibliographical references and index.
  ISBN 978-1-118-09754-0 (cloth); ISBN 978-1-118-12147-4 (ebk);
  ISBN 978-1-118-12148-1 (ebk); ISBN 978-1-118-12149-8 (ebk)
  1. Leadership—Handbooks, manuals, etc. I. Check, Jayme A. II. Pedraza, Jorge E. III. Title.
  HD57.7.B723 2011
  658.4'092—dc22

                              2011014935

Printed in the United States of America

10 9

CONTENTS

PART III
TAKE CONTROL OF YOUR OWN START

PART IV
IMPLEMENT YOUR 100-DAY ACTION PLAN

APPENDICES

The *New Leader's 100-Day Action Plan*, first published in 2006, presents PrimeGenesis's proven solutions, techniques, and suggested action items for each stage of a leader's first 100 days in a new position. Filled with examples, case studies, and tools, the book shows leaders and their sponsors exactly how to build high-performing teams with lasting power that can deliver better results faster. As the concepts of onboarding and transition acceleration continue to take hold and mature, interest in our approach has remained strong with the first two editions of this book having sold more than 50,000 copies worldwide.

Despite the increased awareness and energy around the importance for new leaders to have a comprehensive onboarding plan, leadership turnover continues to be a big problem for organizations and for the leaders themselves. Forty percent of new leaders fail in their first 18 months.[1]

In the context of these general market numbers, over the past eight years PrimeGenesis has been able to lower the failure rate for leaders it has helped around the world from 40 percent down to below 10 percent—a four-fold reduction in risk! The companies that have hired PrimeGenesis to deploy the methodologies discussed in the book have experienced higher rates of retention of senior leaders and higher rates of success on the part of those leaders' meeting goals. The impact on budget, morale, and other employee retention has been significant. Since we finished the first edition of our book in 2005 we've gathered six more years of learning, stories, and methodology enhancements.

---

[1] The 40 percent failure rate came from a 1998 study by Manchester, Inc., confirmed by a Heidrick & Struggles study in 2009.

Thus, it's appropriate to revise *The New Leader's 100-Day Action Plan* again to make it even more valuable to you by:

- *Taking a BRAVE new approach to culture and context.* We have added a new comprehensive approach on how to engage hearts and minds in the intended culture. Now included is explicit guidance on how to assess and manage the business and internal political context and how to use a BRAVE approach to assessing culture, which looks at Behaviors, Relationships, Attitudes, Values, and Environment.

- *Applying social media to onboarding.* To address the changes that social media has brought to communication and leadership, we have shifted the emphasis of the communication chapter to downplay sequential, programmatic communication campaigns and present a current, dynamic, iterative, and interactive approach to conversations across a network of multiple stakeholders, and across a wide variety of media.

- *Incorporating more robust crisis management techniques.* We have added a new appendix on a 100-Hour Action Plan for crisis situations. This iterative approach to crisis management has already been adopted and deployed by the American Red Cross and has enabled it to improve its disaster response time frame significantly by starting to do things on the second day after a disaster that it previously was not doing until the sixth day.

- *Providing advice for the new leader's boss.* For a whole new perspective on onboarding, we have added an appendix on onboarding a new leader, with advice for the new leader's boss drawn from George Bradt and Mary Vonnegut's *Onboarding* book (2009).[2]

- *Including sample 100-Day Action Plans.* In response to clients and readers' requests, we have added an appendix with sample 100-Day Action Plans to show what completed plans might look like.

- *Adding more downloadable forms.* We have added new downloadable forms and updated the existing ones to reflect our updated approach—all available at www.onboardingtools.com.

- *Adding and updating stories, examples, hot tips, and questions.* These illustrate key points and underscore new concepts.

---

[2]Bradt, George, and Vonnegut, Mary, 2009. *Onboarding: How to Get Your New Employees Up to Speed in Half the Time.* Hoboken, NJ: John Wiley & Sons, Inc.

Key Benefits

This book provides several benefits in that it:

1. Reduces the risk of failure (and increases longevity) for new leaders.
2. Provides tools for leaders moving into complex, cross-cultural roles.
3. Provides leaders with an easily deployed yet comprehensive plan for executing on a strategy.
4. Provides several proven tools, techniques, and tricks of the trade that enable leaders to monitor, measure, and keep their success on track.
5. Provides detailed plans for leaders to address essential strategic, operational, organizational, and cross-cultural concerns in their first 100 days.
6. Positions new leaders and their teams to deliver better results faster.
7. Provides a practical look at the top landmines that derail leaders in their first 18 months and supplies remedies to avoid those landmines.
8. Provides a detailed approach to communication that enables leaders to craft and deploy key messages across a network of audiences by using a comprehensive set of media.
9. Provides an onboarding framework (and team management framework) that can be consistently deployed within an organization.
10. Reduces organizations' risk and increases retention rates in hiring or promoting new leaders.

We're excited about this edition and hope you are, too.

ACKNOWLEDGMENTS

We did not *write* this book as much as *discover* it. To a large degree, it is the product of all the transitions that have influenced all the people who have ever influenced us. Throughout our careers, we have learned by doing, by watching, and by interacting with a whole range of bosses, coaches, peers, subordinates, partners, and clients. We end every PrimeGenesis interaction with two questions: What was particularly valuable? How can we make it even more valuable? It is amazing what you can learn by asking.

What you have in your hands was born of continuing to ask those questions.

We would need a separate book to credit the people who have had the most positive influence on us over the years. But we must acknowledge the contributions of our past and current partners in PrimeGenesis. Their fingerprints are all over this book as we all work these ideas every day.

We are indebted to the clients of PrimeGenesis on several levels. We are the first to admit that we have learned as much from them as they have from us. We give our clients complete confidentiality so we have masked individuals and companies' names in the stories involving any of our clients. We are blessed to have the opportunity to work with an extremely diverse group of clients. They run the gamut from the multinational to the small, public company to private, for-profit to not-for-profit. The executives we work with come from many industries, from almost every discipline imaginable, and from many parts of the world. With every client, we have learned something new. Clients inspire, challenge, and teach us on a daily basis, and for that we are grateful. You can learn more about our list of clients on our website at www.PrimeGenesis.com.

We also thank the readers around the world whose enthusiastic embrace of the ideas in this book has kept us motivated to keep it current. We have the good fortune of having truly engaged readers who download tools and then interact with us on a daily basis from around the globe. We thank you for buying the book, passing it on, and reaching out to us to share your ideas, praise, successes, and truly insightful questions.

Finally, abounding gratitude to our editor, Richard Narramore, our agent, Jim Levine, and our friend and sometimes skipper, Philip Ruppel, who introduced us to both of them. Without these three people, this book simply would not exist and you would not have the opportunity to benefit from the perspective and ideas it contains. So you should thank them, too. You will before you're finished.

An Executive Summary
of the Onboarding Process

Are you a veteran CEO taking the reins of your next organization? Or starting a new role as a frontline supervisor? Or are you starting to plan ahead for such a transition? Whether you are joining a new organization from the outside, getting promoted from within, hitting a restart button with your existing team, or mapping out future possibilities, *The New Leader's 100-Day Action Plan* will help you manage your leadership transition so you can take charge, build your team, and deliver better results faster than anyone thought possible.

> *We've found that 40 percent of executives hired at the senior level are pushed out, fail or quit within 18 months. It's expensive in terms of lost revenue. It's expensive in terms of the individual's hiring. It's damaging to morale.*
>
> —Kevin Kelly, CEO of executive search firm
> Heidrick & Struggles, discussing the firm's internal
> study of 20,000 searches.[1]

What do these failed leaders not know or see? What do they not do? Why can't they deliver? In most cases, they dig their own holes by missing one or more of the crucial tasks that must be accomplished in their first 100 days. Some don't understand the impact of their early words and actions and inadvertently send their new colleagues the wrong messages. Some focus on finding a new strategy, but fail to get buy-in and fail to build trust with their new team. Some do a lot

---

[1] As quoted by Brooke Masters in "Rise of a Headhunter," *Financial Times* (March 30, 2009).

of work and expend a lot of energy without accomplishing the one or two things that their most important stakeholders are looking for. All are unaware of some of the important steps required to achieve a successful transition. No leader wants this to happen; but it does, at an alarming rate. This won't happen to you. Not after reading this book! Let's start at the beginning.

Our fundamental, underlying concept is:

> Leadership is about inspiring and enabling others to do their absolute best together to realize a meaningful and rewarding shared purpose.

It's not about you. It's about them—those following your lead. How you set the direction and priorities and what you do to inspire and enable them is important. But what is even more important is what they hear, see, believe, feel, and accomplish together as a team. Leadership is about your ability to create an environment where your team can deliver remarkable results and love doing it. Effective leadership occurs when a team's Behaviors, Relationships, Attitudes, Values, and Environment (per the BRAVE framework) are synchronized to achieve the best results possible.

The Chinese philosopher Lao-tzu expressed this particularly well more than 2,500 years ago:

> *The great leader speaks little. He never speaks carelessly. He works without self-interest and leaves no trace. When all is finished, the people say, "We did it ourselves."*[2]

With that in mind, we have designed this book as an action plan, with a timeline and the key milestones you need to reach along the way to accelerate your own and your team's success in your first or next 100 days. These factors are distilled from insights gleaned from our own leadership experiences and from the work of our firm, PrimeGenesis, whose sole mission is to help executives moving into complex new leadership roles, as well as their teams, deliver better results faster.[3] You will read our own and our clients' stories throughout this book (masked to preserve confidentiality). We hope you will find this to be a practical handbook that helps you know what you

---

[2]Paraphrasing the seventeenth verse of the *Tao Te Ching* by Lao-tzu.
[3]The authors are some of the founders of the executive onboarding and transition acceleration firm PrimeGenesis.

need to know, see what you need to see, and do what you need to do for you and your team to deliver better results faster.

Over the years, we have noticed that many new leaders show up for a new role happy and smiling, but without a plan. Neither they, nor their organizations have thought things through in advance. On their first day, they are welcomed by such confidence-building remarks as: "Oh, you're here . . . we'd better find you an office."

Ouch!

Some enlightened organizations have a better process in place. If you are lucky, you will be associated with an organization that actually puts people in charge of preparing for a leader's transition into a new role. Imagine the difference when a new leader is escorted to an office that is fully set up for her, complete with computer, passwords, phones, files, information, and a 30-day schedule of orientation and assimilation meetings.

Better . . . but still not good enough. Even if the company has done this for you, if you have waited until this moment to start, you are already behind, and you have stacked the odds against yourself. Paradoxically, the best way to accelerate a transition into a new leadership role is to pause long enough to think through and put a plan in place—and then get a head start on implementing it.

We started PrimeGenesis in 2002 having noticed the difference between leaders who have a plan, hit the ground running, and make an impact on their first day, and leaders who wait until Day One to start planning. Since then, we have created and deployed a set of tools and techniques that help executives quickly and effectively transition into new leadership roles. Our work with executives has helped them and their teams deliver better results faster and reduce their failure rate from 40 percent to less than 10 percent at organizations that include American Express, Cadbury, Johnson & Johnson, Kraft, Kimberly-Clark, LexisNexis, MillerCoors, MTV Networks, Novo-Nordisk, Pearson, Playtex, the Royal Bank of Scotland, and UBS, as well as numerous not-for-profit organizations.

The core principles and techniques we deploy to make our impact on senior leaders are the ones described in this book. *The New Leader's 100-Day Action Plan* is the plan we help executives develop and deliver. The tools work for leaders transitioning into new roles at any level. Keep in mind that in today's world, the next 100 days are not going to be anything like the last 100 days. Thus, we are all new leaders all the time and must treat the next 100 days as though they were the first 100 days of the rest of our careers. They are.

The three main ideas are:

1. *Get a head start.* Day One is a critical pivot point for people joining from outside the company. The same is true for the formal announcement of someone getting promoted or transferred from within. In both situations, you can accelerate progress by getting a head start and hitting the ground running. Preparation breeds confidence and a little early momentum goes a long way.

2. *Manage the message.* Everything communicates. People read things into everything you say and do, and everything you don't say and don't do. You're far better off choosing and guiding what others see and hear, and when they see and hear it, rather than letting happenstance or others make those choices for you.

3. *Build the team.* The first 100 days is the best time to put in place the basic building blocks of a high-performing team. You will fail if you try to do everything yourself, without the support and buy-in of your team. As a team leader, your own success is inextricably linked to the success of the team as a whole.

These three core ideas are built on the frameworks of highly effective teams and organizations that we have developed and to which we'll refer throughout the book (see Figure I.1). It's helpful to explain them up front. First, the headlines:

- High-performing teams and organizations are built of *people, plans,* and *practices* aligned around a *shared purpose.*

FIGURE I.I   Core Frameworks

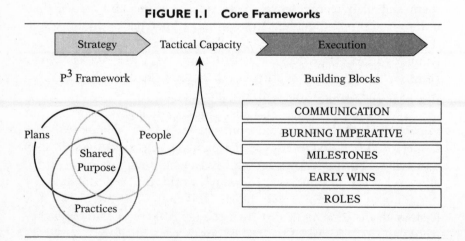

- *Tactical capacity* bridges the gap between strategy and execution, ensuring that a good strategy doesn't fail because of bad execution.
- Five building blocks underpin a team's tactical capacity: *communication, Burning Imperative, milestones, early wins,* and *roles.*

People-Plans-Practices—P³

An organization or team's performance is based on aligning its people, plans, and practices around a shared purpose. This involves getting ADEPT[4] *people* in the right roles with the right support, getting clarity around the strategies and action steps included in *plans*, and getting *practices* in place that enable people to work together in a systematic and effective way. The heart of this is the organization's *purpose*. For that to be genuinely shared, it must be meaningful, clearly understood, and rewarding for each of the people contributing to make its aspiration real.

Tactical Capacity

Tactical capacity is a team's ability to work under difficult, changing conditions and to translate strategies into tactical actions decisively, rapidly, and effectively. It is the essential bridge between strategy and execution. In contrast to other work groups that move slowly, with lots of direction and most decision making coming from the leader, high-performing teams with strong tactical capacity empower each member, communicating effectively with the team and the leader (you), to come up with critical solutions to the inevitable problems that arise on an ongoing basis and to implement them quickly. The goal is high-quality responsiveness and it takes a truly cohesive BRAVE teamwork to make it happen. High-performing teams build on strategy and plans with ADEPT people and practices to implement ever-evolving and acutely responsive actions that work.

> *It is not the strongest of the species that survives, nor the most intelligent, but the one most responsive to change.*
> —Attributed to Charles Darwin

---

[4]Acquire, Develop, Encourage, Plan, Transition.

You have seen this yourself. You have been on teams with members who operate in disconnected silos, incapable of acting without specific direction from above. They may know the strategy. They may have the resources they need, but any variation or change paralyzes them. FEMA actually had run the drill on a major hurricane in New Orleans months before Katrina hit. But the plan collapsed with the first puff of wind because no one could react flexibly and insightfully to a situation that was different from what they had expected.

In contrast, a great example of tactical capacity at work was the way NASA team members came together during the Apollo 13 crisis. Right from "Houston, we've had a problem," the team reacted flexibly and fluidly to a dramatic and unwelcome new reality—a crippling explosion en route, in space. The team went beyond its standard operating procedures and what its equipment was "designed to do" to exploring what it "could do." Through tight, on-the-fly collaboration, the team did in minutes what normally took hours, in hours what normally took days, and in days what normally took months. This teamwork was critical to getting the crew home safely.

If you're lucky, you've been on teams where actions and results flow with great ease, where team members know what is really required and intended and support each other in making those things happen. Those teams have tactical capacity.

As the new leader, it's your job to orchestrate the alignment of people, plans, and practices around a shared purpose. You must convince key people to embrace a Burning Imperative and deliver against it with a great sense of urgency. A Burning Imperative is the antidote to silos and departments that don't cooperate. Tactical capacity is not only about the team responding quickly to changes in external circumstances, it also is about team members working well with each other in support of the team's Burning Imperative.

Building Blocks of Tactical Capacity

The good news is that, as a leader in a new role, you can build tactical capacity into your team quickly by implementing five building blocks:

1. Drive action with ongoing *communication*.
2. Embed a strong *Burning Imperative*.
3. Exploit key *milestones* to drive team performance.

4. Overinvest in *early wins* to build team confidence.
5. Secure ADEPT people in the right *roles*.

The NASA team dealing with Apollo 13 got each of these five building blocks in place, allowing it to react with tactical capacity of the highest order:

1. The culture had been strong. But everyone's *communication* reinforced the message that "failure is not an option" throughout the rescue mission.
2. The team's mission changed from "going to the moon to collect rocks" to the one *Burning Imperative* of "getting these men home alive." This was galvanizing enough (as a Burning Imperative must always be) to transcend all petty issues and focus everyone's efforts.
3. The team's *milestones* were clear: turn the ship around, preserve enough energy to allow a reentry, fix the carbon monoxide problem, survive the earth's atmosphere, and so on.
4. The carbon monoxide fix allowed the astronauts to stay alive and was the *early win* that made the team believe it could do the rest of the things that would get the crew back to earth safely. It gave everyone confidence.
5. Everyone was working with the same end in mind, but they were working in different and essential *roles*. One group figured out how to turn the spaceship around. Another group fixed the oxygen problem. Another dealt with the reentry calculations and the spare crew did whatever it took to complete the mission.

Even though you're unlikely to jump into a situation exactly like the Apollo 13 breakdown, in today's environment almost all leadership transitions are "hot landings," where you must hit the ground running to have a chance of success. Often you will need to fix something, maybe a few things, fast. Sometimes you will have more time to plan. In most onboarding situations, you will have at least a few days to create an onboarding plan—especially if you give yourself a head start. Time is like air (without carbon monoxide!) to breathe and a head start gives you time. Your first plan gets you moving in the right direction; it will evolve as you learn more and things change—which they will.

The 100-Day Action Plan

Here are the steps in our onboarding process. They are the chapters in this book. As Dr. Seuss advised, "be dexterous and deft, and never mistake your right foot for your left!"[5]

> *Part I*   **BECOME** the Best Candidate for the Job
>
> *Part II*   **DISCOVER** Your New Role: It's Always More Than You Think It Is
>
> *Part III*   **TAKE CONTROL** of Your Own Start
>
> *Part IV*   **IMPLEMENT** Your 100-Day Action Plan

Part I Become the Best Candidate for the Job

Chapter 1: Position *Yourself for a New Role*

Positioning yourself for a leadership role is about connecting values with goals, and crossing strengths and communication. You must supplement your talent with learning and practice to build your knowledge and sharpen your skills over the short, mid, and long term. Then, when you're ready, you need to communicate those strengths to secure the promotion or new leadership role you deserve.

FIGURE I.2   The 100-Day Action Plan

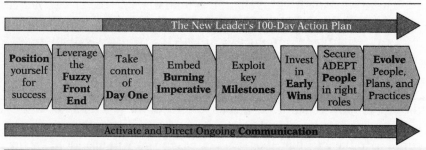

---

[5]"Congratulations! Today is your day, you're off to great places, you're off and away. You have brains in your head, you have feet in your shoes, you can steer yourself in any direction you choose. You're on your own and you know what you know, and you are the guy who'll decide where to go. So be sure where you step, step with care and great tact, and remember that life's a great balancing act. Just never forget to be dexterous and deft, and never mix up your right foot with your left!" (Dr. Seuss, *Oh, the Places You'll Go,* New York: Random House, 1990).

Leadership is personal. Your message is the key that unlocks personal connections. The greater the congruence between your own BRAVE Behaviors, Relationships, Attitudes, Values, and the Environment you create, the stronger those connections will be. This is why the best messages aren't crafted—they emerge. This is why great leaders live their messages not because they can, but because they must. "Here I stand, I can do no other."[6]

Chapter 2: Sell *before You Buy: Answer the Only Three Interview Questions*

You cannot turn down a job you have not been offered. So first put your energy into getting the job offer. Remember that there are only three fundamental interview questions and be prepared to talk about your (1) *strengths*, (2) *motivation*, and (3) *fit* with the organization and the position. Remember also that interviews are not about you. They are about what you can do for those doing the interviewing. Selling is about positioning your strengths, motivation, and fit characteristics in terms of their needs.

Part II Discover Your New Role: It's Always More Than You Think It Is

Chapter 3: Map *and* Avoid *the Most Common Land Mines*

In general, you'll want to mitigate *organization*, *role*, and *personal* land mines before accepting a job, and jump-start *relationships* and *learning* even before Day One so you can concentrate on successful *delivery* and *adjustment* after you start. We've seen way too many people join organizations and discover that what they are really expected to do does not match what they thought they were signing up to do. There are ways to avoid finding yourself in that situation.

Chapter 4: Do Your Due Diligence *before You Accept the Job Offer*

The ability and willingness to assess and deal with risk is often a critical differentiator between success and failure. Once you've been offered the job—and only after you've been offered the job—do in-depth due diligence to make sure it is right for you. This involves

---

[6]Attributed to Martin Luther at the Diet of Worms, 1521, when asked to recant his earlier writings.

mitigating organization, role, and personal risks by answering three questions:

1. What is the organization's sustainable competitive advantage?
2. Did anyone have concerns about this role; and, if so, what was done to mitigate them?
3. What, specifically, about me, led to your offering me the job?

With those answers in hand, you can then decide if you've got a *low level of risk* that requires no extraordinary actions, *manageable risk* that you'll manage as you go, *mission-crippling risk* that you must resolve before going forward, or *insurmountable barriers* requiring you to walk away.

Part III   Take Control of Your Own Start

Chapter 5: Choose the Right Approach for the Business Context and the Culture You Face

Be careful about how you engage with the organization's existing business context and culture. The business context is a function of the business environment, organizational history, and recent business performance. Together, these factors indicate the relative importance and urgency of the change required.

An organization's culture underpins "the way we do things here" and is made up of Behaviors, Relationships, Attitudes, Values, and Environment, which all feed into the culture's readiness for change.

Crossing context and culture can help you decide whether to Assimilate, Converge, and Evolve (fast or slow), or Shock. Then map contributors, detractors, and convincible watchers so you can move each of them one step by altering their balance of consequences.

Chapter 6: Embrace and Leverage the Fuzzy Front End before Day One

The time between acceptance and start is a gift you can use to rest and relax or to get a head start on your new role or next 100 days. Our experience has shown that those who use this Fuzzy Front End to put a plan in place, complete their prestart preparation, and jump-start learning and relationships are far more likely to deliver better results faster than those who choose to rest and relax. Five important steps:

1. Identify the most important stakeholders up, across, and down—both inside and out.
2. Plan your message, Fuzzy Front End, and first or next 100 days.
3. Manage your personal setup so you have less to worry about after you start.
4. Conduct prestart meetings and phone calls to jump-start important relationships.
5. Gather information and learning in advance to jump-start learning.

MasterCard's Ajay Banga did this well. He leveraged the time after he had been announced as CEO but before he started by casually, but pointedly, interacting with key stakeholders with a simple introduction: "Hi, I'm Ajay. Tell me about yourself."[7]

Chapter 7: Take Control of Day One: Make a Powerful First Impression

Everything is magnified on Day One, whether it's your first day in a new company, or the day of a big announcement. Everyone is looking for hints about what you think and what you're going to do. This is why it's so important to seed your message by paying particular attention to all the signs, symbols, and stories you deploy, and the order in which you deploy them. Make sure that people are seeing and hearing things that will lead them to believe and feel what you want them to believe and feel about you and about themselves in relation to the future of the organization.

The Sierra Club's Executive Director Michael Brune did a particularly good job of managing his Day One. He thought through his message in advance and then communicated it live, face-to-face, and via social media on his first day so that everyone would know what was on his mind. He smartly utilized several communication methods to reach a wide range of people in their own preferred way of communication.[8]

---

[7]Bradt, George, "The New Leader's Playbook," *Forbes* (February 23, 2011).
[8]Bradt, George, "The New Leader's Playbook," *Forbes* (March 2, 2011).

Chapter 8: Motivate and Focus Your Team with Ongoing Communications (Including Social Media)

Where the emphasis used to be on logical, sequential, targeted, ongoing communication campaigns, the communication revolution has made it essential to manage multiple, concurrent, ever-evolving conversations across an ever-changing network of stakeholders. Leverage your core message as the foundation for those conversations by seeding and reinforcing communication points through a wide variety of media with no compromises on trustworthiness and authenticity.

The American Red Cross's head of disaster services, Charley Shimanski, does this as well as any executive. His message flows from every pore of his being. Before his first major conference with 140 disaster relief directors from around the country, Charley asked himself: "What do I want them to feel when they're done hearing from me?" He knew the answers: "I wanted them to feel that they are at the core of what we do, that our success is on their shoulders. I wanted them to feel proud."[9]

Part IV Implement Your 100-Day Action Plan

Chapter 9: Embed a Burning Imperative by Day 30

The Burning Imperative is a sharply defined, intensely shared, and purposefully urgent understanding from each of the team members of what they are "supposed to do, *now*," and how this works with the larger aspirations of the team and the organization. While mission, vision, and values are often components of the Burning Imperative, the critical piece is the rallying cry that everyone understands and can act on. Get this created and bought into early on—even if it's only 90 percent right. You, and the team, will adjust and improve along the way. Don't let anything distract you from getting this in place and shared—*in your first 30 days!*

Sam Martin has a lot of experience in this area. As he describes his early days as CEO of supermarket chain A&P:

> *It was essential to have an articulated plan available to share robustly around the organization and with all our stakeholders. . . . If our employees are not properly armed with the right information, they will give the wrong message . . . they're going to give a message anyway. So getting the right message in the right hands quickly is important and essential to getting off on the right foot and having any chance of success in the outcome.*[10]

---

[9]Bradt, George, "The New Leader's Playbook," *Forbes* (March 9, 2011).
[10]Bradt, George, "The New Leader's Playbook," *Forbes* (March 16, 2011).

Chapter 10: Exploit Key Milestones to Drive Team Performance by Day 45

The real test of a high-performing team's tactical capacity lies in the formal and informal practices that are at work across team members, particularly around clarifying decision rights and information flows.[11] The real job of a high-performing team's leader is to inspire and enable others to do their absolute best, together. These leaders spend more time integrating across than managing down. The milestone tool is straightforward and focuses on mapping and tracking and what is getting done by when and by whom. High-performing team leaders take that basic tool to a whole new level, exploiting it to inspire and enable people to work together *as a team!*

Royal Caribbean's CEO Richard Fain explains it this way:

> *If you don't establish early on key milestones—long-term milestones rather than the short-term milestones—you get caught in the "next week" syndrome . . . everybody says, "We're going to know so much more next week or the week after" . . . so the focus shifts to next week or the week after and we all desperately wait for that period. Meanwhile the longer-term milestone goes by the wayside.[12]*

Chapter 11: Overinvest in Early Wins to Build Team Confidence by Day 60

Early wins are all about credibility and confidence. People have more faith in people who have delivered. You want team members to have confidence in you, in themselves, and in the plan for change that has emerged. You want your boss to have confidence in you. Early wins fuel that confidence. To that end, identify potential early wins by Day 60 and overinvest to deliver them by the end of your first six months—*as a team!*

The head of IBM's alliance with Oracle, Sue Hed, gets the early win concept. Sue overinvested in a few early pilot programs by going out into the field to better understand her teams' challenges, make key contacts, establish relationships, close deals, and oversee the implementation of the programs. She proved that the programs worked locally and her efforts gave the team confidence and momentum to extend the programs elsewhere. As Sue describes it, "The buy-in

---

[11]Neilson, Martin, and Powers, "The Secrets to Successful Strategy Execution," *Harvard Business Review* (June 2008): 60.

[12]Bradt, George, "The New Leader's Playbook," *Forbes* (March 23, 2011).

has been great in other countries because they saw the success and had testimonials from their peers."[13]

Chapter 12: Secure ADEPT People in the Right Roles and Deal with Inevitable Resistance by Day 70

Make your organization ever more ADEPT by Acquiring, Developing, Encouraging, Planning, and Transitioning talent:

- *Acquire:* Recruit, attract, and bring onboard the right people.
- *Develop:* Assess and build skills and knowledge.
- *Encourage:* Direct, support, recognize, and reward.
- *Plan:* Monitor, assess, and plan career moves over time.
- *Transition:* Migrate to different roles as appropriate.

This is one of the most important things you do. Jump-start this by getting the right people in the right roles with the right support to *build the team!*

As a case in point, Chiquita's CEO, Fernando Aguirre, met an employee, Leo Urzua, during his stint on CBS's show *Undercover Boss*. Leo was a harvest coordinator who tried to teach Fernando how to pick and prune lettuce. Through the process, Fernando learned of and was inspired by Leo's quest to become a U.S. citizen. Fernando committed to helping Leo achieve his goal. When Leo got sworn in as a citizen in Yuma, Arizona, several months later, the keynote speaker at that ceremony was . . . Fernando Aguirre.[14]

Chapter 13: Evolve People, Plans, and Practices to Capitalize on Changing Circumstances

By the end of your first 100 days, you should have made significant steps toward aligning your people, plans, and practices around a shared purpose. Remember, this is not a one-time event, but, instead, something that will require constant, ongoing management and improvement.

Monitor the situation over time. Identify and classify the impact of surprises as major or minor, enduring or temporary, and be ready to react as appropriate. It's important to panic early and stay panicked.[15] For major, temporary events, follow the basic flow of

---

[13]Bradt, George, "The New Leader's Playbook," *Forbes* (March 30, 2011).
[14]Bradt, George, "The New Leader's Playbook," *Forbes* (April 6, 2011).
[15]Jonathan Garrity, CEO of Cambridge Hanover, gave us the "panic early" part of this. We discovered the need to stay panicked on our own.

prepare—understand—plan—implement—revise or prepare. For major, enduring changes, redeploy or restart with a relentless focus on the message throughout.

- Manage your strategy (plans) as a cycle, ensuring that you are looking at your situation, customers, collaborators, capabilities, competitors, and conditions on a regular basis and reflecting changes in them in your ever-evolving strategies and plans.

- Manage your operations (practices) by continually tracking, updating, and adding milestones. Disciplined, integrated execution doesn't happen unless you demand it, monitor it, and reinforce it over and over again.

- Manage your organization (people) by deploying the ADEPT tool for ongoing talent development. You don't have to use this tool. But you do have to have a complete and disciplined way to strengthen your organization on a continuous basis over time.

Walmart's CEO Mike Duke knows that we are all new leaders all the time. That's why organizational change management is an ongoing part of his life. When Walmart's merchandising failed to deliver the expected results over the 2010 holiday season, Mike replaced his head merchandiser and completely revamped their holiday merchandising approach in time to be able to announce the changes in their next quarter's earnings call.[16]

Make This Book Work for You

By now you should be aware that there may be a better way to manage transitions than just showing up on Day One or charging into your promotion announcement or newly merged team and doing what "they" tell you to do. Similarly, there may be a better way for you to tackle this book than just starting on page one and reading straight through until you lose steam.

You might want to start with the 100-Day Checklist (Tool 6.1) at the end of Chapter 6. You might want to begin with the chapter summaries at the end of each chapter. Or you may prefer to read straight through the main body of the book. Use the book's elements in the

---

[16]Bradt, George, "The New Leader's Playbook," *Forbes* (March 1, 2011).

way that works best for you. Just bear in mind that there really is a logical order of thinking and acting here, and it is helpful to have this clear in your mind before you do anything. Don't read this book over your first 100 days. Read the most appropriate parts now, and then dip back in repeatedly over your first 100 Days and beyond.

We have designed this as a flexible handbook split into a main body, a set of appendices, and downloadable tools.

The main body (Chapters 1 through 13) is highly structured and practically oriented, with ideas, examples, tools, forms, and checklists in the book. In this main body, we are highly prescriptive and directive: "Do this," "Do that," "Don't do the other."

The appendices provide more depth on some subjects like leadership and communication and get at specific situations like internal and international moves, merging teams, leading through a crisis, and guidance for the new leader's supervisor. We've included some sample 100-Day Action Plans at the end.

We have posted easily editable versions of all the downloadable tools at www.onboardingtools.com. They are included in the price of the book. Use them. Additionally, we add bonus tools, chapter updates, and new chapters as we think them up. So, shame on you if you don't visit that site from time to time—starting with now.

People often tell us, "This is just common sense. But I like the way you've structured it." (One person said, "You brought together all of the critical thinking sessions I had with myself in the shower every morning before work!" We'll let you imagine that in your own way.)

As you set out to follow our structure, understand that we have a bias to push you to do things faster than others would expect. This timetable is based on the needs of our clients, who typically are moving into demanding, complex new leadership roles, and who need to meet or beat high expectations fast; but it may not be appropriate for your situation without some customization. We present you with options and choices. You are in charge. We wish you success in your new leadership role. We hope this book will help you and your team to deliver better results faster than anyone thought possible!

PART I

BECOME THE BEST CANDIDATE FOR THE JOB

Position Yourself for a New Role

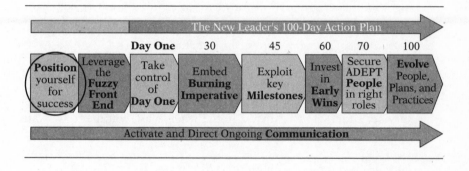

There are three components to activating your leadership potential. The first is knowing your own leadership qualities and capacities. The second is building a career plan. The third is interacting effectively with others in such a way that this becomes a part of an organization's or a market's perception of you. Know yourself, create a plan, and then help others know you. We've mapped out three concrete steps you can take to position yourself for leadership roles and promotions.

1. *Know your leadership potential.*

   Begin with the first dimension—know yourself as a leader. A title or promotion does not make anyone a leader. Leadership emerges from the character, qualities, and capacities of the individual. Make no mistake about it, authentic leadership is personal. It starts with identifying the characteristics, values, attitudes, strengths, and preferences that you hold at your core that will be the foundation for your leadership style. Without knowing these it's possible that your leadership style will be ineffective or seem hollow. Knowing oneself is the foundation of all true leaders.

2. *Build a career plan.*

Great leaders are not made in a day. Leadership is built over time. You start with your preferences, identify your strengths and opportunities for growth, reach down to your core values, and then build, methodically and intentionally, toward developing the skills, connections, and momentum that will help you realize you personal goals.

3. *Communicate your readiness for leadership.*

The best way to communicate that you can lead is to lead. Step up and lead something. It could be a major project. It could be an extracurricular cross-functional effort like a community service effort or a team outing. Either way, volunteer to lead something and lead.

Let's go into more depth on these three steps.

Know Your Leadership Potential

We have developed a tool called BRAVE: Behaviors, Relationships, Attitudes, Values, and Environment to start the process. This tool provides a quick and effective way to help you break out the elements of what makes you tick professionally and then, guided by a deep understanding and focused intent, design a career trajectory for yourself. Use it to get to know your preferences and your values and to help you align your professional choices and behavior with those qualities.

We will be returning to this tool at later points in this book, each time with a slightly different purpose in mind, and each one effectively building off this first analysis and assessment. BRAVE becomes the core connection between you and your team, your team and the larger organization. We encourage you to think of it as a foundation, a pivot, off which all your actions and intentions will move, into the future, and into success. This foundation is your core ethical being—who you are. It drives what you say and what you do. Or as one of our clients summarized it: "Be. Do. Say." It will also be the framework by which you evaluate your leadership opportunities and challenges. Be, Do, Say. We will be coming back to these over and over again.

We have designed a suite of tools for you and in a number of cases you will be asked to use them more than once. These are, after all, tools. They are designed to be used and reused. Like any craftsperson with a tool, you will get better and better at using them with repetition.

There is a copy of the BRAVE Tool 1.1 at the end of this chapter and a downloadable, printer-friendly copy of this tool (along with many of the tools in this book) at www.onboardingtools.com. You may find it more effective to write things down on these tools than to write in the book.

BRAVE PREFERENCES

Behave: How do you prefer to act, make decisions, control business, and so on?

_____

_____

_____

Relate: How do you prefer to communicate (including mode, manner, and frequency), engage in intellectual debate, manage conflict, assign credit and blame, and so on?[1]

_____

_____

_____

(continued)

---

[1]Ben Dattner explains in *The Blame Game* how credit and blame are key determinants of corporate cultures: "When credit and blame are managed properly, people are willing and able to experiment, learn and grow. When credit and blame are mismanaged and unfair, people shut down, become demotivated, and focus more on covering their rears rather than moving forward" (Ben Dattner, *The Blame Game*, Free Press, 2011, p. 17).

Ben then went on to explain to me that it's not necessarily that differences in the way credit and blame are used are good or bad, but that they are different. Do not assume that your new culture will use credit and blame the way your old culture did. You can just as easily err on the side of taking too much credit and not enough blame as on the side of taking too little credit and too much blame.

Attitude: What's your ideal organization's purpose, mission, vision, identity, basis for power, and so on?

_____

_____

_____

Values: What are your underlying beliefs, approach to learning, risk, time horizons, and so on?

_____

_____

_____

Environment: What is your preferred environment in terms of office space protocols, decor, and so on?

_____

_____

_____

Answer these questions for yourself for now. This framework will come back in subsequent chapters as a way to approach the "fit" interview question, do due diligence on that after you've been offered a job, and then determine your approach to engage the organization.

The point of this process is to have you look at your own preferences or habits and then work from there to identify your strengths, your values, and your goals. If you're quite honest with yourself, you may find that there are some preferences that may not work as strengths, or even truly connect with your values.

For example, you might be a highly motivated perfectionist, and find that you would rather "do things yourself" than work with a team. In some environments that combination might fit perfectly well, in others, not at all. Or you may find that in your perfectionism you tend to be as severe with others as you are with yourself, which undermines a deeper value you hold to serve as a mentor for others.

Once you have completed this exercise, you'll want to let your leadership intention be known by declaring it. The *declaring* part is important, because this is what best enables you to commit to your career path. Start by declaring this to yourself. Commit yourself. Your commitments become more real as you share them with others.

Select a listener (a buddy or two) and declare your intentions and your commitments to them. Your commitments are suddenly that much more real. It actually works, try it. If you feel uncomfortable declaring your commitment to someone else, it's a good sign that your commitment as you've defined it might not be authentically yours. Keep refining it until you feel more comfortable. Make it real!

Build a Career Plan

Having used the BRAVE tool to analyze the basic elements of your leadership potential, you are now ready to design your career plan. Your career plan will have a short-term positioning dimension and a longer-term strength-building dimension. The short-term dimension starts with our Five-Step Career Plan tool—Tool 1.2—which can also be found at the end of this chapter and online.

Five-Step Career Plan Tool

This tool provides a quick and effective way to help you understand what makes you tick professionally and design a career trajectory for yourself. Use your BRAVE preferences as input and then align your professional choices with those preferences.

Let's walk through the main steps of the Five-Step Career Plan tool:

1. *Likes/dislikes.* This is your raw data. Take a hard look at your BRAVE preferences to guide you and then go through your past activities and jobs and lay out everything you liked and didn't like. This is about specifics, not generalities.

   It may help to use the third person pronoun when making your list. (He. She.) She liked: planning, thinking, getting a sense of accomplishment, working with people. She liked: having some freedom, the support system in a big company, having a short commute, not working on weekends. He didn't like: being pushed too hard, not being able to take Sunday off, dealing with things that didn't work right, having colleagues let him down, feeling as if he worked at a company of second-class citizens.

   People tend to enjoy doing things they are naturally strong in. This exercise will help you understand your strengths.

2. *Ideal job criteria.* With your BRAVE preferences and these likes and dislikes in mind, lay out your ideal job criteria. If you could wave your magic wand, what would that dream job look like? Explore what features of these criteria are meaningful or important

to you. Test, challenge, and shape your answers. Make sure the job criteria you've come up with line up with your preferences and likes or strengths.

3. *Long-term goals.* Next, consider your long-term goals. It may help to start with the end in mind. Start at retirement and work back 5 years, then 10 years, then 15 years, and so on to start laying out an entire career line. What do you want to achieve? Think about your professional life and about your personal life, and especially about the ways these are connected. At every point in the process, you should be thinking about whether your strengths, motivations, values, job criteria, and goals match. You may feel that you have a good sense of these before you start. Or you may feel that these are too removed from the practical job at hand. Either way, go through this exercise, and open yourself to these questions: "What matters to me, now? What will matter to me over time?"

4. *Options.* The idea of options triggers widely different responses in people. Some people become oddly passive, or even fatalistic. "What will be, will be." Or, "Well, it was meant to be." Others panic, get jumpy. We urge a different approach. We are convinced that the mind-set that generates a sense of possibilities, of options, is the mind-set that creates real opportunities and fosters success. We encourage you to read Appendix 1—Deploy Six Basic Elements of Leadership. This should enrich your sense of how to create leadership options for yourself.

   Do not create just one option! Options energize potential. Create parallel options for yourself. Real ones. Even if your second option is not nearly as attractive as the main option at hand, having a viable alternative is crucial to your success. A second option also allows you to gain a greater perspective on the first option, thus seeing it in a better light. Remember: Create options in parallel!

5. *Choices.* If you follow these suggestions, sooner rather than later an opportunity will come your way. If you've done your homework, you will have at least two real options to choose from when the moment comes to make a decision. Go back to your list of BRAVE preferences, ideal job criteria, and long-term goals. Look at your options. Think through what they are likely to bring you. Compare options by weighting your criteria and evaluating each option's results.

Gut check: Once you've made your choice, write it down and go to sleep. If you wake up in the morning feeling good, then you've probably made a good decision. If you wake up in the morning with your gut indicating that you have made a mistake, you misled yourself. Most likely, you erred in weighting your ideal job criteria. It's okay to have misled yourself, just so long as you have the maturity and mechanism to make yourself aware of it. Your gut is that mechanism.

The Five-Step Career Plan exercise should be reviewed periodically throughout your career as your parameters change. By doing so you will continue to: (1) understand yourself and your goals, (2) create options, and (3) select the best option that best matches your strengths, values, interests, and goals. You can consider this exercise over a short-term, midterm or long-term time frame.

Over the *short term*, you can't change your strengths. You are what you are and where you are and you should focus on creating options that can take advantage of your existing strengths and position. This means that you should concentrate on understanding your own strengths and helping others understand them.

Over the *midterm*, you can expand and sharpen your strengths and take a measured approach to deploying them and creating real leadership momentum. Look for ways to develop them by getting involved in projects both inside the company and outside that afford you the opportunity to stretch, learn, and practice those skills. If you are proactively building your strengths, people often take it as a sign that you are meant for leadership.

Over the *long term*, decide what strengths you'll need to have to achieve your long-term goals. Continually use the tools in this chapter to discover what you need to learn to move to the next level. As Charon and Drotter discuss in *The Leadership Pipeline*, different strengths are required to manage yourself, to manage others, to manage managers, to manage functions, or to manage an entire business.[2]

Virtually all the leaders we've ever talked to readily admit that along the leadership path they continually learned . . . that they had more to learn. Thus, if you want to move to different levels of leadership

---

[2]Charan, Ram, Drotter, Stephen, and Noel, James. *The Leadership Pipeline* (San Francisco: Jossey-Bass, 2001).

over time, you're going to have to build new strengths, supplementing your existing talents with new knowledge and skills. With a long-term view you can and should invest in appropriate learning and in getting yourself into positions and assignments that allow you to practice new leadership skills.

Crucial Strengths

Yes, we have told you to pick roles that match your strengths and that allow you to leverage them best. But that doesn't mean you should ignore key skill sets that do not fall into your strengths bucket. Some strengths are nice to have, others are must-haves if you are in a leadership role. Different roles require different strengths.

One undeniably crucial skill for all leaders is communication. Leadership and communication are inextricably related. If communicating is not one of your strengths, you *must* put a plan in place to improve your abilities in this area. Buying a lottery ticket might give you a better chance at winning than trying to succeed with poor communication skills. To increase your muscle in this area, you'll have to become aware what your limitations are so you'll know how to extend yourself beyond them in the future.

Each role will have a few crucial skills that will be required for a leader to possess to be successful. As you complete the Career Planning exercises it is essential that you know the crucial strengths required for the role you are seeking. Once they are known you must honestly assess whether there is a match with your strengths. The moment you find that you are lacking in a crucial strength, start working on a plan to develop that skill as best you can and have an augmentation plan in place if you can not get that particular strength to the level required for the role. It is essential that you are thorough in determining the crucial strengths required for a role and that you are honest in your self-assessment match.

Communicate Your Readiness for Leadership

Warning: You should only move on to this next step after you have thoroughly and honestly completed the earlier exercises.

Once you've begun to know yourself, the next step is to help others know you. Now that you've gotten a good handle on your strengths, values, and goals, you are ready to think through positioning them in a proactive and methodical way. The simple exercise of knowing your strengths and goals will set in motion a leadership dynamic where you signal your leadership qualities to others, they attribute these qualities to you, others still begin to see these qualities, and opportunities for leadership emerge. The point here is to make this a deliberate and conscious plan, something you control rather than wait for random luck to fall your way.

We've broken down the components of communicating leadership into a set of six basic elements that you can deploy deliberately and consistently. Here are the headlines. See Appendix I on leadership for more discussion.

1. Listen and observe first.
2. Talk in order to listen and connect better.
3. Imagine the leaders' or key stakeholders' perspectives.
4. Identify potential areas for leadership.
5. Lead through actions that communicate.
6. Carpe Diem.

Communication Pillars

Before you even accept a job, your communication plan should begin to take shape. As you position yourself for leadership in a new role, you should already be fortifying the foundations of what will eventually become your comprehensive communication plan. We will ask you to think strategically about communication through this book and in great detail in Chapter 8, but as a start you will want to be aware of the three pillars of a comprehensive communication plan. Just as a computer program calls up subroutines on a regular basis in the background to make sure that things are always running smoothly, this book refers to these pillars in several different places. The three pillars are:

1. *You.* You can't communicate anything meaningful to anyone anywhere anytime until you know who you are and what's important to you. The exercises in this chapter are designed to help you develop that awareness. What you say is only credible and sustainable if it's delivered in your own voice backed up by your actions and your values. Be. Do. Say.
2. *Target audience.* Communication must be received to have any impact. Knowing whom you are communicating with, what's

important to them, and how they will receive that communication is just as important as knowing who you are.

3. *Message.* You can't get people to do anything differently unless they believe there is a reason for them to do that (platform for change), they can picture themselves in a better place (vision), and they know what to do to be part of the way forward (call to action). These are the basic points from which your message will be derived and that you'll be driving over and over again in your communication.

At this point you should begin thinking about each of these pillars as essential elements to your communication campaign. The first pillar you'll want to solidify is you, but be aware that every interaction you have will provide key information on your target audience and your message. Do not miss those opportunities.

This is another tool we will return to again in the communication chapter. We introduce this tool now with a focus on positioning yourself for leadership. It is never too early to begin to develop your message. As you position yourself for leadership you'll want to develop a message that is true and that communicates your leadership potential and style.

Let's go into a little more depth on the tools and on your message that you can use as you position yourself for leadership.

Identify Them—Your Target Audience

Start by getting clear on whom you are communicating with, what they are thinking, doing and know.

- With whom are you communicating? Be as specific as you can and include everyone and all groups that can have an impact, including your targets, their primary influencers, and other influencers. Answer each of the following questions with your entire target audience in mind.
- What are they currently thinking and doing? What's most important to them?
- What do they need to stop doing, keep doing, or change how they are doing it?
- What do they need to know to move them from their current state to the desired state?

Choose the Right Message for You and for Them in Your Particular Context

Think through the platform for change, vision, and call to action. Then distill them down to one driving message and your three communication points.

1. *Platform for change.* The things that will make your audience members realize they need to do something different than what they have been doing.
2. *Vision.* Picture of a brighter future—that your audience members can picture themselves in.
3. *Call to action.* Actions the audience can take to get there.

To illustrate these points, imagine a pack of polar bears. They are playing on an ice flow. It's melting! It's drifting out to sea! They're either going to drown or starve to death. Either scenario is not good. [Platform for change.] The good news is that there's some food nearby that's sitting on land. The bears could play there, be safe, and get food. [Vision.] So, the lead polar bears come up with a plan to depart the drifting ice and safely swim to land. [Call to action.]

Keep in mind that everyone who is affected by your leadership will want to know the same thing: "How will the changes impact me?" So, when you are crafting your communication points, be sure to be able to explain (1) how the changes will affect them, and (2) how they enable them to be more successful themselves.

Great communication pivots off a central message. For example, "We're going to be ranked 1 or 2 or we're going to get out" was one of Jack Welch's early messages at GE. Or, "a car in every driveway" was the overarching message Ford deployed early in the twentieth century. The purpose of an overarching message is to anchor everything else in your communication plan. A good place to find it is in your vision of the future.

Writing about Rochester, New York's former school superintendent at the time of his hiring, Jean Claude Brizard and Meaghan McDermott said,

> His message for Rochester is that we must "make education personal."
>
> "I read somewhere once that every child is a work of art," he said.

"Our task is to help create a masterpiece out of each. We need to get teachers and principals to a place where they can track the progress of each student and create the proper enrichment and intervention for each."

He said he wants to create an environment in the district where if he asks a school principal about a specific student and their dreams, aspirations, struggles and achievement, he and school leaders will be able to have a meaningful dialogue about that child's future.[3]

Voice

Find your voice, the outward expression of your underlying attitudes and values appropriate for the context you're facing. This will come to life in your behaviors, the way you relate to others, and the environment you create. If you're using a voice that is not authentically yours, it won't work. Make the effort to discover your own voice.

Your message and voice are inextricably linked—if not the same thing.

The greatest impact comes when three things intersect:

1. You and what's important to you in terms of behaviors, way of relating to others, attitudes, values, and environment.
2. Your audience's character or culture and its readiness for change.
3. The situational context and the importance and urgency of the need for change.

When you get those in line you will find the message and the voice you need to inspire and enable others to feel the way you want them to feel and do the things you need them to do.

Position Yourself: Summary and Implications

Don't underestimate the value of investing in your own positioning.

- Know your leadership potential: identify your preferences and existing strengths and talents that you can turn into strengths appropriate to meet your long-term goals.

---

[3]Meaghan M. McDermott, "Brizard takes city school district's reins today," *Rochester Democrat and Chronicle*, January 2, 2008. (Brizard has since moved on to head up Chicago's schools.)

- Build a career plan—short-, mid-, and long-term goals. Showcase your strengths, develop your skills, stretch yourself.
- Demonstrate your readiness for leadership: lead something, whether it's a major project or just the team outing.
- Be aware of the communication pillars and work to solidify you first while constantly gathering information to help to identify your target audience and message.

QUESTIONS YOU SHOULD ASK YOURSELF

- Do I understand my strengths?
- Am I aware of the crucial strengths required for the roles I am seeking?
- Do I understand what motivates me?
- Do I understand my own preferences so I can determine fit?
- Am I ready to lead?
- Am I prepared to demonstrate that readiness to lead?

TOOL 1.1
BRAVE Preferences*

Behavioral Preferences

ACTIONS   more   ......|......|......|......|......|......   more
                 individual   team-based

DECISION   hierarchical   ......|......|......|......|......|......   collaborative
  MAKING

CONTROL   written/   ......|......|......|......|......|......   verbal/
  POINTS   systematic   face-to-face

OTHERS _____

Relationship Preferences

COMMUNICA-   formal   ......|......|......|......|......|......   informal
  TION

INTELLECTUAL   surface-level......|......|......|......|......|......   in-depth
  DEBATE

CONFLICT   avoided/   ......|......|......|......|......|......   welcome/
                 destructive   constructive

OTHERS _____

Attitude

BUY-IN TO   not much   ......|......|......|......|......|......   fully committed
  PURPOSE

IDENTITY   subgroup bias   ......|......|......|......|......|......   one-team bias

POWER   controlled   ......|......|......|......|......|......   diffused

OTHER OBSERVATIONS _____

TOOL 1.1   (continued)

Values

LEARNING   directive   ......|......|......|......|......|......   collaborative/
                                                                          shared

RISK   protect what is ......|......|......|......|......|......   risk more/gain
  APPETITE   more

TIME   shorter term   ......|......|......|......|......|......   longer-term,
  HORIZON   multiyear

UNDERLYING BELIEFS _____

Environmental Preferences

OFFICE LAYOUT   walled   ......|......|......|......|......|......   open

OFFICE DECOR/   formal   ......|......|......|......|......|......   casual
  DRESS

OTHER INSIGHTS: _____

_____

TOOL 1.1b
BRAVE Preferences Guide

Behaviors

ACTIONS: Do you prefer to act more on your own or with a team?

DECISION MAKING: Do you prefer bosses to make decisions and tell subordinates what to do or more team-based collaborative co-creation and consultation?

CONTROL POINTS: Do you prefer a business that is managed in writing systemically or more verbally and face-to-face?

OTHER: Note any other behavioral preferences that give you clues as to "The way you prefer things to be done around here."

Relationships

COMMUNICATION: The scale goes from more formal to less formal modes and manners.

INTELLECTUAL DEBATE: Are you more comfortable with surface-level, polite conversations or more in-depth probing, discussion and debate?

CONFLICT: Do you prefer to avoid conflict because it is destructive or welcome it as a constructive way to move ideas forward?

OBSERVATIONS RE USE OF CREDIT & BLAME, ETC. other uses of credit and blame.

TOOL 1.1b   (continued)

Attitude

BUY-IN TO PURPOSE: How important is purpose to you?

IDENTITY: Are you more comfortable identifying with yourself, a sub-group, a group/division or the organization as a whole – one-team?

POWER: An organization's attitude to power is closely related to the way it makes decisions.   Whether power is institutional, personal, or resource-based, figure out how tightly you prefer it to be controlled or diffused.

OTHER OBSERVATIONS: Note other things about your attitudes.

Values

LEARNING: Determine if you prefer to be directed around what and how to learn or whether you prefer learning to be more collaborative and shared.

RISK APPETITE: Determine whether you're happier in an organization that cares more about protecting what it is or gaining what it doesn't have, but could have – risking more to gain more.

TIME HORIZON: Determine whether you prefer an organization that is more focused on shorter time-frames or longer time-frames.

UNDERLYING BELIEFS: Note any other core beliefs that are relevant.

Environment

OFFICE LAYOUT: Do you prefer more formal walled offices vs. more casual open spaces?

OFFICE DÉCOR: Preferences re: formality vs. casualness of dress and work spaces.

OTHER INSIGHTS: Note other environmental preferences.

TOOL 1.2
Five-Step Career Plan*

1. List your LIKES and DISLIKES

Activities

_____

_____

Jobs

_____

_____

Situations

_____

_____

Lifestyle

_____

_____

Other

_____

_____

2. List your IDEAL JOB CRITERIA categorized as follows

Good for others (impact on others, match with personal values, influence on organization)

_____

_____

Good for me (enjoyable work/activities, fit with life interests, reward, recognition, respect)

_____

_____

TOOL 1.2   (continued)

Good at it (match between activities and strengths, learning, development, resume builder)

_____

_____

Life interests:
Application of technology
Quantitative analysis
Theory development, conceptual thinking
Creative production
Counseling and mentoring
Managing people and relationships
Enterprise control
Influence through language and ideas

3. Identify your LONG-TERM GOALS

_____

_____

4. Build a broad range of OPTIONS that meet your long-term goals

_____

_____

5. Make CHOICES by evaluating your options against your criteria

_____

_____

Finally, perform *a gut check.*

_____

CHAPTER 2

Sell before You Buy

ANSWER THE ONLY THREE INTERVIEW QUESTIONS

The New Leader's 100-Day Action Plan								
		Day One	30	45	60	70		100
Position yourself for success	Leverage the **Fuzzy Front End**	Take control of **Day One**	Embed **Burning Imperative**	Exploit key **Milestones**	Invest in **Early Wins**	Secure **ADEPT People** in right roles		**Evolve** People, Plans, and Practices

Activate and Direct Ongoing **Communication**

You can ace any interview if you remember three things during the process:

> Thing 1: You cannot turn down a job offer that you have not received.
>
> Thing 2: There are only three fundamental interview questions—ever.
>
> Thing 3: There are only three fundamental interview answers—ever.

Thing 1

Before you accept a job, you must first get an offer. Then, and only then, can you decide if you should accept it. Do not do these steps out of order. Your initial focus should be solely on getting the job offer. If you start to imagine or assume you have the job before you have the offer, you have diverted some of your focus away from reality and are wasting your time. Once you have received the offer, your approach should change.

Everything you do in the interview process should be designed to get the company to offer you the job. This includes not only your answers to their questions, but also your questions to them. At this stage in the process, your questions are not about helping you decide if you want the job. They are about helping them decide to offer it to you. Sell yourself first. Next, secure the offer. Then, after you have the offer, and only then, figure out if it's right for you.

Thing 2

There are only three interview questions.

Every question you've ever been asked, and every question you've ever asked in any interview is a subset of one of these three fundamental questions:

1. Can you do the job?
2. Will you love the job?
3. Can I tolerate working with you?

That's it. Those three: strengths, motivation, fit. The questions may be asked in different words, but every question, however worded, is just a variation on one of these. As each question comes, it is your task to determine which of the three is really being asked.

Thing 3

There are only three fundamental interview questions, so there are only three fundamental interview answers.

Every answer you give in an interview should be a subset of these three answers:

1. My strengths are a match for this job.
2. My motivations are a match for this job.
3. I am a good fit with this organization.

That's it. Those three. Your answers to questions will be more elaborate, but your answers should always be dressed-up versions of one of the three.

Since there are only three interview questions and three interview answers, all you have to do is to prepare three answers in advance and recognize what question you are being asked. Then you are ready to ace any interview. If Question 1 is asked, you should lead your response with an Answer 1. Question 2 indicates that you lead with an Answer 2. You're probably catching on by now, but a Question 3 requires you to lead with an Answer 3. Simple. Isn't it? After you lead with the proper answer you can embellish your response with either of the other two answers.

The bad news is that it is going to be a lot more work than you might think to prepare these answers in advance of each interview. Interviews are exercises in solution selling. They are not about you, they are about them—their needs, their problems. You are the solution. Think of the interview process as a chance for you to show your ability to see, hear, and solve the organization's and the interviewer's problem.

It interviewers know what they are doing, they will be looking beyond a narrowly defined problem (and solution) and understand that beyond a technical expertise a broader set of criteria matter: strengths, motivations, values—a general fit. When they don't really know what they're doing, they can be brought around to seeing things the right way. Still, in every case the solution must be presented as much as possible from their perspective. Thoughtful preparation can often be the deciding feature between a yes and a no. This is tricky stuff, but it is worth the investment of time.

Question 1: Can you do the job? Or more likely: What are your strengths? (Strengths)

Answer 1: Prepare three situation/action/results examples that highlight your strengths in the areas most important over the short term and long term to the people interviewing you.

Question 2: Will you love the job? Or more likely: What are you looking to do? (Motivation)

Answer 2: Position the role and the organization you are applying for in terms of your values and what you like to do.

Question 3: Can I tolerate working with you? Or more likely: What sort of people do you like to work with? (Fit)

Answer 3: Position the organization you're interviewing with in terms of the BRAVE framework discussed in Chapter 1. Answer by telling how your preferred Behaviors, Relationships, Attitudes, Values, and work Environment is a match with the organization.

Imagine that you are interviewing for a job where a new leader and a new team are being put together to solve a specific problem or to address a specific need or goal. The parties doing the interviewing may not fully understand the problem; and if they do, they may not fully articulate it to you during the interview. In many cases, organizations think and learn about what they want as they conduct the hiring process. You can have a greater impact than you realize on what the organization needs and what the job should be at this point. The winning candidate is often the one who, acting as a management consultant, helps the decision makers and team members get a better sense of what the problems, or needs, really are, and then conveys confidence that under the candidate's supervision the right things would get done.

Let's return to the three interview questions and answers. You have done your homework, so all you have to do is figure out which of the three questions you are really being asked, and respond to it with the corresponding answer. You should always lead with the corresponding answer to the question, but from there you can move on to other answers. Skillful candidates can transition smoothly from the topic at hand, whatever it is, to the key points they want to cover. The key points should always indicate that the candidate is a solid fit for the role. You want to talk in terms of strength, motivation, and fit, but you may not want to use those words or reveal your approach. In fact, we recommend that you don't. Think of this approach as a secret code.

The powerful part of this approach is that the interviewer will never know that you are deploying it and your answers will tell an impressive story, regardless of the interviewer's skill level. By knowing this secret code of interviewing, you can control the process without anyone realizing you are doing so. Don't be afraid to lead the interview by deciphering the real questions beneath the actual questions and then providing the corresponding answers. All this has the further advantage of giving you confidence in the interview situation, confidence tied into acute listening skills, a great combination.

For example, "Tell me about yourself." Make no mistake about it, this is a "strengths" question and you should lead with a strengths-based answer. This common but somewhat dauntingly open-ended question can also be leveraged as a setup for all three of your answers. The joking-chatting time is over; you've been given the reins for a bit. Be ready to lead the interview process with your strengths and let the interviewer guide you to motivation and fit.

"What do you know about me/us?" This is a motivation question if there ever was one. Prove that you cared enough to do some homework. You should know, or have surmised, enough about their current situation to put you in a position to discuss your strengths and fit as well.

The good news is that the Internet and social media make it much easier to learn about organizations and people than it was before. The bad news is that it makes it easier for everyone. Plan to go beyond a simple Google search. Understand the facts of the business, its situation and priorities. Then learn about the individuals you'll be talking to. A partial list of tools includes Bloomberg, Hoovers, Edgar, Seeking Alpha, industry-specific blogs, the organization and individuals' LinkedIn and Facebook pages, Twitter streams, and the like.

Chart 2.1 lists some common interview questions and classifies them in their proper categories.

The "strengths, motivation, fit" concept is a good organizing tool for your interview preparation. But remember that you probably don't want to show your organizing tool to interviewers unless it reinforces one of the strengths they are evaluating.

Champion athletes know that the race begins long before the starting gun is fired. Although this is a cliché in the world of

CHART 2.1   The Questions Behind the Questions

Common Question	Real Question	Lead Answer
Tell me about your career transitions.	Will you love the job?	Motivation
Tell me what you did at_____?	Can you do the job?	Strengths
Tell me about your favorite boss.	Can I tolerate working with you?	Fit
Why should we hire you?	Can you do the job?	Strengths
What is your greatest weakness?	Can you do the job?	Strengths
Are you a team player?	Can I tolerate working with you?	Fit
Why did you leave your last job?	Can I tolerate working with you?	Fit
Where do you see yourself in 5 years?	Will you love the job?	Motivation
Why does this job interest you?	Will you love the job?	Motivation
What would your last team say about you?	Can I tolerate working with you?	Fit

sports, it's barely recognized in the business world. It is startling how rarely executive leaders make the most of the early stages of onboarding and particularly those first contacts with the new organization.

So here's our tip: Your new assignment started as soon as you learned you were a candidate. Act accordingly. Be prepared. Strategize. Caucus with trusted friends. Spend the time and effort that you would if you had already started the job. You wouldn't walk into a presentation to the board of directors unprepared, would you? Each interaction with the people involved in hiring, evaluating, and working with you should bear the marks of careful and thoughtful preparation, delivery, and follow-through. You are making many critical first impressions. Patterns of perception and behavior are being set as soon as you become a candidate. You should be the one to script them. Carefully plan and prepare for each of your meetings during the hiring process.

If you've been involved in hiring a new leader then you know that those involved in the decision can have wildly different ideas about what to look for in the candidate. If you're lucky, you have experienced seeing a great candidate emerge from an interview process. You're even luckier if this person ended up being what people had hoped.

How does a great candidate emerge and why? What usually happens is that the candidate somehow manages to hit the right buttons for two or more people in the process, usually early on, and those interviewers begin to influence the process on the candidate's behalf. How did that happen? Chance? Possibly, but skill is also likely to have been involved. The candidate presented strengths and motivation in a way that directed the discussion onto the question of fit. How do skillful candidates do this? A standard technique is to structure the interview as an exchange where as much information is being given as is being put out. As in any selling situation, there needs to be a back-and-forth flow of queries, expressions of interest, thoughtful answers, refinements, and enthusiasm.

Great job candidates foster enthusiasm in the people who are interviewing, and that enthusiasm gives those candidates a lot of insight and allows them to sell themselves more effectively. How do you foster enthusiasm? By presenting yourself with confidence and professionalism, certainly, but also by being enthusiastic. Great candidates enjoy the interview process. They come across as if they really enjoy talking about work, management styles, the opportunities at hand, and other related topics. This is not to be confused with an attempt to behave like a cheerleader waving pom-poms. A skillful interviewer helps set up the conditions for discussing things that matter. What's important to you and what's important for them, coupled with what really motivates you and what really motivates them are what matter. For your interview to be successful, you must find a way to compellingly and enthusiastically connect with and communicate the things that matter.

Come prepared, present with confidence, be enthusiastic (talk about what matters), and brim with a sense of possibility and opportunity. These qualities will quickly attract an inside ally, which is often the way opportunities get offered to you.

HOT TIP

Everything is part of the interview: You won't go too far wrong if you imagine that everything you do and say is being videotaped to be shown to the final decision maker. This is why you must use every part of every interaction with everybody in the organization as an opportunity to reinforce your strengths, motivation, and fit. Until you've been offered a job, it's all about getting the offer.

Be "On" at All Times When Being Considered for a Promotion from Within

Management people will be looking at your strengths, motivation, and fit when they are considering you for promotions from within as well. So you'll want to use the same strategy as previously discussed when you are being interviewed. But, and it's a big but, they may not ever interview you. Instead, they may get answers to questions in these areas by observing you in your job, or through a series of casual conversations with you or with others. So, if everything is part of the interview when you're joining from the outside, it's equally true that everything is part of the overall evaluation when you're up for a promotion from within. Often this evaluation will be going on before you even know that you're up for a promotion. So, our prescription is to assume that you're always being evaluated for the next promotion. More information on getting promoted from within and other tactics for different transition situations can be found in Appendix VI.

Negotiate for Success

You got the offer! Congratulations! You're done! Accept it and move forward. Right?

Wrong! Don't relax yet.

First of all, you should have been working to create more than one option. Leadership is about creating options and in this situation you should have been working all along to create options, real ones, for yourself. Even if your second option is not nearly as attractive as the main option at hand, having a viable alternative is crucial to your success with negotiating the first option and it can help you see the apparently preferred option in a better light.

Second, there's often a real sense of urgency on the part of the hiring organization to move as quickly as possible from offer, to acceptance, to start. It is a huge trap that can be detrimental to you should you get caught up in it. Even with the initial offer in hand, there are things you need to do to set yourself up for success. The goal is to set things up for a successful outcome over the long term. As any mogul skier knows, if you're focusing only on the bump you're just going over, the next one can throw you off. Lean forward and look ahead.

You may have to shape that offer to turn it into a recipe for success. First you sell to get an offer. Then, you negotiate to get the right offer. Then, you do a thorough due diligence to decide whether you should accept. It is important to do these in sequence so that you don't muddle your thinking or send mixed messages. With the offer in hand, selling is over. Now it is time to negotiate. We'll tackle due diligence in Chapter 4 after we lay out the seven major onboarding land mines. (In the real world, negotiating and due diligence often overlap. That's okay. Just don't start either until you're done selling.)

You must negotiate a win-win package that factors in all the different forms of short-, mid-, and long-term compensation, benefits, termination rights, and the like. It is equally important to negotiate the details of the role as well as responsibilities, expectations, and authority. There are generally more dimensions open to negotiation than are readily apparent. Take a hard look at the position's responsibilities and relationships. Make sure they line up with appropriate authority and resources. If there's a mismatch, negotiate to correct it before you accept the offer or pay the price later.

Although it's great to get any offer, the first offer may be just one step toward crafting the right offer.

Many people find negotiating for job terms unpleasant, possibly even distasteful; it makes them nervous. In the face of this nervousness, people may resort to uncharacteristic behavior. They become oddly passive. Or oddly aggressive, playing out some imagined role from the Godfather. We could write a separate book about negotiating; but for now, suffice it to say that it can and should be done in a positive, constructive, collaborative atmosphere and tone. It is about clarifying needs and desires for both parties. Successful negotiations typically leave both parties energized, and there is no situation where this is more important than in negotiating for a new job responsibility.

Negotiating Worksheet

Once you've been offered your new position, the negotiating begins. To ensure that you address all the issues that are essential to your success, follow our six-step process on negotiating.

1. *Make a plan.* (Identify the dimensions of the negotiations by answering these questions: What are my needs and concerns? What are the employer's needs and concerns?)
2. *Get started.* (Identify areas of agreement.)
3. *Clarify positions.* (State, support, and listen.)
4. *Find alternatives.*
5. *Gain agreement.* (Study proposals, make concessions, summarize, test the agreements.)
6. *Implement.* (Communicate, deliver, and monitor.)

Make a Plan

There are two parts in making a plan: map out your needs and concerns, and map out their needs and concerns. Both should be done across all the critical dimensions of the negotiation. Your dimensions reflect your ideal job criteria and long-term goals. It's important to know what you want and what you're willing to give up to get it. To complete this process, identify your walkaway, minimum, expected, and opening points for each critical dimension for you and for the employer.

For You

"Walkaway" is the minimum you'll even begin to talk about. If the other party opens with something below that point, you walk away without even countering.

"Minimum" is the minimum acceptable.
"Expected" is where you think a deal will be done.
"Opening" is what you'd say first, if asked.

For Them

"Walkaway" is the maximum they'll even begin to talk about. If you open with something above that point, they walk away without even countering.

"Maximum" is the maximum acceptable.
"Expected" is where they think a deal will be done.
"Opening" is what they'd say first, if asked.

In this example, on the dimension of base salary, there is a deal to be done. You, the new leader are expecting a base salary of $225,000, but would take as low as $205,000. The company is expecting to pay you $210,000, but would pay as much as $230,000. Thus, there is a deal to be done somewhere between $205,000 and $230,000.

The dimensions are important. The more dimensions you can negotiate on, the more room there is for give and take. For many people, a $200,000 straight salary is not as good as a $190,000 salary with a $10,000 per year travel allowance, or a salary of $190,000 and a bonus of up to $25,000. As the level of the role increases, the degrees of freedom on negotiations increase as well. A good way to learn what's possible is to use the Internet to research recent employment contracts for senior leaders of the company.

One executive got bored with his retirement. He applied for and was offered a job in a consulting group with compensation of a straight salary. His response was, "That's much less than I've been used to earning. But, given my stage in life, I could be happy with that annual salary if you gave me 20 weeks' vacation a year." They did.

We've used a base salary example because it's easy to illustrate. You will want to map out on similar scales all the important dimensions of short-, mid-, and long-term compensation, benefits, termination rights, role, responsibilities, expectations, and authority (see Figure 2.1).

FIGURE 2.1   **Negotiating Position Map**

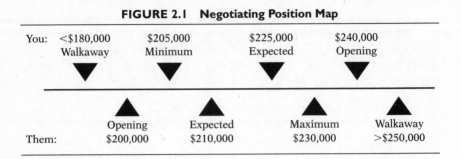

You:	<$180,000 Walkaway	$205,000 Minimum	$225,000 Expected	$240,000 Opening

	Opening	Expected	Maximum	Walkaway
Them:	$200,000	$210,000	$230,000	>$250,000

Sell Before You Buy: Summary and Implications

Get the offer first. You cannot turn down an offer you have not received.

Prepare for an interview by being ready to position your strengths, motivation, and fit in the context of the interviewing organization's articulated and unarticulated needs.

In the interview, make your points fully, but succinctly, and then shut up and listen.

Don't shy away from negotiations. Negotiations are not just about compensation, but are also about crafting the details that lead to the right offer.

In your normal day-to-day work, act and talk as you would if you were being evaluated for a promotion. (Because you are.)

QUESTIONS YOU SHOULD ASK YOURSELF

- Have I thought through multiple examples of how I can answer the three key questions?
- Have I done enough research to understand what's most important to the people I'm talking to?
- Have I taken a thoughtful approach to acceptance and negotiation?
- Is this job right for me in terms of strength, motivation, and fit?
- Have I crafted the right offer or am I accepting any offer?
- What would a videotape of my interview say about me?

TOOL 2.1

Negotiating Prep and Guidelines*

(For each dimension)

My opening: _____

My expected: _____

My minimum: _____

My walkaway: _____

Their walkaway: _____

Their maximum: _____

Their expected:_____

Their opening: _____

Get started

Somehow negotiations are always easier if you can start by agreeing. Find the areas that you agree on and discuss those first.

Areas of agreement:

_____

_____

_____

Areas for debate

There's a framework for areas where there's a difference as well.

1. State your position.

2. Support your position with other information.

3. Listen to the other person's position and probe for understanding. Don't challenge at this point. Just seek to understand.

---

*Copyright © PrimeGenesis® LLC. To customize this document, download Tool 2.1 from www.onboardingtools.com. The document can then be opened, edited, and printed.

TOOL 2.1   (continued)

Areas for debate:

_____

_____

_____

Find alternatives

Look for ways to meet everyone's needs. Often this involves bringing another dimension into the picture.

_____

_____

_____

Gain agreement

Again, there's a process for managing this:

1. Receive and make proposals

_____

_____

2. Receive and make concessions on different dimensions

_____

_____

3. Summarize the situation

_____

_____

4. Test agreements

_____

_____

_____

(continued)

TOOL 2.1   (continued)

5. Circle back to concessions until there's a complete agreement

_____

_____

Implement

Implementing is all about following through. You need to do what you say you're going to do. You need to communicate steps along the way. You need to deliver. You need to monitor all the parties so you know they are delivering as well.

_____

PART II

DISCOVER YOUR NEW ROLE
IT'S ALWAYS MORE THAN YOU THINK IT IS

CHAPTER 3

Map and *Avoid* the Most Common Land Mines

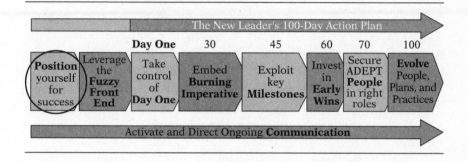

Land mines—we read about them every day in the news as IEDs (improvised explosive devices) are everywhere. They are easy to create, seldom detected, and can cause significant damage and surprise when triggered. In August 2005, *BusinessWeek* magazine reported that there is great hope in using bees to detect these land mines by conditioning the bees to associate the explosive chemicals of land mines with food, thereby providing a safe way to indicate where land mines may be buried. Who would have thought that simple bees would lend hope to defeating such a horrible explosive weapon?

The first 100 days of your transition are also rife with land mines and just like the real thing, they are usually hidden and are often undetected until it is too late. Being aware that land mines exist and learning how to anticipate them will limit their devastating potential. Learning how to deactivate them safely will help you sail straight through to success.

This chapter provides a map showing where those onboarding land mines might exist, how they are created, when they are most likely to occur, and, most importantly, what to do to avoid them. Our 100-Day Plan provides you with a land mine deactivation methodology. Each step suggested in our 100-Day Plan has taken into account the most common derailing land mines that leaders like you are liable to encounter.

The Deadly Seven

There are seven major onboarding land mines that you are likely to come across as a new leader. They can be encountered at any time, but there are specific points in the first 100 days where you are most likely to encounter them.

Chart 3.1 summarizes the seven most deadly land mines and indicates the best time to deactivate them.

We have segmented these into three phases:

Phase 1: Before accepting the job (offer to acceptance).

Phase 2: The Fuzzy Front End (acceptance to Day One).

Phase 3: Day One and beyond (after Day One and always).

Don't be fooled by our suggestion of a phased approach. The purpose of the phases is only to help guide you on what land mines to tackle first and when. Once you have completed all three, not to mention any one phase, your work is not done. Land mines will always exist but they are most easily hidden from you in the first 100 days. Know that you must always be mitigating all of these land mines well beyond your transition. In fact, you should always be doing it. The chart below depicts the best time to mitigate in your first 100 days.

Start before the beginning! By the time you have started you should have identified and begun to address five of the seven deadly land mines! Chapter 6 focuses on developing a systematic and appropriately thorough approach to assessing the risk posed by the Phase 1 land mines. Here we review all seven of the land mines together to provide you as clear a view as possible of the overall land mine landscape and the skills and tools you need to deploy to deactivate the land mines.

The mitigation and deactivation of the most common onboarding land mines is best started early in the process.

CHART 3.1   Deadly Seven Onboarding Land Mines

Land Mines	Description	Best Stage to Mitigate/Deactivate	Deactivation Method
Phase 1			
1. Organization	Lack of a winning strategy or the inability to implement that strategy.	Before accepting job	Ask tough questions.
2. Role	Expectations and resources or key stakeholders are not aligned.	Before accepting job	Listen for inconsistencies. Pursue.
3. Personal	Gaps exist in your strengths, motivation, or fit.	Before accepting job	Ask yourself tough questions. Get a third (fourth, fifth) opinion.
Phase 2			
4. Relationship	Failure to build or maintain key relationships, up, across, or down.	Fuzzy Front End	Activate a 360 relationship compass and use it to help guide your potential challenges and landmines.
5. Learning	Failure to gain adequate information, awareness, or knowledge of customers, collaborators, capabilities, competitors, or conditions.	Fuzzy Front End	Activate an ongoing learning campaign to thoroughly master the 5Cs. Keep your learning sharp.
Phase 3			
6. Delivery	Failure to build a high-performing team or deliver results fast enough.	First 100 days	Identify and validate clear and genuine winning deliverables and timetable. Empower and execute with team.
7. Adjustment	Failure to see or react to situational changes.	As appropriate	Monitor business conditions and results actively. Understand the causes of change. Replan and execute quickly.

WARNING!

We are going to talk about these land mines one by one, but they frequently come in multiples and often interact with each other. Exposure to one risk heightens others, and failure has a way of gaining its own terrible and often unstoppable momentum.

Land Mine 1: Organization

The lack of a clear, concise, differentiating, and winning strategy creates an organizational land mine.

You do not want to get on a ship that has already sunk. Some people thrive on this risk and want to be part of the turnaround. It is one thing to be a turnaround expert going into an organization that knows it needs to make significant changes fast. It is a recipe for disaster if you are not a turnaround expert and you're going into an organization that needs those skills but doesn't actually realize it.

Louisa had been looking for a job for 18 months. She took a job with a growing division of a major player in the software business. They were trying to expand into a completely new area and asked her to come in as VP of marketing for the new group. She had been lobbying for the general manager role, but settled for the marketing job because she was so excited about the new division's prospects. She should not have been.

As it turned out, the division had no competitive advantage and was competing against an entrenched competitor that had quickly stepped into the gap on which Louisa's new company had staked the division's future. Six months into the job, Louisa recommended that the company abandon the effort and focus on other things. It was the right recommendation for the organization, but bad for Louisa as she was out of a job again.

Deactivation method: Ask tough questions.

Organizations without a winning strategy often don't really know they're in trouble, so figuring this out can take some cool-headed and hard-nosed investigation. You will need to ask tough questions about winning strategy at a time when everybody wants to feel good, including, maybe especially, you. The excitement of the new job, bigger paycheck, or better title can bring your guard down and overpower your reasoning skills. A key sign of a winning strategy is a widespread ability among key players to articulate it with conviction.

Land Mine 2: Role

If expectations, resources, or key stakeholders are not aligned you will encounter a role land mine. Often new leaders step into jobs that are virtually impossible from the start because the expectations that exist are unrealistic or cannot be delivered for whatever reason.

One new president had done a great job of negotiating his title and package, but had failed to consider reporting lines and resources. He soon learned that none of the heads of marketing, finance, information, or human resources reported to him. His only direct reports were the heads of sales and business development. By taking the title of president—without the appropriate authority—all he had managed to do was to paint a target on his back for his peers to shoot at so they could get him out of the way and strengthen their own positions.

Deactivation method: Listen for inconsistencies or uncertainty, pursue with questions.

Listen carefully for contradictions, changing representations, slipperiness or uncertainty, any signs of some unspoken friction or disagreement. Pursue these telltale signs with more questions! Make sure that key stakeholders are aligned around your: (1) role and responsibilities, (2) deliverables, (3) timetable, (4) authority, (5) interactions, and (6) access to essential resources. Asking about these in the right way is an art. You do not want to convey anxiety, a lack of confidence, or a lack of trust. But you can, with full confidence and a comfort-inducing sense of "let me understand better what success looks like here," bring out the alignment (or lack of it). It is critical for you to know exactly what your boss expects you to deliver and what resources can be controlled and influenced to deliver against those expectations.

Land Mine 3: Personal

Personal land mines are the ones that you bring to the new job. They are activated when significant gaps exist in your strengths, motivation, or fit for the job. Often executives assume that their strengths are well matched to a particular role, when in fact they are not. Assumptions about strengths usually are based on prior success without a true in-depth strength assessment. Although a new job may sound like your former job, there will be a whole new range of dynamics that may require significantly different skill sets. By missing this factor, leaders often fail to realize that they may not possess certain strengths that are essential for success in the new role. But not you.

After years of working at large consumer product companies, Alice moved to Santa Monica, California, to join a start-up social networking site as the chief marketing officer. She was thrilled to be moving into a "hot new company," and she was thrilled with her promotion in title. Alice was hired to bring her experience in traditional marketing to the start-up. On her first day in the job, she called the marketing team together to ask for the market research studies, the most recent membership feedback, focus group results, brand positioning strategy, and the current marketing strategy and category spend. She was shocked that none of that existed in the typical format and depth that she had grown accustomed to, if at all.

Alice knew that she had to make quick decisions on some key marketing areas, but she had no idea how to do that without her traditional tools or how to motivate a staff that was far different from the traditional marketing staff that she had worked with in the past. She struggled with the entrepreneurial environment and discovered that just being an expert in brand management was not enough to survive in a fast-paced, broken-field run start-up. She struggled in almost everything she did and soon realized that the hot new company was not a fit for her motivations, her strengths, or her basic temperament. "I had the marketing skills, but I did not have any clue about the skills required in a start-up environment."

Deactivation method: Ask yourself the tough questions. Get a third opinion. Get a fourth and fifth.

There are some people who ignore their own symptoms of illness or disease and who avoid going to a doctor for another opinion. In this situation that behavior can get you in a lot of trouble that could have been avoided. If you've been offered the job it's easy to trust the implied opinion that you have everything it takes to succeed. Ask yourself the tough questions about whether you really have the strengths and motivation for a true fit. If you have a nagging feeling, find people whose opinions you trust and create conditions for a fair assessment.

Land Mine 4: Relationship

If you fail to identify, establish, or maintain key relationships up, across, or down, you will encounter relationship land mines (there may be clusters of these and they can set each other off in succession, watch out!). These key relationships are those that have a stake in or can impact your success. We refer to these people as *stakeholders* and they can be found up, down, or across the organization from you.

When you miss the needs or agendas of other key stakeholders or outside influencers, there is a good chance that some impact will be felt. The problem is you won't necessarily know that this has started to happen, but it can get a life and a momentum of its own, outside of your presence or even awareness. If you lend an insufficient or ineffective effort to building a productive teamwork environment with direct reports, land mines are often the result. If expectations of up stakeholders are not clearly understood, go unchecked, or frequently change, this is certainly dangerous territory for land mines. Finally, poor preparation and communication follow-through are often key culprits in activating these land mines.

Relationship land mines catch many executives completely unaware. These are especially tricky because sometimes the results of stepping on one do not show up for months, or longer. What is worse, you can get caught by these land mines just by pure neglect of a key stakeholder or someone that you didn't even know should be a key stakeholder: "I was just too busy to reach out to her." "He has a role in all this? He's just the head of Investor Relations!"

Relationship risks are particularly severe for people who are brought in as change agents. Often those people come in with a hero mentality, thinking they are the organization's savior. This is not necessarily a problem and sometimes they're right. The problem occurs when new leaders *act* as if they are saviors. Nobody wants to see that, especially those who have been part of the situation that needs saving. Don't be a savior. Be a team leader. History is littered with many dead heroes who never made it home.

Sebastian came into the organization to create a new ventures group. He mapped out most of the key stakeholders and was building relationships with them. After a while, it became apparent that Suri, the head of another division, was undermining his efforts. Sebastian did not understand why, since he had never come in contact with Suri.

Eventually, Sebastian learned that Suri was upset that he had not seen her as important enough to establish a relationship with early on.

She watched as he built relationships all around her and left her out. She felt he was purposely snubbing her. Suri was upset, not because of something Sebastian had done or said, but because he had not said anything to her at all. Her efforts to undermine him were an immature way of showing her disappointment, but she wanted him to know that she could make things difficult for him. Sebastian overlooked her when he built his key stakeholder list and it cost him months later.

Deactivation method: Activate a 360-relationship compass and use it to help guide you to potential challenges and land mines.

Land Mine 5: Learning

Fail to grasp key information in any of the 5Cs: Customers, Collaborators, Capabilities, Competitors, or Conditions and you have effectively created learning land mines. Executives often miss the importance of certain Cs or diminish the importance of one or more. If you don't have a learning plan in place for each and every C, the likelihood of undetected land mines greatly increases.

If you don't know what you need to know or—worse yet—don't know what you don't know, then land mines will surely be plentiful. So what do you need to know? At the very least, you need to know critical information about each of the 5Cs, especially about the real value chain of your business. If you use our guidelines or your 5Cs analysis (see Appendix II), the information you gather will significantly diminish the risk of learning land mines.

Learning is essential. Being perceived as wanting to learn is almost as important as learning itself. You have heard it before: "Seek first to understand,"[1] "Don't come in with the answer,"[2] "Wisdom begins in wonder."[3] You hear it repeatedly in many different ways, because it is proven advice. Heed it. You need to learn and you'll want to be perceived as being hungry to learn.

Harold joined a company that was helping companies take advantage of favorable tax treatments for new technologies. He had done his homework well across most of the 5Cs. He liked the team. They liked him. He knew exactly how he could add value to the group and to its customers. What he had failed to learn about was that

---

[1]Covey, Steven, *The 7 Habits of Highly Effective People* (New York: Simon & Schuster, 1989).
[2]Watkins, Michael, *The First 90 Days* (Watertown, MA: Harvard Business School Press, 2003).
[3]Attributed to Socrates.

the government was about to change the law and take away the favorable tax treatments. So, a few months into the job, the company effectively got legislated out of business.

Deactivation method: Activate an ongoing learning campaign to thoroughly master the 5Cs.

Keep your learning sharp.

Land Mine 6: Delivery

In the end, it boils down to delivery. It's not what you do; it's the results you deliver. Strategies and plans always can work great on PowerPoint presentations, but they often fail to work when they meet reality. If you get everything else right but fail to deliver, you fail. If you deliver, the organization can tolerate many other faults. If you are leading a team, you cannot deliver if the team does not deliver. At the end of your first 100 days, the most dangerous land mine is failing to build a high-performing team fast enough to deliver the expected results in the expected time frame.

Steve was hired as the head of business development for a venture-backed technology company that had developed a cutting-edge digital rights management (DRM) software. Steve was excited about the opportunity because he knew that the technology was one of the best and the market was screaming for such a DRM product that was easy and reliable to use. Steve's main priority was to enter into long-term agreements with the major entertainment studios.

Steve made inroads with the studios quickly but he became frustrated by their notoriously slow movement. While keeping his eye on the studio business, he began to concentrate on other industries that required DRM technology and was able to secure a strong deal flow.

A year later Steve was fired after a meeting with the venture capital company. Although Steve was pleased with his inroads at the studios, he had not yet closed any deals with a major entertainment firm. He felt that the deal flow from other industries compensated, but he didn't understand that his up stakeholders thought he was concentrating 100 percent on studio business and felt that that business was far more valuable than the other industries that Steve had mined. He delivered, but he delivered off strategy.

Deactivation method: Identify clear and genuine winning deliverables and timetable. Validate with key stakeholders. Empower and execute with the team.

To be clear, this is about *real* delivery. It is not about manipu-
lating expectations to get the base low. It is not about picking the
wrong battles. It is not even about the process to get there. It is about
putting points on the board with real impact. Delivery comes in all
forms, but it is only valuable if it is what was ordered. It's easy. Know
what's expected. Validate what's expected. Deliver what's expected. Do
that, and you win!

Land Mine 7: Adjustment

You can do everything correctly to this point, but if you do not see or react
to the inevitable situational changes, then new land mines will certainly
be created. The act of planning and managing is not a static exercise.
You must be keenly aware of the fluid dynamics of your team's situation.
Missing the need to constantly survey the environment and adjust accordingly is just like a skipper setting sail for a destination and never adjusting
his sails for the ever-changing seas and weather conditions.

Things change and you and your team need to change when they
do. Sometimes you can get away with minor adjustments. Sometimes
a complete restart is required. The risk lies in not seeing the need
to change, not understanding how to change effectively, or in being
too slow to react to the changes you do see.

Tony was hired by Victor to run the operations of the division that Victor headed. Tony reported directly to Victor and soon
after joining, he realized that the division was significantly underperforming. Tony embraced the challenge and made great gains in
operational efficiencies in a short time; but while operations were
improving, other aspects of the division continued to falter. As a
result, Wendy, one of Victor's counterparts from a sister division
was promoted to head both divisions. So now, Tony was reporting to
Victor who was now reporting to Wendy. Tony thought that this move
represented no big change for him.

He was wrong. He was sure that Victor would represent his
work to Wendy and he had assumed that his style and approach
would be embraced because it was producing results. What he did
not know is that Wendy's division had been run under a completely
different operational style and her division's results were far stronger
than Victor's ever had been.

For Tony, the change was a sea change, which usually indicates
that a huge adjustment is also required. Tony missed that what had

happened was a sea change and therefore it never crossed his mind that a "huge adjustment" might be required. Any change in structure requires a relook at what is going on, if not a complete restart. Tony did not do that. He kept soldiering on, assuming that Victor would make his case to Wendy.

Two months later Victor and everyone he had brought in to work for him, including Tony, were fired.

Deactivation method: Monitor business conditions and results actively. Understand the causes of change. Replan and execute quickly.

Map and Avoid the Most Common Land Mines: Summary and Implications

There are seven deadly onboarding risks: Organization, Role, Personal, Relationship, Learning, Delivery, and Adjustment.

Almost every one of these land mines is created or reactivated by actions or inactions of the executive. So, at a basic level executives are in almost complete control of how many land mines they may create, reactivate, or detonate along the way.

Be aware that the mitigation of land mines begins far sooner than most executives think. Your land mine deactivation approach is important and must start early:

Phase 1: Before accepting the job (offer to acceptance). Uncover and manage Organization, Role, and Personal land mines before accepting the job. Chapter 4 will address this particular phase in greater, more systematic detail.

Phase 2: The Fuzzy Front End (acceptance to Day One). Learn what you need to know and use the 5Cs as your guideline. Learning early is essential. Be sure to jump-start your relationships as early as you can. Keep close attention to up, down, and across stakeholders. Be careful not to miss anyone who can have an impact on your career.

Phase 3: Day One and beyond (after Day One and always). Build a high-performing team to execute and deliver. Keep an eye on the landscape and adjust as needed.

Land mines will always exist but they are most easily hidden in the first 100 days. Know that you must always be mitigating all of these land mines well beyond your transition. In fact, you should always be doing it.

Inevitably, no matter how good of a deactivator you are, you will step on a land mine at some point. The goal is to avoid as many as you can and be in a position to react decisively when you detonate one. When a land mine rears its ugly head, keep yours and hit the restart button. Who needs bees?

QUESTIONS YOU SHOULD ASK YOURSELF

- Have I uncovered all the land mines?
- Do I understand those land mines' root causes and implications?
- How will I continue to mitigate land mines beyond my first 100 days?

CHAPTER 4

Do Your *Due Diligence* before You Accept the Job Offer

wish I'd read this chapter before I accepted that job!"

We hear that a lot.

In Chapter 3 we mapped out the seven deadly land mines with a view to sensitizing you to areas of potential danger and then presenting you with deactivation methods you can use to mitigate the risk. In this chapter we focus more particularly on Phase 1, because this ultimately brings up the question: Should I really take this job? To know the answer to the question, you need to make an informed assessment of the degree of risk.

So, for Phase 1, we exhort you to take a systematic approach to mitigating the three major potential land mines or risks that could derail your onboarding. Those are, as we discussed earlier, organizational risk, role risk, and personal risk. We suggest a process that will uncover and help you assess those risks. Finally, we suggest a framework for mitigating those risks once you've understood them better. You may want to follow our suggestions. Or, later you can send us an e-mail saying, "I wish I'd read this chapter before I accepted that job!" You won't be alone.

It is important to understand that a comprehensive risk assessment is a vital step in opening crucial communication channels that are likely to be mutually valuable down the road.

See relationship and learning land mines from Chapter 3. We have more structured thoughts on communication planning and practice later in the book.

How to Uncover Risk

So you have to do your due diligence. Almost nobody wants to do due diligence. Almost nobody likes to do due diligence. Almost nobody knows how to do due diligence well. It's as though people don't want to do anything to spoil the moment of getting a job offer and knowing that somebody else appreciates them. Ignorance can be bliss . . . until the things you didn't see, show up and conk you in the head.

You may wonder if due diligence is really necessary. Or you may be uncomfortable asking the tough questions that are required to uncover potential risks. Know that due diligence is absolutely essential and that it is not as painful or time-consuming as you may think. It is the same skill set that you've deployed when you've done situation analyses for business plans or hired people and done reference checks or bought cars or houses or picked a college or made decisions based on incomplete information. At the core, due diligence is an exercise in collecting and analyzing information from multiple sources to reduce the risk inherent in a decision. As with just about everything discussed in this book, a carefully thought-out and methodical approach will help. Without such an approach, you are leaving yourself open to significant risks.

We suggest three steps:

1. Decide what information to collect.
2. Identify (multiple) potential sources of information.
3. Gather and analyze the information.

We have combined gathering and analyzing because they are iterative. Your analysis will help you decide how much more information you need.

Three main questions drive your lines of investigation:

1. What is the organization's sustainable competitive advantage? (To get at organizational risk.)
2. Did anyone have concerns about this role; and, if so, what was done to mitigate them? (To get at role risk.)
3. What, specifically, about me, led the organization to offer me the job? (To get at personal risk.)

Decide What Information to Collect

To avoid trying to boil the ocean, you've got to focus your risk assessment on exploring the few most important areas. Before accepting a job, you must gather information in the following areas to answer three fundamental questions around organization, role, and personal risks. The Due Diligence Tool at the end of this chapter can help you keep track of the answers to these questions.

Organizational Risk

The main questions you are trying to answer here are:

- What is the organization's sustainable competitive advantage?
- Are there any risks with the current *Customer* base?
- Are there any risks with relationship with significant *Collaborators* of the organization?
- Does the organization have the *Capabilities* required for long-term success?
- Do *Competitors* pose significant risks to the viability of the organization?
- Are there any outside *Conditions* that will impact the viability of the organization?

When looking to mitigate organizational risk, be sure to assess risk elements across the 5Cs: Customers, Collaborators, Capabilities, Competitors, and Conditions. The good news is that you probably have a significant head start on understanding many of these or you wouldn't even have been considered for the job. But do not rely on what you think you know. Appendix II provides more detailed guidance for your 5Cs analysis. Go through the exercise and see what new things you can learn. In particular, you need to understand all these in the light of the specific job you've been offered. Here are some headlines about the 5Cs.

The 5Cs

Build an understanding of Customers, Collaborators, Capabilities, Competitors, and Conditions.

> **Customers**: First line, customer chain, end users, influencers
>
> **Collaborators**: Suppliers, allies, government/community leaders
>
> **Capabilities**: Human, operational, financial, technical, key assets
>
> **Competitors**: Direct, indirect, potential
>
> **Conditions**: Social/demographic, political/government/regulatory, economic, market

See Appendix II on situational assessment, for a more detailed explanation and useful worksheets including a SWOT (Strengths, Weaknesses, Opportunities, and Threats) analysis.

Role Risk

The main questions you are trying to answer here are:

- Did anyone have concerns about this role; and, if so, what was done to mitigate them?
- Why does the position exist? Why did they need to create it in the first place?
- What are the objectives and outcomes? What are you supposed to get done? By when is it supposed to be done?
- What will the impact be on the rest of the organization? What kind of interactions can you expect with key stakeholders?
- What are your specific responsibilities, including decision-making authority and direct reports?

To mitigate the first risk (internal concerns about the role), you should:

- Find the people who had concerns.
- Understand those concerns.
- Understand what has changed to make those concerns go away.
- Believe that those people will support the role (and you) going forward.

This may require some iterative conversations. Most likely, somebody had concerns. Almost certainly somebody internally wanted the job or part of the job. There is always somebody who wanted things realigned in a different way. You should find those people and understand their concerns. Then, you need to know if and how they were made to feel better. Knowing who is *not* onboard with your new role and why is often as important as knowing who is onboard (and why).

To mitigate the remaining risks and understand key elements about the role itself, you should ensure that the key stakeholders:

- Are aligned around the role's reason to exist.
- Understand and are in agreement with the objectives of the role.
- Understand the impact that the role will have on them and the organization.
- Are clear on the responsibilities of the role.
- Understand the interdependencies that the role requires.
- And their relevant constituents will have the elements of the new role communicated to them in an appropriately thorough way.

Personal Risk

The main questions you are trying to answer here are:

- What, specifically, about me, led the organization to offer me the job?
- Is this the company and role that can best capitalize on my strengths over time?
- Will I look forward to coming to work weeks, months, or years from now?
- Will I fit with the culture?

The goal is to find out if your strengths, motivation, and fit are a match for what is required to deliver the expected results. Knowing what you know, would you hire yourself for the job? If there are significant differences, probe and explore and keep the option of walking away open in your mind. Not taking a job due to lack of fit is usually one of the best career moves a leader can make.

We strongly believe that a strong "fit" match is essential for a leader's long-term success. You may have already noticed that theme coming up a few times already. If your research is indicating that there might not be a fit match, you should seriously consider walking away. We often see executives convincing themselves that they can "make themselves fit" but that approach rarely works.

Fit is so important that we suggest you spend as much time as needed to get clarity on whether it exists. In addition to the questions here, we encourage you to go back to the BRAVE exercise in Chapter 1 and use it as an overlay to what you have learned about the new role. If you honestly answered the BRAVE questions, those results alone will bring you a long way toward answering the role fit question.

If you still don't have an answer, we suggest that you flip forward to Chapter 5 for some clues as to how you can assess your new organization's culture. Pay particular attention to the BRAVE tool for assessing the organization's culture and the Be, Do, Say section. If you feel you can Be, Do, and Say along with the organization, than it's a good sign that there is a match. If you still don't know, something is just not right and we'd bet that you should walk away.

Identify Potential Sources of Information

Many successful and competent people are weak in this skill. First, know yourself on this point. If you are lost, is it really difficult for you to stop and ask for directions? If so, extend this impulse to your work situation. How good are you at getting information from third-party sources? Many people shut down what they consider *gossip* with the feeling that it is an inefficient use of time and is morally suspect. A lot of it is, to be sure, but the fact is that people like to talk about what matters to them and a lot of what they say is deeply informative about the organization. Even if you feel uneasy with malicious gossip, some clearheaded thinking about how information works in organizations can help you realize that there is virtuous gossip, or informal discussion, that is absolutely vital to your ability to understand your environment. In fact, these informal information networks will be vital to your ongoing success in your role. You will fail if you underestimate or disregard this fundamental truth.

So, you need to identify sources of information. You'll need scouts, seconds, and spies to help you. Scouts are people outside the company who can give you a view of what's going on inside the company. Seconds are people who want to help you succeed. Spies are people on the inside who can give you special insight into what's going on.

One of the advantages of information gathering is that it can be a good way to start to open mutually valuable communication channels for use down the road. This is where this starts to happen, and these are some of those people with whom who you want to have those open channels in the future.

If you cross the 5Cs with scouts, seconds, and spies, you can come up with a pretty good list of potential sources of information. The key word here is *potential*. You're not going to talk to everybody on the list. You're not going to gather every possible bit of information. You're going to start with the most important information sources and then iterate between gathering and analyzing until you've satisfied yourself with the answers to the three key questions.

With that in mind, Chart 4.1 provides a list of potential sources of information.

Be aware that the first valuable data you get from your information-gathering efforts may be the degree of comfort your new company shows about your search. If the company is open to your learning everything you can before you accept, that is a very good sign. If the company absolutely blocks you from learning anything, be careful. It says something about their commitment to mutual understanding.

Your information gathering should likely start by laying out your due diligence plan with the person(s) who offered you the job. Let them know what you want to learn and how you want to do it. Position this along the lines of your wanting to learn as much as you can before you accept because you're anticipating this being a long-term relationship and you want to make absolutely sure the fit is right.

Gather and Analyze the Information

Gathering information is an art, a skill honed with practice. Like all aspects of communication, some of us are better at it than others. You could identify all the right information to collect, line up all the right sources of information, and then fail miserably at getting what you need if you go about it in the wrong way. If you're lucky,

CHART 4.1   Potential Sources of Information for Uncovering Risks

Areas of Risk	Roles	Sources
Customers	Scouts	Customers and analysts who follow customers or the industry and can provide insight about the organization.
	Seconds	Internal and external mentors and coaches who know customers.
	Spies	People who call on customers from within your new organization.
Collaborators	Scouts	Suppliers, agencies, allies, and analysts who provide insight about the organization by following suppliers, agencies, and allies.
	Seconds	Internal and external mentors and coaches who know suppliers, agencies, and allies.
	Spies	People who work with suppliers and allies within your new organization.
Capabilities	Scouts	People inside the organization, former employees, and analysts following the organization or the industry who can provide insight about capabilities and how things work inside the organization.
	Seconds	Internal and external mentors and coaches who know the organization.
	Spies	People at multiple levels in the organization who can tell you the truth (especially good sources are future direct reports, peers you have not yet met, board members as appropriate, and other key players). People in similar positions in other organizations with the same ownership.
Competitors	Scouts	Customers, suppliers, agencies, allies, and analysts following the competition who can provide insight about competitors.
	Seconds	Internal and external mentors and coaches who know competitors.
	Spies	Be careful here. Even though you have not yet accepted a job with your new organization, the right thing to do is to start behaving as though you are a part of that organization with regard to spying on competitors. Don't do anything you wouldn't want blown up on the front page of the *Wall Street Journal* later.
Conditions	Scouts	Social, demographic, political, government, regulatory, economic experts, analysts, and journalists who cover these areas.
	Seconds	Internal and external mentors and coaches who understand general conditions.
	Spies	People at multiple levels in the organization who can tell you unvarnished truths about the impact of conditions on the organization (especially good sources are future direct reports, peers you have not yet met, board members as appropriate, and other key players).

all you need to do is ask and you shall receive. But, communication is rarely that simple or easy. Trust is the grease that lets communication work and conversely communication is what builds and sustains trust.

Especially when you're new, you need to create "trust effects" quickly and easily. Self-awareness will go a long way here. Are you good at helping people feel comfortable, and do they open up to you? If not, you need to work on this skill. If you are, you still should seek to get better at it as you move up the leadership ladder.

The quickest and most effective tip we can give is that a genuine concern about the organization's ability to succeed will start opening the doors of communication. That concern, coupled with a sensitivity and concern for the person you are seeking information from, will further open those doors. If you can portray both of those trust effects, people will want to help you. For many leaders, especially new leaders, the Achilles' heel is their own pride and aspiration. If you ask for help or information in a genuine way, people will give it to you and it will actually make them feel good doing so. This is especially true in the information-gathering phase, so take advantage of it and don't be afraid to ask for information or help. If you do it correctly, you will gather the information you need, you will make your sources feel good, and you will begin to develop trusting relationships.

What? So What? Now What?

You've gathered your information (what). You've analyzed it and thought about it (so what). Now what do you do? We suggest categorizing the risk as low, manageable, mission-crippling, or insurmountable and then taking appropriate action.

Low Level of Risk

Don't confuse this with a low level of risk found. If you've neglected to gather the required information and therefore have either not found risk, or classified it incorrectly as a low risk, then you deserve whatever pain comes your way. If you come away from this effort with the assessment that there is no risk, you probably did a lousy job in your information gathering or you are about to walk into a rare situation.

Why do we say that? Because there are always risks. That's why we are so keen on proper information gathering. If the risk isn't there now, it will show up later. But if the organization has a sustainable competitive advantage for now, and if key people are aligned around a common, clear definition of the role you're going to take, and if you would hire yourself for that role in this organization at this time, you should be in good shape at the start. Go on to Chapter 5. Do the rest of the things we suggest and enjoy the ride. Just keep your eyes open for the inevitable changes and their inherent risks.

Manageable Level of Risk

None of this is an exercise in eliminating risk. It is an exercise in identifying risk so you can manage it. If your efforts uncover a manageable level of risk, you should feel good for two reasons. First, you've found the risks even before you accepted the job. Second, you're confident you can manage them. This would include the following situations:

- The organization has a competitive advantage, but it's being threatened.
- The organization knows how to create a sustainable competitive advantage, but it hasn't locked it in yet.
- The role is clear, but not all are aligned.
- You don't exactly have the strengths that the organization thought you did, but you know how to compensate for that gap.

In these situations, go ahead and accept the job and manage these risks as you go.

Mission-Crippling Risk

This is where the fun stops. This is where you've uncovered something that is going to keep you from being successful unless you can change it. The critical judgment in this whole exercise is separating manageable risk from mission-crippling risk. By classifying something as manageable, you are saying that you can make things work. By classifying something as mission-crippling, you're saying that you cannot be successful with a change. So before you accept this role, you should be certain that you have the authority and can implement the necessary changes to resolve or mitigate this risk. If not, you should walk away.

If you have not yet accepted the job, you're in a strong negotiating position because you can choose to try to figure out a mitigation plan or walk away. No organization you'd ever want to be a part of wants to set you up for failure. If there's a mission-crippling risk, it is in everyone's best interest to resolve it.

Typical mission-critical risks include:

- Lack of resources required for you or the organization to achieve its objectives.
- Lack of clarity and alignment on your role and its responsibility and authority vis-à-vis others.
- Insufficient support from your team, your boss, or key stakeholders.
- Severe conditional changes without a plan to weather the storm.

A Broad-Based Lack of Fit

If you're already in the job and discover a mission-crippling risk, things are a little tougher, mostly because it's harder to walk away. This means you'll have a bias to classify things as manageable that may be mission-crippling. As painful as it may be over the short term, if you cannot succeed without something changing, devote the time and effort to get it changed before you try to move forward.

Insurmountable Barrier

An insurmountable barrier is a mission-crippling risk that cannot (or will not) be resolved. As painful as it is to find these, finding them before you accept the job is dramatically less painful than finding them later. If it feels insurmountable, it is. Listen to your intuition.

HOT TIP

Manageable versus mission-crippling risk: The difference between manageable and mission-crippling risk is a judgment call. Be confident in your own judgment. If you don't think the risk is manageable, it isn't. Change things as quickly as possible. Mitigate the risks or walk away.

The other land mines relationships, learning, delivery, and adjustment will be dealt with in later chapters. It's not that organization, role, and personal risks are any more important than these other land mines, it's that those three need to be addressed before accepting the job.

Due Diligence: Summary and Implications

The most opportune time to complete your due diligence is between the offer and acceptance phases. Waiting until later or ignoring this step can be devastating to your potential for success. During this step, you should be making sure that the job is right for you. Mitigate organization, role, and personal risks by answering the key questions outlined in this chapter.

In assessing these risks, three steps can help:

1. Decide what information to collect.

2. Identify potential sources of information: Scouts, Seconds, and Spies across Customers, Collaborators, Capabilities, Competitors, and Conditions.

3. Gather and analyze the information.

Then:

If you're facing:	You should:
A low level of risk	Do nothing out of the ordinary (but keep your eyes open for the inevitable changes to come).
Manageable risk	Manage it in the normal course of your job.
Mission-crippling risk	Resolve before accepting the job or mitigate before doing anything else if already in the job.
Insurmountable barriers	Walk away

QUESTIONS YOU SHOULD ASK YOURSELF

- Is this the right organization and role for me? Do I fit?
- Am I the right person for this organization and role at this point in my career?
- What is my information-gathering approach?
- What are the risks and how can I mitigate them?

TOOL 4.1

Risk Assessment Checklist*

Following are key questions to answer during due diligence to help mitigate risk.

Mitigate ORGANIZATIONAL RISK.

1. What is the organization's sustainable competitive advantage?

_____

_____

_____

_____

2. Are there any risks with the current Customer base?

_____

_____

_____

_____

3. Are there any risks with relationship with significant Collaborators of the organization?

_____

_____

_____

_____

(continued)

TOOL 4.1 (continued)

4. Does the organization have the Capabilities required for long-term success?

_____

_____

_____

_____

5. Do Competitors pose significant risks to the viability of the organization?

_____

_____

_____

_____

6. Are there any outside Conditions that will impact the viability of the organization?

_____

_____

_____

_____

Mitigate ROLE RISK.

1. Did anyone have concerns about this role and, if so, what was done to mitigate them?

_____

_____

_____

_____

2. Why does the position exist? Why did they need to create it in the first place?

_____

_____

_____

_____

TOOL 4.1   (continued)

3. What are the objectives and outcomes? What are you supposed to get done?

---

4. What will the impact be on the rest of the organization? What kind of interactions can you expect with key stakeholders?

---

5. What are your specific responsibilities, including decision-making authority and direct reports?

Mitigate PERSONAL RISK.

1. What, specifically, about me led the organization to offer me the job?

---

2. Is this the company and role that can best capitalize on my strengths over time?

(*continued*)

TOOL 4.1　(continued)

3. Will I look forward to coming to work three weeks, months, or years from now?

_____

_____

_____

_____

_____

4. Will I fit with the culture?

_____

_____

_____

_____

_____

Overall Risk Assessment

If You Are Facing	You Should
A low level of risk	Do nothing out of the ordinary (but keep your eyes open for inevitable changes).
Manageable risk	Manage it in the normal course of your job.
Mission-crippling risk	Resolve before accepting the job or mitigate before doing anything else, if you are already in the job.
Insurmountable barriers	Walk away.

PART III

TAKE CONTROL OF YOUR OWN START

CHAPTER 5

Choose the Right Approach for the Business Context and the Culture You Face

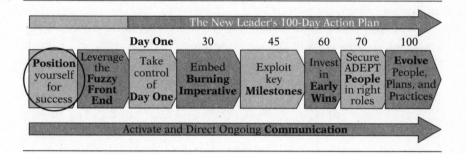

You have important choices to make before Day One. One choice that you must make in advance is how best to engage with the existing culture. Cultural engagement is extremely important in a successful transition; and it is essential that executives know what their cultural engagement plan will be before walking in the door for Day One. We have developed an ACES model, which lays out three cultural engagement choices: (1) Assimilate, (2) Converge and Evolve (either fast or slow), and (3) Shock. After the decision to take the job in the first place, this may be the most important decision you make in your first 100 days.

You must pick the right approach if you are to have any hope of a successful transition. It is difficult, if not impossible, to recover from a wrong cultural engagement choice. Making the right pick is dependent on the context you're walking into and the existing culture's readiness for change. We recommend that you think this through early, test your hypothesis during your Fuzzy Front End, and then relook at your choice just before Day One.

Don had had a successful career as a management consultant, venture capitalist, and most recently as a COO of a mortgage company that he helped turn around. So when he was hired as COO of a high-growth company to bring in better management controls, more process, and organizational focus he was looking forward to making an impact quickly.

On his arrival, Don quickly analyzed the various divisions of the company and gave each of them their marching orders. He rebuilt their processes, tightened up their controls, and sharpened their goals. He saw signs of early wins in some areas and, of course, resistance in others.

Don had a mandate from the CEO and board to build in a more comprehensive strategic long-term approach to running the business and he set about it as if he had been hired to save a failing company, something he had been hired to do a number of times in the past.

The problem was that no one, other than Don, considered it a failing company. Nor did anyone believe he—who was this guy anyway?—should "save" it. As a result, almost everything he had done had rubbed somebody the wrong way. But Don never noticed it. He felt the culture was ready and waiting for the right person to come and implement heroic change.

In fact, all they were looking for was a more mature and systematic approach to the way they were already doing business. Don didn't realize that he didn't have real buy-in from his key stakeholders—above, below, and laterally—and as a result they were determined to ignore or undermine the marching orders that Don had given. Four months after his arrival, the company posted its worst results ever. Don was history.

Don's mistake was that he had violated the organization's core cultural "code" of decision making and management. He had made a fundamental miscalculation of how to engage the organization, failed to build important alliances with key stakeholders, and misread the CEO's and board's directive. The key component that he failed to read was that the management, and especially the CEO, had coalesced around a culture of consensual decision making and tactical management that revolved entirely around slow and steady structural change that focused on routinely, even religiously, maintaining monthly results. He tried to shock the organization instead of converging and evolving.

Be careful about how you engage with the organization's existing business context and culture, carefully thinking through whether you should Assimilate, Converge and Evolve, or Shock it at the start. Make this choice early on because it will determine your approach to your Fuzzy Front End, Day One, and first 100 days.

The business context is a function of the business environment, organizational history, and recent business performance. If those items are solid and well positioned, there is not a context for change. However, if they are shaky or unsustainable, some degree of contextual change is required. The key question is: How significantly and how fast does the organization need to change given its current context?

An organization's culture underpins "The way we do things here" and is made up of Behaviors, Relationships, Attitudes, Values, and Environment—BRAVE. Somewhere between Attitudes and Values lies what is perhaps the most important dimension: the culture's readiness to change (see Figure 5.1).

Determine if you're a group entering a time of smooth sailing, unstable calm, ready to accelerate, or facing disaster:

FIGURE 5.1   Context and Culture

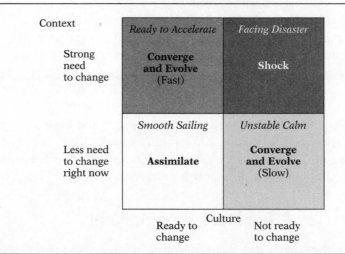

1. *Smooth sailing.* If the context *does not require* urgent changes and the culture is *ready* to change, Assimilate in. You can figure out the minor changes you need to make over time together with your team and your stakeholders.

2. *Unstable calm.* If the context *does not require* urgent changes and the culture is *not ready* to change, Converge and Evolve *slowly*. (Remember Don!) Changes will be required eventually. But you have time to become part of the organization and then start to develop the team so it is ready to change when it's required. Often a way to start this change is with a series of carefully thought-out minor shocks deployed over time.

3. *Ready to accelerate.* If the context *does require* significant changes and the culture is *ready* to change, Converge and Evolve *quickly*. You may be the catalyst that helps the organization wake up to the urgent need for change. Quickly is the word, too slow and failure will catch you.

4. *Facing disaster.* If the context *does require* significant changes now and the culture is *not ready* to change, then, well, you have a truly challenging situation. You must Shock the system for it to survive, you must do it immediately, and the going will be tough.

It is critical to get this right. Use the tools below to properly assess the context and culture—that is, to determine if it finds itself in smooth sailing, unstable calm, ready to accelerate or facing disaster—in terms of business environment, organizational history, and recent business performance.

If you've been following our book step-by-step you will have already performed a risk analysis for organizational risk, role risk, and personal risk using the 5Cs as directed in Chapter 4. You can use these same materials to ask the same set of questions from a slightly different perspective. Assuming that the risk level to *you* was acceptable (or tolerable?), you'll also need to assess where in the spectrum of needing versus being ready to change does the organization lie. The higher the organization risks you assessed earlier, the more the organization requires change. Also, a higher role risk often indicates that the organization is *not* ready for change.

Business Environment

We start then with the 5Cs—this time with a particular focus on how these affect the current context and culture of the organization.

Given how different this new line of inquiry is from the earlier one, it's probably a good idea literally to go through step-by-step, asking each time: What does this tell me about the context and the culture?

(See Appendix II on situational assessment, for a more detailed explanation and useful worksheets including a SWOT analysis.)

The 5Cs

Customers, Collaborators, Capabilities, Competitors, and Conditions all influence the context.

Customers: First line, customer chain, end users, influencers.

Collaborators: Suppliers, allies, government/community leaders.

Capabilities: Human, operational, financial, technical, key assets.

Competitors: Direct, indirect, potential.

Conditions: Social/demographic, political/government/regulatory, economic, market.

Be sure to look for trends within each C. Analyzing these will give you a picture of what's going on in the business environment and how that sets the context. Smooth sailing will be quite different from facing disaster.

Organizational History

Understanding how the organization got to its current state can give you invaluable insight into the roots of why people think and feel the way they think and feel and, from there, the organization's readiness or willingness to change. Go back as far as you can to understand things like the founder's intent, heroes along the way, and the stories and myths that people carry around with them. If Don had paid a little more attention to some of these myths rather than playing out his own, he might have learned something valuable.

Recent Business Performance

Dig below the obvious. Understand the components of the over-all numbers to get at what is working well and less well. We've seen a number of cases where overall revenue growth masked

underlying problems in one or more core business units or irre-
versible rises in cost. Get at absolute and relative results, recent
trends, and positive and negative drivers. This will give you a
sense of the kind of a time frame. "Choosing" Converge and
Evolve slowly when it should have been quickly (not to mention
immediate Shock) can be, well, fatal.

These calls can be tricky. If what's going on in the business environment and what's impacting recent business performance is going to have only a temporary impact, but more
fundamental drivers predict future stability or growth, you'll want to
downplay or manage through it. If what's going on will have an
enduring impact, you'll need to make more significant changes. In
Chapter 13 we discuss evolving (in response to changing circumstances at the 100-day mark) in greater detail. If this will be your
approach from the start, we recommend reading it carefully "ahead
of schedule" as it were.

Cultural Readiness for Change

Next, assess the organization's cultural readiness and ability to adapt
to changing circumstances. Readiness to change requires a combination of self-awareness, will, and skill. Members of the organization
must understand the need for change, want to change, and be able
to change. We don't need to revisit Newton's three laws of motion to
know that "change don't come easy." The best way to determine the
readiness and ability to change is to use the BRAVE tool. Again, we
(naturally) expect you to have followed our suggestion in Chapter 4
and performed a BRAVE analysis on the organization already. Review
this work, or better, do it again (it's amazing what happens when you
do these exercises a second, third, or fourth time!), this time from the
point of view of assessing cultural change. The BRAVE tool is Tool 5.2
at the end of the chapter.

An organization's culture underpins "The way we do things
here" and is made up of the same elements we discussed in Chapter 1
under the BRAVE Preferences tool. Just as an individual has preferences, so, too, does an organization. The BRAVE tool can be used to
give you a strong sense of the true culture underneath the surface or
stated culture. It is common in organizations, especially those facing
challenges, for the stated culture not to be practiced. The key

elements of BRAVE—Behaviors, Relationships, Attitudes, Values, and the Environment—help you understand the way people really do think and talk about things.

> **Behave**: How people act, make decisions, control the business, and so on.[1]
>
> **Relate**: How people communicate with others (including mode, manner, and frequency), engage in intellectual debate, manage conflict, assign credit and blame, and so on.[2]
>
> **Attitude**: How people feel about the organization's purpose, mission, vision, identify with the subgroup, group, organization as a whole, basis for power, and so on.
>
> **Values**: The underlying assumptions, beliefs, intentions, approach to learning, risk, time horizons, and so on.
>
> **Environment**: The work environment in terms of office space protocols, decor, and so on.

People generally learn about culture starting with the most superficial (what people say about their culture), but it is rooted in what people really are, their core assumptions and beliefs. "Be. Do. Say." This approach can be applied to people individually and to organizations on a whole. Let's take a deeper look at each element.

> **BE**: The underpinning of culture (and integrity) is what people really are, their core assumptions, beliefs, and intentions. These show up in Attitudes and Values.
>
> **DO**: These are behavioral, attitudinal, and communication norms that can be seen, felt, or heard such as signs and symbols like physical layouts, the way people dress, talk to each other, and interact with each other. These show up in Behaviors, Relationships, and the work Environment.

---

[1]This is described in Schein, Edgar. 1985. *Organizational Culture and Leadership*. San Francisco: Jossey-Bass.

[2]Dattner, Ben, *The Blame Game*, Free Press, 2011, p. 17.

SAY: What people say about their culture can be found in things like mission statements, creeds, and stories. As Edgar Schein points out, these get at the professed culture.[3]

For a culture to be sustainable, the BRAVE elements and what people say, do, and are must be in sync. It is easy to see when people's behaviors don't match their words. It is far more difficult to figure out when their words and behaviors match each other, but don't match underlying values. Yet, when that happens, those people's behaviors, relationships, and attitudes will change over time. Just as your own values, actions, and words need to line up, the same is true for those of an organization.

HOT TIP

Look well beyond the professed culture: It's not what people like about their preferences. It's just that value statements and creeds are often aspirational. You must understand the resting, steady state norms of behaviors, relationships, attitudes, values, and the work environment that people default to "when the boss is not around."

Political Advice for a New Leader: Strategies for Winning Hearts and Minds, and Dealing with Feet-Draggers and the Openly Hostile

The ACES model of Assimilate, Converge and Evolve (either fast or slow), or Shock should guide your overall approach to engaging with your new organization. At the same time, be mindful that each individual will have a different view of the situation and a different readiness for change. Inevitably you will have some people who support what you're trying to do, some who resist it, and some who will

---

[3]See Edgar Schein, *Organizational Culture and Leadership* (San Francisco: Jossey-Bass, 1985).

sit on the sidelines and watch for a while. We identify these three types of influencers as Contributors, Detractors, and Watchers:

Contributors: These are the people who share your vision, and have been working for change. Often they are new to the company or role so they see that there's more to gain by going forward with the new leaders than by holding on to the past.

Detractors: These are the people who are comfortable with the status quo, fear looking incompetent, perceive a threat to their values/power, fear negative consequences for their key allies, have been in the position for a long time so they have more to lose in giving up the current state than they have to gain in supporting a risky change.

Watchers: These are the people that are on the fence, generally the silent majority.

Note that people with high levels of current power have a bias to resist change because they have more to lose than to gain. It's not always the case, but it is true in enough situations for you to be particularly careful in dealing with these people.

Our overall prescription is to move every influencer one step in the right direction. Don't try to turn Detractors into Contributors in one fell swoop. In general, start by turning your Contributors into team leaders, then move the convincible Watchers into Contributors, and get the Detractors out of the way. Sound like a neat trick? It is, and here is a four-step process to get it done:

1. Identify each team member's *Power Interests*. Power interests can be institutional, personal, or resource-based.

   - *Institutional* power is based on formal position and reporting lines (who manages whom). This is generally hierarchical and often monarchical.

   - *Personal* power is based on relationships, persuasiveness, and expertise. This is different from institutional power because it comes from individuals' strengths as opposed to their formal position in the organization.

   - *Resource*-based power comes from control of information/ knowledge, funding, and people (both formal and informal), either in general or as it relates to one specific task.

2. Identify each team member's perceived balance of consequences.

   Whether they know it or not, or admit it or not, people have a perceived balance of consequences. A perceived balance of consequences is how people think that the impact of following the new leader versus the impact of resisting change will benefit or harm them. It comes down to a perceived balance of risks and rewards. The basic question you need to ask is: Do they think they will be better off over time supporting your new leadership or resisting it (probably passively)?

   After your thoughtful analysis, simply answer this question: Is their likelihood of change high or low? You should have a response for each key member.

3. Based on your answers to the questions above determine if each team member is likely a *Contributor, Detractor* or *Watcher* by properly positioning them in Figure 5.2.

4. Actively change the *Balance of Consequences*. Make it less risky and more rewarding to follow and at the same time more risky and less rewarding to resist.

   • Increase positive consequences of good behaviors.

   • Increase negative consequences of bad behaviors.

   • Decrease negative consequences of good behaviors.

   • Decrease positive consequences of bad behaviors.

FIGURE 5.2   Power and Change

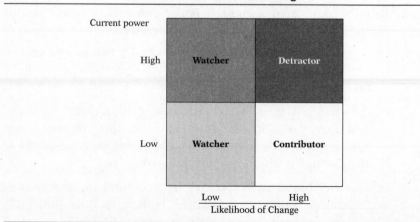

This last step is a big one, but it can be done. Many leaders can get through the first three steps but then they do nothing but hope that people will eventually move in the right direction (i.e., contributors into team leaders, the watchers into contributors, and the detractors out of the way). Hope will not get the job done. Here are three ways to grease the wheels to get the team moving in the right direction:

1. Change the balance of incentives including recognition and rewards to support the desired culture in light of the context.

2. Change the organization, and/or resource allocation to support the desired culture in light of the context.

3. Make sure that everyone understands the changed balance of consequences.
   - Drive your message.
   - Set up action-forcing events (milestones, regular meetings/updates, etc.).
   - Leverage small commitments into larger ones, most likely starting with Contributors who step up and then expanding to convincible Watchers.

Shocking the System

History is full of heroes who went out on a quest, paved the way for the future, and died. Think about the Greeks at Thermopylae, holding off a much larger force of Persians long enough to give the rest of Greece the belief that they could win in the end.

Like those dead heroes, leaders shocking a culture often come to a bad ending. Sometimes, that initial shock paves the way for their successor to complete the cultural transformation. So, even if the first transformational leader fails to change the organization, all may not be lost.

Successfully shocking a culture requires support. If you do it on your own, you're setting yourself up to be a dead hero. Shame on you if you try to shock a culture without support. You will fail. The people you bring in will be in trouble. The organization will lose time.

Instead:

- *Get a head start* by building a base of support for your plans with key constituencies in advance.

- *Manage your message* throughout the transition, knowing that some people will not want to hear what you have to say. In some cases, it may be better to let others deliver the bad news. Candidates could include your predecessor, established insiders who see things the way you do, people brought in on a temporary basis, or outside consultants.

- *Build the team* by identifying and cultivating early supporters. It's essential to get those early supporters to bring in a critical mass of convincible watchers before the detractors drag the watchers their way.

Choose the Right Approach for the Business Context and Culture You Face: Summary and Implications

Be careful about how you engage with the organization's existing business context and culture. The business context is a function of the business environment, organizational history, and recent business performance. This adds up to the relative urgency of change.

An organization's culture underpins "The way we do things here" and is made up of Behaviors, Relationships, Attitudes, Values, and the Environment (BRAVE), which all indicate the true culture and the readiness to change.

Crossing context and culture can help you decide whether to Assimilate, Converge and Evolve (fast or slow), or Shock. Then map contributors, detractors, and watchers so you can move each of them one step by altering their balance of consequences.

QUESTIONS YOU SHOULD ASK YOURSELF

- What is the organization's business context?
- How ready is the culture to change?
- Who are the likely contributors, detractors, watchers?

TOOL 5.1

Context Assessment Sheet*

___

Business Environment

CUSTOMERS	low satisfaction	.....|.....|.....|.....|.....|.....	highly satisfied
COLLABORATORS	combative	.....|.....|.....|.....|.....|.....	supportive
CAPABILITIES	lagging industry	.....|.....|.....|.....|.....|.....	leading industry
COMPETITORS	ahead of us	.....|.....|.....|.....|.....|.....	behind us
CONDITIONS	unfavorable	.....|.....|.....|.....|.....|.....	favorable

Organizational History

FOUNDER'S INTENT:

___
___
___

ORGANIZATIONAL HEROES:

___
___
___

GUIDING STORIES AND MYTHS:

___
___
___

(continued)

___

*Copyright © PrimeGenesis® LLC. To customize this document, download Tool 5.1 from www.onboardingtools.com. The document can then be opened, edited, and printed.

TOOL 5.1   (continued)

Recent Business Performance

ABSOLUTE AND RELATIVE RESULTS:

_____

_____

_____

_____

RECENT TRENDS:

_____

_____

_____

_____

POSITIVE DRIVERS:

_____

_____

_____

_____

NEGATIVE DRIVERS:

_____

_____

_____

_____

Need to change: LESS URGENT   ......|......|......|......|......|......   URGENT

_____

TOOL 5.2
Culture Assessment Sheet*

Behaviors

ACTIONS   more individual ......|......|......|......|......|...... more
                                                                team-based

DECISION   hierarchical   ......|......|......|......|......|...... collaborative
    MAKING

CONTROL   written/   ......|......|......|......|......|...... verbal/
    POINTS   systematic   face-to-face

OTHER NOTABLE PRACTICES _____

Relationships

COMMUNICATION formal   ......|......|......|......|......|...... informal

INTELLECTUAL   surface-level ......|......|......|......|......|...... in-depth
    DEBATE

CONFLICT   avoided/   ......|......|......|......|......|...... welcome/
                    destructive   constructive

OBSERVATIONS RE: USE OF CREDIT AND BLAME, AND SO ON

_____

Attitude

BUY-IN TO   not much   ......|......|......|......|......|...... fully
    PURPOSE   committed

IDENTITY   individualistic ......|......|......|......|......|...... one-team

POWER   controlled   ......|......|......|......|......|...... diffused

OTHER OBSERVATIONS _____

                                                            (*continued*)

_____

*Copyright © PrimeGenesis® LLC. To customize this document, download Tool 5.2
from www.onboardingtools.com. The document can then be opened, edited, and printed.

TOOL 5.2   (continued)

Values

LEARNING   directive   ......|......|......|......|......|...... collaborative/
                                                                            shared

RISK APPETITE   protect what ......|......|......|......|......|...... risk more/
                          is   gain more

TIME HORIZON   shorter term ......|......|......|......|......|..... longer-term,
                                                                            multiyear

UNDERLYING BELIEFS_____

Environment

OFFICE LAYOUT   walled   ......|......|......|......|......|...... open

OFFICE DECOR   formal   ......|......|......|......|......|...... relaxed

HOW PEOPLE DRESS formal   ......|......|......|......|......|...... casual

OTHER INSIGHTS:

Readiness for change   not ready ......|......|......|......|......|...... ready

---

TOOL 5.2b
BRAVE Culture Assessment

Behaviors

ACTIONS: Observe whether people have a bias to act more on their own as individuals or as a team.

DECISION MAKING: Observe whether bosses make decisions and tell subordinates what to do or tend toward more team-based collaborative co-creation and consultation.

CONTROL POINTS: Observe whether the business is managed in writing systemically or more verbally and face-to-face.

OTHER NOTABLE PRACTICES: Note any other notable practices that give you clues as to "The way things are done around here."

Relationships

COMMUNICATION: The scale here goes from more formal to less formal modes and manners.

INTELLECTUAL DEBATE: Look to the difference between surface-level, polite conversations and more in-depth probing, discussion, and debate.

CONFLICT: Determine if people have a bias to avoid conflict because it is destructive or welcome it as a constructive way to move ideas forward.

OBSERVATIONS RE: USE OF CREDIT AND BLAME, AND SO ON: Note other uses of credit and blame.

(continued)

Attitude

BUY-IN TO PURPOSE: Dig into the level of commitment to the organization's purpose.

IDENTITY: Probe where people fall on the scale of identifying with themselves, their subgroup, their group/division or the organization as a whole—one-team.

POWER: An organization's attitude to power is closely related to the way it makes decisions. Whether power is institutional, personal, or resource-based, figure out how tightly it is controlled or diffused.

OTHER OBSERVATIONS: Note other hints about people's attitudes.

Values

LEARNING: Determine if people are directed around what and how to learn or whether learning tends to be more collaborative and shared.

RISK APPETITE: Determine if the organization cares more about protecting what it has or gaining what it doesn't have, but could have—risking more to gain more.

TIME HORIZON: Determine whether the organization is more focused on shorter time frames or longer time frames.

UNDERLYING BELIEFS: Get at the beliefs and assumptions underlying the organization's choices.

TOOL 5.2b   (continued)

Environment

OFFICE LAYOUT: Note the bias to more formal walled offices versus more casual open spaces.

OFFICE DECOR: Note the formality of work spaces.

HOW PEOPLE DRESS: Note the formality versus casualness of the way people dress.

OTHER INSIGHTS: Note other clues from the environment.

Readiness for change:

This is the main question. Organizations with more dimensions on the right are generally more ready to change than organizations with more dimensions falling to the left of these scales.

TOOL 5.3
Context and Culture Map*

STRONG
NEED TO
CHANGE

NO NEED
TO CHANGE
RIGHT NOW

CULTURALLY   CULTURALLY
READY TO   NOT READY TO
CHANGE   CHANGE

TOOL 5.4

Contributor/Watcher Map*

HIGH LEVEL
OF CURRENT
POWER

LOW LEVEL
OF CURRENT
POWER

UNLIKELY   HIGH LIKELIHOOD
CURRENT STATUS   CURRENT STATUS
WILL CHANGE   WILL CHANGE

CHAPTER 6

Embrace and Leverage the
Fuzzy Front End before Day One

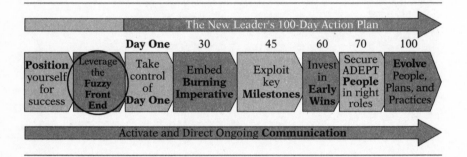

WARNING!

If you have already started your new role, this chapter may upset you. It is full of ideas for people to implement before they start. The best way to take charge, build your team, and get great results faster than anyone thought possible is to create time by starting earlier than anyone thought you would.

But even if you have already started your new role, read this chapter. If you have yet to tackle the things presented in this chapter, start doing them immediately. Read on to find out where you need to catch up. Truth is, many of the ideas in this chapter are useful throughout and well beyond Day One and your first 100 Days. There's a Fuzzy Front End to just about every major initiative.

Create Time, Take Action

Many leaders fall into the trap of thinking that leadership begins on Day One of a new job. Like it or not, a new leader's role begins as soon as that person is an acknowledged candidate for the job. Everything new leaders do and say and don't do and don't say will send powerful signals, starting well before they even walk in the door on Day One.

If you embrace this concept and do something about it, you increase your chances of success. This one idea can make or break a new leader's transition. New leaders who miss the opportunity to get a head start before the start often discover later that organizational and/or market momentum was working against them even before they showed up for their first full day at the office.

We refer to this bonus time between acceptance and start as the Fuzzy Front End. It often comes at the worst possible time, interfering with the last days of an old job, time earmarked for taking a vacation, catching up with personal errands postponed for too long, or just unwinding a little before the big day.

The good news is that, more often than not, the key elements of the Fuzzy Front End can be addressed in relatively short order. Even so, strive to stretch out the time between acceptance and your start date and get as much done as you can. Adding days before your official start is one of the best ways to get more done during your first 100 days. This is the only opportunity you'll ever have to create extra time and valuable white space before jumping into your new role.[1]

Choose the Right Day to Be Day One

One subtle way of creating time is to take control of the start date. You can:

- Negotiate a start date to allow for a longer Fuzzy Front End and therefore more time for helpful activities before Day One. Start dates are often arbitrarily set by organizations eager to get a new leader started sooner. Often their roles have been open for months, and another week or two will not make a difference.

---

[1]See Gladwell, Malcolm. 2005. *Blink*. Boston: Little, Brown.

Yes, in some instances they are set in stone; and if that's the case, then you'll have to rely on other ways to create time.

- Keep the identified start date, but agree with your boss and HR to announce the official start date as some later point in time (usually a week or two later). Your new organization and traditional thinking defines Day One as your first official day on the job, but this doesn't mean that you have to accept that same definition. By having a private Day One that only your boss knows about and a later public Day One that is made in the official announcement, you are in effect stretching your Fuzzy Front End.

Game Changing

At first, Nathaniel did not buy the concept that he should start before his official Day One. He wanted to take some time off so that he could show up at his new job rested and relaxed. Further, he felt uncomfortable asking for meetings before he was officially on the job. Eventually he agreed to try several of our suggested actions before Day One. Here is exactly what he wrote to us in an e-mail one week later:

> I've already reached out to some future colleagues and some agency counterparts just to introduce myself. You're right—it is game changing. Everyone has reacted with warmth and candor, and it will make the first few weeks far more effective and enjoyable.

Communication Matters in the Fuzzy Front End

We have discussed communication strategy throughout this book. It is at the core of your actions as a leader. Here, in the Fuzzy Front End, is a particularly critical moment for setting your communication strategy in motion. Many of your key first contacts will occur in this period. This is when your team, your colleagues, and the broader organization begin to shape a sense of you, your personal BRAVE (Behaviors, Relationships, Attitudes, Values, Environment), whether it seems to be in sync with theirs, and what is likely to happen in the coming weeks and months. It may be premature to have developed a formal communication plan, but you should already be on the path with a communication strategy.

Your Fuzzy Front End has several elements. It's a combination of very mundane things—managing your office setup—intermixed with some really crucial high-level work preparing how you are going to tackle your first day and beyond. It's fuzzy, but boy does it matter.

You should use your Fuzzy Front End to:

- Identify key stakeholders.
- Craft your message.
- Manage your office setup.
- Manage your personal/family setup.
- Conduct Fuzzy Front End meetings and phone calls.
- Deploy an information-gathering and learning plan.
- Plan your first 100 days, starting with making your final decision about how to approach the context and culture you face.

Identify Your Key Stakeholders

Step one is to identify your key stakeholders up, across, and down both in your organization and outside. Key stakeholders are those people who can have the most impact on your success in your new role. Many transitioning executives fail to think through this process or look in only one direction to find their key stakeholders. Others make the mistake of treating everyone as key stakeholders and end up trying to please all of them. Both of these approaches are doomed to fail.

Up stakeholders may include your boss, your indirect boss if there is a matrix organization, your boss's boss, the board of directors, your boss's assistant, or anyone else who resides further up in the organization.

Across stakeholders might include key allies, peers, partners, and even the person who wanted your job but didn't get it. The across stakeholders that executives often forget are key clients and customers (external and internal).

Down stakeholders usually include your direct reports and other critical support people who are essential to successful implementation of your team's goals. Your executive assistants should be high on this list, as they can often serve as an additional set of eyes and ears.

Former stakeholders. If you're getting promoted from within or making a lateral move, make sure to take into account your former stakeholders up, across, and down from your former position. (More on this in the appendices.)

Internal board. Your internal board is made up of the people you are going to treat differently because of their influence or impact regardless of their explicit roles in the hierarchy. You're going to treat them like board members, never surprising them in meetings and making sure that they get the chance to give you informal, off-the-record advice. Set the stage early and position yourself as an executive who is eager for and welcomes feedback from your internal board.

Candidates for your internal board are people who are going to have an undue influence on your boss or your ability to get things done. Think in terms of your key peers. Think in terms of people who have been with your boss for a long time, of people who seem to enjoy the mentor role, of people who are trusted advisors within the organization, or of key founders who may not have a significant role in the day-to-day operations, but still wield significant influence. Once you have identified them, develop individual relationships with them. If you are in the position to do so, play the same role for them, when appropriate.

Just figuring who all these people are can be a daunting task all its own. Fortunately, this is not something new executives have to do by themselves. Generally, there will be a human resource contact, a boss, or an internal mentor who can help to identify these people.

You can often get good hints about key stakeholders from the persons who previously held your role. If they were successful, they might provide some insight. If they were not successful, they probably missed or underserved a key stakeholder, so it is important to figure out who that was and why the person was underserved. Some key stakeholders will be apparent, yet others are often hidden from view, so do not be afraid to ask when you are building your list.

Although it is important to keep the key stakeholder list to a manageable size, if you are not sure initially whether someone is a key stakeholder, keep the person on the list until you can get an answer. Ignoring a key stakeholder can have a devastating impact on a new leader and might kill any chance of a successful transition. Similarly, if you are likely to confuse where stakeholders fit, have a bias to upgrade them. You are not going to get in much trouble treating an "across" like an "up" or a "down" like an "across." The opposite is not true.

Craft Your Message

Per what we said in Chapter 1, you'll need to clarify your thinking about your message before you start talking to any of your stakeholders. If you're not sure about your going in message at this point, stop and think it through. You don't have to stick with it. You can evolve it as you learn. But you must have a going in point of view if you're going to lead. Your message is the keystone of your communication. It should be enough to satisfy your key stakeholders' curiosity while optimizing your opportunities for learning.

Everything you do communicates, especially in the Fuzzy Front End and the first interactions with people after your official Day One. Again, everything you do and say and don't do and don't say sends powerful signals to everybody in the organization observing you and everyone in the organization who is in communication with those who observe you. Be, Do, Say. People and organizations intuitively shape a sense of your BRAVE orientation from the get go. Crafting and deploying your message has to do with the words you use (and don't) and the actions you take (and don't) and who you are. Be conscious of your choices. When we say everything, we really do mean everything communicates. If you have a clear foundation of your BRAVE orientation, much of this will come naturally. Nonetheless, think it through as an intentional message.

In Chapter 8 we discuss the importance of developing and launching ongoing communications to drive your actions in the first 100 days and beyond. Many of the elements of the plan will be finalized and launched after Day One, but there are key foundational elements that you will want to work out now, in the Fuzzy Front End. Make no mistake about it, your communication starts in the Fuzzy Front End (if not before) whether you realize it or not.

Everything that communicates works in both directions. This not only applies to everything you do, but to everything everyone else does as well. So throughout the Fuzzy Front End, be keenly aware that everything you experience is, or should be, communicating something to you as well. Hard data, relationships, inferences, your intuition, existing communication material, and what you might see "between the lines" all provide clues as to how you should begin to craft your message. Not only are you communicating your BRAVE to your new environment, you are absorbing theirs. Your future success lies in calibrating the contact between these carefully.

To get started on laying the foundation of your communication plan, you'll want to leverage all the information you have collected to this point to begin crafting your key communication points. Then, with those in hand, you can begin the initial seeding phase of your communication. Know that every interaction you have is an opportunity to seed your message. If you're not seeding the message you intend, what message are you unintentionally seeding?

Seed. You generally do not want to start with a big launch that catches everyone by surprise. Instead, you'll want to seed your message with an ever-growing set of stakeholders before your launch. The seeding process gives you an excellent opportunity to test your message and delivery, observe individual reactions and subsequently sharpen your message. Do not underestimate the power of seeding. In the Fuzzy Front End your seeding should be subtle and not aggressive. As you learn later in the chapter, the Fuzzy Front End is more about listening than it is about talking. So keep it subtle. Now is not the time to be planting earth-shattering messages.

If you follow the steps of our prototypical 100-day plan (not that anyone does exactly), this seeding phase runs from well before your start through to your Burning Imperative workshop.

In Chapter 8, we'll guide you through the steps of a communication campaign, but for now focus on laying the foundation of your communication plan by (1) understanding your audience, (2) leveraging all that you've learned thus far, (3) crafting your overarching message, and (4) begin testing and seeding your message throughout the Fuzzy Front End. Your choice comes down to controlling your message or to letting unintended messages control you. One approach sets you up for success and the other could sink you early on. We'll let you decide which approach is best.

HOT TIP

Get your message vaguely right immediately. Of course, you're not going to go preach your message on or before Day One. You're going to evolve it over time. But you can't avoid inadvertently sending the wrong message until you know the right message for you, for them, for the mission, and for the moment.

Manage Your Office Setup

The perfect office that is fully stocked and completely set up to your liking does not just suddenly appear. If you are lucky, you will have a place to call your own on your first day, but most likely it will not be tailored to fit your needs or your style. Leaders in new roles often underestimate the time, planning, and thinking required to get their office space right for what they need. Many leaders make one of two mistakes when setting up their space.

One mistake is to focus energy and attention in the first week on getting the office just right. What kind of message does that send? The other mistake is to work in a less than suitable environment for months while trying to find the time to get the office right. More often than not, that time never comes and as a result may hamper performance. Neither option is good. The alternative solution is to get this nonmission critical yet important job done during the Fuzzy Front End.

You will need a place to work. This will involve, at a minimum, some sort of desk and chair. But think beyond that. Do you want an office? Do you want your predecessor's office? Do you want that office to have chairs, tables, or couches? Think through how you like to work and what messages you want your workspace to communicate. Should it say, "I'm the boss? I am powerful. Enter at your own risk?" Or should it say, "Come on in, flop yourself down and tell me what's on your mind?" Big desks, with formal chairs facing them say the former. Couches and comfortable chairs around a coffee table say the latter.

There is no right answer to any of this. But part of preparing to lead is thinking through how you want to lead and the messages you want to send. Your physical workspace says a lot about you—even before people meet you.

Other physical things about your workspace to think about include cabinets, whiteboards, flip charts, audiovisual equipment, personal computer/laptop (with e-mail access), phones, cell phones, stationery, files, and business cards. Our checklists (Tools 6.1 to 6.4) at the end of this chapter will make it easier for you or an assistant to get the job done for you before Day One.

Get Your Space Right for Your Best Productivity

Gerry had worked at this new company for six weeks before, in an odd turn of events, his former company decided to exercise a noncompete clause that it had with Gerry that required him to resign from his new job and wait it out for 12 months. Luckily for Gerry, the second company wanted to hire him back after his noncompete expired.

We met Gerry a few weeks before he was about to reenter the second company and took him through the PrimeGenesis onboarding, or in his case, reboarding preparation. When we got to the point about personal setup, Gerry excitedly interrupted us.

"That's it!"

"That's what?"

"That's why I was so uncomfortable. I'd worked at my previous company for 23 years and never really thought about my office. Then I got here and felt uncomfortable. I always thought it was just the newness. But it's because I've always had a whiteboard in my office. I think on a whiteboard. My office here didn't have one."

The HR person sitting in promised to make sure there was a whiteboard in Gerry's office before he got there, so Gerry could "think"!

Everything Communicates . . . And Not Always as Intended

Robert had joined a high-tech consulting company as the general manager of delivery and operations. Robert was tasked with professionalizing the firm's project management approach, and he smartly figured out that his task would require a significant amount of interaction with his staff of talented but young project managers. He meticulously set up his office to be inviting and relaxing, knowing that the methodologies that he would be introducing would take awhile for his staff to understand and grow accustomed to. His office was set perfectly for the task, and the environment he envisioned was set almost immediately.

Robert decided to put some personal touches in his office, and he thought it would be fun if he hung one of his detailed model planes from the ceiling of his office. Several of his project managers had expressed an interest in aviation, and Robert was certain that this would foster an even more creative atmosphere.

The problem was that Robert chose to hang a World War II Nazi fighter plane. For Robert, that plane symbolized the beauty of efficient project management, but for others in the company it symbolized something quite different. Robert was genuinely shocked that some of his people had found the plane offensive. He immediately took it down and apologized, but the damage that it did to Robert was drastic and an excellent start was quickly derailed.

Everything communicates and not always what you may have intended. Be careful.

Address Technology and Security Issues Early On

As long as we are on the subject of personal setup, it is worthwhile to make sure someone is getting you access to the things that you will need. In today's technology-dominant, security-driven world, many things are essential yet we often forget their importance. Without these things, it is often impossible to get work done. Think about items such as identification cards, garage or elevator passes, computers, network access, voicemail, e-mail address, and any number of passwords. It is best if all these things are taken care of in the Fuzzy Front End.

Know What You Can Expect in Support

Also, it is worthwhile to identify who can help you get set up. Usually it is helpful if someone other than yourself notifies the key support staff that you will be requiring their assistance before Day One. If you have not already negotiated this up front, it is important to know whether you will have an assistant.

Do you want an assistant? What should be her skill set? Will you be sharing her with someone else? What is her current workload? Will you have an assigned mentor or HR representative to help you navigate the existing culture in the early days?

One of our most enlightened clients requires new senior leaders to come into the office two to three weeks before they start so they can physically see their space and pick things like layouts and color schemes. That is an organization that truly embraces the Fuzzy Front End!

Theresa went one-step further when she joined a different firm as CEO. She had her new administrative assistant meet her at the office on Saturday, nine days before her official Day One. At Theresa's request, her assistant brought a map of the office, with everyone's name on the spot where their work area was located with each department color-coded. Together, they walked around the office so Theresa could get a feel for the lay of the land. Finally, the two of them decided on how Theresa's office would be laid out and furnished and submitted the proper work orders to get it completed before Theresa started. On Day One, Theresa didn't have to ask anyone where anything was because she was fully able to navigate the office with ease.

Manage Your Personal and Family Setup

No matter how much you try, you cannot give the new job your best efforts until you get comfortable about your family's setup. Taking the time to figure out housing, schools, transportation, and the like is not a luxury. It is a business imperative. The more drastic the move, such as an international move, the more issues you'll need to solve. There is no better time to get this resolved than during the Fuzzy Front End. If you wait, all these decisions will distract you at a time when everyone is making those first and last impressions of your performance. The first 100 days are your most important test, and you can't afford to take your eye off the ball any more than is absolutely necessary. Executives often make the mistake of assuming that their significant other will take care of all the personal and family issues, but that is usually unrealistic. The more of these issues that you can get resolved before Day One the better.

Also, whether you admit it or not, having a settled place to come home to as you transition into a new role can make a significant difference in your ability to recharge at the end of the day and on weekends. Moving and starting a new job are two of the most stressful things that can happen to you and your family, so why not make sure that the two Day Ones (office and personal) do not start at the same time?

The checklists at the end of this chapter should help guide you through both your office and your personal setup. Don't underestimate the distraction that both of these tasks can cause and strive to address as much as possible in the Fuzzy Front End.

The main point about personal setup, both at home and in the office, is that you can get it in motion well before you actually show up. There will be enough other things to worry about in the early days of a complex transition that you do not want to be rummaging around for a computer, door key, or school for your children. Get those things settled well in advance.

Conduct Prestart Meetings and Phone Calls

Everything communicates. This includes whom you talk to, in what forum, and in what order. People will view the order in which you talk to people as a sign of their relative importance. Starting Day One, that order is indelible. The people you talk to early will feel valued. The people you talk to later will feel slighted. These early conversations can make a huge difference.

There is a physical limitation to how many people you can talk to on Day One or Week One, and so on. If the people you talk to on Day One feel valued, the people you talk to before Day One will feel even more valued. So be selective in the order in which you approach and talk to people. Before making your calls, think about what you might say or indicate to those folks holding a spot on your key stakeholder list. Be thoughtful, plan, and know that you are communicating even without saying a word.

The most important stakeholders are the ones who are going to be most critical to your surviving and thriving in the new role.

These might include:

- Your new boss.
- The most influential board members.
- Critical peers—especially ones who were candidates for your new job.
- Critical customers and clients.
- Critical direct reports—especially ones who were candidates for your new job or who are considered to be flight risks.

The impact you can make by reaching out to these critical stakeholders before you start is incalculable. Yet we are often surprised at how reluctant some executives are to set up those meetings. They often expect to encounter resistance, but rarely do. To make the process easier, here are some suggestions for starting a conversation.

"Hi Jack, I'm Jill. I'll be starting in two weeks as president. Stuart has told me that you're an absolutely critical part of the team. I didn't want to show up without getting a chance to meet you in advance."

"Bob . . . since you're such a valued customer of my new company, I can't imagine starting work without getting to know you first. I'll meet you anywhere in the world that's most convenient for you, anytime that's most convenient for you over the next month. I'd really like to have your perspective on what's going on before I start."

"Andrew . . . since you weren't on the board's search committee, we haven't met. But I'd like to spend some time with you before I start."

Leverage the Fuzzy Front End to Get Real Answers

Another reason to start communicating with key stakeholders early is that the answers you get to questions before you actually start will be different from the answers you get after you start. You are a different person before you start. You are not yet an employee or boss. You are just someone looking to make a connection and learn. The answers you get during the Fuzzy Front End almost always prove to be exceedingly valuable after Day One.

What You See as Possible Just Might Define You

You should have meetings with the most important key stakeholders up, across, and down as well as phone calls with other stakeholders, if at all possible. This is so important that we encourage you to expand your concept of possible. For some reason, executives often think meeting with the most important stakeholder is not possible if it involves taking a flight or crossing time zones. We've had executives fly halfway around the world for hour-long meetings, and we've had them meet key stakeholders on ski lifts, cruise ships, Little League baseball fields, and the hinterlands just to get those meetings done before Day One. Possible can encompass many arrangements if you are willing and creative.

There are times when Fuzzy Front End meetings may not be possible or a potential stakeholder may be unwilling, but it is still important to make a concerted effort to set them up. Just asking for the premeeting makes a favorable impact.

Prestart Conversations Have a Cascading Impact

Bill was joining a company as head of sales. Jairu, the previous, beloved, head of sales had switched over to head up client relations with the firm's largest customer. We were brought in to help Bill with his onboarding, but not until the Friday before he started. We talked to him between his son's Little League baseball games on Saturday and identified Jairu as someone Bill should reach out to if possible. He agreed, and he had what he thought was a nice, but not particularly important conversation with Jairu on Sunday.

The next day, Bill's Day One, six of his eight direct reports said that Jairu had called them the evening before. They each told Bill that Jairu had told them that he thought Bill was a "good guy" who would be an asset. Jairu could have made the transition difficult. Instead, Bill had turned him into a supporter—even before Day One.

Do Not Miss the Importance of New or Hidden Stakeholders

Stuart was joining a large bank to head up its Asian operations. He had met most of the key corporate headquarters stakeholders in Zurich before he accepted the job. We were talking to him about stakeholders and job responsibilities and discovered that Stuart's new company had just bought another, smaller bank located in Germany with several product lines that would fall under Stuart. Not surprisingly, as the transaction had just been completed, Stuart had never met anyone at the acquired bank.

At our suggestion, he got on a plane and spent two days at the acquired bank getting to know its key players before he actually started his job. The people he met were amazed that he came to visit them on his own time. Even if they were concerned about other people at the headquarters, they knew they were on Stuart's radar screen. Stuart learned later that his visit calmed anxieties at the acquired bank and put a temporary and eventually permanent halt to a planned mass exodus that, if it had occurred, would have directly impacted Stuart's success.

If They Can Have Early Influence, It Is Better to Meet Them Now

Ben had been offered a job as chief marketing officer of a fast-growing Internet company. He asked if he could meet some members of the board because they were playing an active role in the company.

"What if they don't like you? We've already made you an offer."

"If they don't like me, I want to know before I accept. I'd rather have you withdraw the offer than fire me later. Plus, by letting them weigh in now, they'll have some ownership over my entry. This will help me down the road."

So Ben met them. They did not withdraw the offer and things went well. By doing this, Ben eliminated a potential risk and sent a strong message to the board that he thought their buy-in was important.

Discover Problems Early On

Elliot was about to join a high-growth company as VP of marketing. In parallel to the search for the VP position, the CEO had met with two directors of marketing that he planned to hire to work on recently acquired product lines. Both of these new hires were positioned to report to Elliot.

At our suggestion, Elliot requested that he interview the two before they were extended offers. This turned out to be a good idea because Elliot was not impressed with either one. He went back to the CEO and explained the risks he saw in hiring the intended candidates. It came out that the CEO really had not been all that impressed with them either but was trying to get a team in place for Elliot before he started. Elliot convinced the CEO to extend the search to get better candidates to fill the roles. The CEO agreed and Elliot got rid of two significant problems even before he started.

HOT TIP

Meet with critical stakeholders before you start.

This one idea is worth a gazillion times whatever you paid for this book. Contacting key stakeholders before you start always makes a huge difference. It is a game changer.

Deploy an Information Gathering and Learning Plan

Now that you have your prestart conversations set, it is important to have an approach for those conversations. Make no mistake; these conversations are most successful when you are talking as little as possible and listening as attentively as possible. They are about building relationships, gathering information, and learning. Listen and observe.

In a wonderful TED (Technology, Education, Design) Talk, researcher/storyteller Brene Brown explains that making a connection with someone else requires us to let him or her really see us, leaving ourselves vulnerable to harm.[2] These early prestart conversations are your first best chance to let your guard down, be vulnerable, and make connections with your most important stakeholders by asking for their help in terms of their read on the situation, priorities, and, "How things are done around here."

---

[2] Brown, Brene, talk at TED, Houston, July 2010.

Because this is about relationships first, your first question is probably something along the lines of, "Tell me about yourself." You want to connect with your key stakeholders individually. You want to understand their personal wants and needs as well as their business issues. This may also be a good time to take your crafted message out for a test drive; but keep in mind this is not about you, so keep your message short and on point. Because you are here to build relationships and learn, it is not the time to tell your life story or to offer opinions on "How things should be done."

Structuring the conversations is useful. Come into these conversations with an open mind and actively listen to what your key stakeholders have to say. Doing so in a planned and thoughtful way is fundamental to maximizing the value of these conversations. We suggest breaking the conversations into learning, expectations, and implementation.

Learning

Under the learning part of your conversations, you should focus on two key areas: perceptions and strengths. Perceptions have to do with understanding each stakeholder's assessment of the situation at hand. Once you've learned a stakeholder's view of the situation, you also want to get their input in terms of the 5Cs described earlier: Customers, Collaborators, Capabilities, Competitors, and Conditions. Use each of these Cs as a guideline for your questions.

Different stakeholders will have different views of the same situation. Some will think things are going well. Some will look at upside opportunities for the future while others will tell you that things are not going well and need to be turned around quickly to prevent the impending disaster. This is not a search for the one truth. This is an exercise in understanding the different stakeholders' perceptions so that you can figure out how to work best with each of them.

The second part of the learning phase is the identification of strengths. It is useful to understand the different stakeholders' perceptions of what strengths exist in the organization and what strengths need to be developed for the organization to be even more successful. Feel free to ask these questions directly. The answers will provide valuable information about the organization and may offer some insight into your key stakeholder as well.

When you receive answers to your questions, ask for examples that might reinforce the answers. These examples will provide further depth to your understanding and will also enable you to quickly switch the "we" in your stories from being about your old company (which rubs everyone the wrong way) to being about your new company (which makes people feel like you're starting to fit in).

Expectations

Early on, it is important for you to develop an understanding of how your stakeholders view the priorities (high, low, and untouchables) of the situation. Just by learning what they consider a high or low priority will give you a valuable perspective on how to best interact with them and how their priorities may affect your ability to deliver against your own goals.

Stated priorities are not real until they have resources attached to them. So for you to determine your own and to decipher your key stakeholders' priorities, you should focus on finding out what resources (human, capital, or otherwise) are allocated to the most important and urgent priorities.

This is also an excellent time to figure out if there are any "untouchables." Untouchables are those things that may seem odd or do not have a natural fit with the larger goals of an organization or division, but might be pet projects or protect people that you should not touch. Most organizations have them; and they can be the third rail for executives who don't recognize them as untouchables. Identify them early and let them be.

The learning objectives of the conversations with your stakeholders will be different up, across, and down. Therefore, your questions will also be different for each group. With the "up," you're looking for direction. With the "across," you're looking to build mutual understanding. From the "down," you're looking to learn about their current reality and needs.

Throughout this process, your objective should be to understand. Ask questions, listen well, and remember, don't offer your opinion yet. At this point, you just don't know enough to offer an opinion, and most likely you cannot provide any reasonable direction to anybody. So don't try. Take the pressure off yourself and just ask and listen using the preceding frameworks.

Implementation of Communication

At this part of the conversation, you're looking to understand (1) how people communicate; (2) how decisions are made; and (3) what the control points are (what things are measured, tracked, reported, and how).

You need to understand stakeholders' communication preferences in terms of mode, manner, frequency, and disagreements.

Mode

Different people have different communication mode preferences. Is it e-mail, voicemail, in person, memos, or something else? Sending voicemail to e-mail people is as unproductive as sending e-mail to voicemail people. Communication is useless unless and until it has been received. Many executives mistakenly assume that everyone communicates the same way they do.

Charlie had two bosses. One boss prided himself on never reading his mail, but he checked his voicemail regularly. The other boss so detested voicemail that he had his assistant type out his voicemail messages and forward them to him via e-mail, which he read regularly. So, to accommodate the different communication preferences, Charlie would leave an update for his first boss via voicemail and would update his second boss with the exact same message, but would do so via e-mail.

Manner

Manner is similar to social behavior or style. In what way or style does the stakeholder like to receive his information? Two people might say they prefer face-to-face meetings. One might want you to stop by anytime, put your feet on the desk and share early ideas. The other might want you to make an appointment with his assistant at least two weeks in advance and make sure that all the key players have provided input into your PowerPoint deck before you share it with him. Each of these is a face-to-face meeting (mode), but their manner is very different.

Frequency

Shame on you if you wander in for your monthly update with your boss and she says, "Where have you been? I expect weekly updates." Shame on you if you come in for your third weekly update and your boss says, "Why are you here every week? You are a senior player. I hired you to run your operations. Come to me if there's a problem or update me monthly." Like the other elements of communication, frequency preferences will vary greatly, so ask in advance.

Disagreements

Different people prefer being disagreed with in different ways, ranging from:

- Never disagree with me.
- Challenge me one-on-one, but only in private.
- Challenge me in team meetings, but never let anyone outside "the family" know what you're thinking.
- Challenge me in any meetings, but gently.
- Gloves off, all the time, because public challenges communicate the culture we want.

Ask about this, but don't believe the initial answers you get. Initially, start at the top of the list and wait to see how your key stakeholders (and especially your boss), respond to disagreements and challenges from others before you start disagreeing with them or challenging them.

Decisions

Decisions can be made in a variety of ways, and it's important that a new executive understand how the key stakeholders like and expect to make decisions. Again, it comes down to asking. Chart 6.1 provides a helpful scale for understanding how decisions between you and another person can be made.

In general, you want to push things to Levels 2 and 4 (either you or your key stakeholder makes decisions with input from the other). Input is helpful whether it is veto rights, consultation, or information. Shared decisions have a nasty tendency not to be made by anyone. Avoid putting yourself in that scenario.

By the way, it is not good enough to think you know how this process should play out, or to assume that your stakeholders are on the same page with you on this. Make the effort to define the major decisions clearly and know how they will be made. Whether you make a decision that your boss thought was his or your direct report is making a decision that you felt was yours, it usually leads to uncomfortable circumstances at best and exploding land mines at worst.

CHART 6.1   Decisions

Type	Decision Process
1	I decide on my own
2	I decide with input from you
3	You and I decide together
4	You decide with my input
5	You decide on your own

How to Manage the Process with Stakeholders	
Up	You ask how major decisions are made
Across	You negotiate how major decisions are made
Down	You inform how major decisions are made

That's the easy part. The trickier, and perhaps equally important, part is understanding where decision power resides in the organization. The three key sources of power are the Deciders, the Influencers, and the Implementers. It is important to consider how they interact and how they impact the organization when you are establishing your decision-making process.

Deciders: The formal decision maker as described in the organizational chart. Makes decisions. Sets rules.

Influencers: People and things that influence the formal decision maker. This may include information, experts, trusted advisors, political access, staff/team support, tradition, reputation, and professional credibility.

Implementers: People who control resources required to implement decisions and impact the consequences of the decisions both inside and outside the organization.

Control Points

Different organizations use different metrics and processes for controlling what is really going on. You need to know what they are so you can track what is happening. What are the key measures of success along the way? How are they tracked? How often are they tracked? How are they reported? How can you get access to them? Meetings? Reports?

There are always metrics that are important, but are not formally captured or distributed. There are always additional key indicators that are used that you won't find out about early on. Keep an eye out for those shadow control points because often they turn out to be some of the best indicators around.

In addition to control points, there is a whole set of information you should have and review before you show up for Day One. These may include key documents, financials, customers, competitors, collaborators, current capabilities, market information, business environment, macro trends, share, distribution, pricing, merchandising, advertising, promotion, packaging, product, presence, public relations, operations, and key contacts.

Use Your Learning to Draft Your 100-Day Plan before Day One!

There is a lot to learn—the 5Cs analysis and the conversations format previously suggested are solid tools to guide you along the way, but they are not designed to be all-inclusive. Instead, think of this process as a starting point for your entry into your new role. If you follow the process to this point, you will have completed a reasonably in-depth dive into your new organization's people, plans, practices, and purpose.

It is important not so much to have learned everything before you show up, but to have a plan to learn in place. Your learning plan, like all plans, will evolve as you get more knowledgeable.

The knowledge gathered from your due diligence and your own self-study coupled with what you learn in your prestart conversations should enable you to begin to put things in context and help you figure out what you want to do on that first day, during that first week, and during those first 100 days. With this knowledge base, you can use Tool 6.1 at the end of this chapter to begin the outline of your 100-day plan. One of the most important choices you must make is how to approach the context and culture you face. So reconfirm that choice at the end of your Fuzzy Front End, just before you head into Day One.

Fuzzy Front End: Summary and Implications

During the Fuzzy Front End, you should:

- Identify key stakeholders.
- Craft your message.

- Manage your office setup.
- Manage your personal/family setup.
- Conduct prestart meetings and phone calls.
- Deploy an information-gathering and learning plan.
- Plan your first 100 days.
- Listen, listen, and listen.

The prestart meetings and phone calls are a great chance to jump-start relationships by opening yourself up and asking for help around learning, expectations, and implementation. You should do these tasks. The benefits are huge.

QUESTIONS YOU SHOULD ASK YOURSELF

- Do I have the time I need before I start? (If not, can I create it?)
- Have I optimized the time I've got?
- Should I consider a different start date?
- What am I communicating during my Fuzzy Front End?
- Do I understand my audience?
- Have I leveraged what I know to craft my message?
- Am I controlling my message?
- Am I comfortable with my before Day One objectives?
- Is my learning plan strong enough?
- What other resources can help with my office and family setup?

TOOL 6.1
100-Day Checklist*

STAKEHOLDERS

UP

_____

_____

ACROSS

_____

_____

DOWN

_____

_____

(FORMER**)

_____

_____

MESSAGE

PLATFORM FOR CHANGE

_____

_____

VISION

_____

_____

CALL TO ACTION

_____

_____

_____

TOOL 6.1   (continued)

FUZZY FRONT END

PERSONAL SETUP

_____

_____

JUMP START LEARNING

_____

_____

MEET LIVE IN ADVANCE

_____

_____

_____

PHONE IN ADVANCE

_____

_____

(ANNOUNCEMENT CASCADE**)

_____

_____

DAY ONE

_____

_____

_____

_____

_____

FIRST WEEK

_____

_____

_____

_____

_____

(continued)

** If promoted or moved from within

TOOL 6.1 (continued)

TACTICAL CAPACITY BUILDING BLOCKS

BURNING IMPERATIVE (BY DAY 30)

_____

_____

MILESTONES (BY DAY 45)

_____

_____

EARLY WINS PLANS (BY DAY 60)

_____

_____

TEAM ROLES (BY DAY 70)

_____

_____

COMMUNICATION STEPS

_____

_____

TOOL 6.1b
100-Day Checklist—Sample: New Company*

To help you understand how this plays out, this sample new leader kept a weekly journal through his Fuzzy Front End and first 100-days. You can find it at www.primegenesis.com/blog/category/new-leaders-journal.

STAKEHOLDERS

UP: JACK (BOSS), SUSAN (BOSS'S BOSS)

ACROSS: ANDREW (HEAD OF SALES), BARNEY (HEAD OF PRODUCT DEVELOPMENT), CHESLEY (CFO), GERALD (AD AGENCY), HAL (PR AGENCY)

DOWN: DAVID (BRAND X DIRECTOR), ELLEN (BRAND Y DIRECTOR), FAITH (MEDIA DIRECTOR)

(FORMER**)

MESSAGE: OUR TIME!

PLATFORM FOR CHANGE INITAL PUBLIC OFFERING HAS GIVEN US INCREMENTAL RESOURCES

VISION: MARKET LEADER IN OUR CATEGORIES

CALL TO ACTION: RESEARCH, DEVELOP, SELL, IMPLEMENT MARKETING INVESTMENT PLANS

FUZZY FRONT END

PERSONAL SETUP: GET FAMILY SETTLED IN RENTAL HOUSE, OFFICE, PHONE, COMPUTER, ETC.

JUMP START LEARNING: CONSUMER RESEARCH, CUSTOMER USAGE AND ATTITUDE, BASE PLANS

(continued)

TOOL 6.1b (continued)

MEET LIVE IN ADVANCE: DAVID, ELLEN, ANDREW, BARNEY

PHONE IN ADVANCE: GERALD, HAL, CHESLEY, FAITH

(ANNOUNCEMENT CASCADE**)

DAY ONE: (JUL 1) ORANGE JUICE WITH FULL TEAM, NEW MANAGER ASSIMILATION, IN-STORE VISITS

FIRST WEEK: REVIEW BASE PLANS, 1:1S WITH ALL MARKETING PEOPLE, AGENCY ORIENTATIONS

TACTICAL CAPACITY BUILDING BLOCKS

BURNING IMPERATIVE (BY DAY 30–JUL 31)—WORKSHOP WITH MARKETERS, AGENCIES, SALES, PDD

MILESTONES (BY DAY 45–AUG 15)—SET DAY II OF WORKSHOP

EARLY WINS PLANS (BY DAY 60–AUG 31)—TBD (LIKELY NEW ADVERTISING CAMPAIGN)

TEAM ROLES (BY DAY 70–SEP 10)—TBD (LIKELY SHIFTING RESOURCES INTO ADVERTISING)

COMMUNICATION STEPS—START INTERNAL BLOG, SHARE BASE PLANS WITH WHOLE ORG

** ASTERISKED SECTIONS ARE PRIMARILY FOR INTERNAL MOVES

TOOL 6.2
Stakeholder Map*

		NAME	POSITION	INTERACTION PLAN
UP	MANAGEMENT, BOARD			
ACROSS	KEY PEERS, INTERNAL ALLIES			
	CUSTOMERS, SUPPLIERS			
DOWN	DIRECT REPORTS			
	INDIRECT			
OTHER				

TOOL 6.3

Onboarding Conversation
Framework*

Key questions to ask during onboarding conversations (in addition to all the questions you would normally ask).

1. LEARNING

What is your read on the general SITUATION?

_____

_____

_____

_____

What STRENGTHS/CAPABILITIES are required?

_____

_____

_____

_____

Which STRENGTHS/CAPABILITIES exist now? Examples?

_____

_____

_____

_____

2. EXPECTATIONS

What do you see as key PRIORITIES? Lower priorities? Current UNTOUCHABLES?

_____

_____

_____

_____

*Copyright © PrimeGenesis® LLC. To customize this document, download Tool 6.3 from www.onboardingtools.com. The document can then be opened, edited, and printed.

TOOL 6.3 (continued)

What RESOURCES are available to invest against these priorities?

_____

_____

_____

_____

3. IMPLEMENTATION

Tell me about the CONTROL POINTS (metrics and process: meetings, reports)

_____

_____

_____

_____

Tell me about some of the key decisions we make. Who makes them? How?

Who	1. A on own	2. A w/B's input	3. Shared	4. B w/A's input	5. B on own

What is the best way to COMMUNICATE with you? (Mode/manner/frequency/disagreements?)

_____

_____

_____

_____

Relocation Checklist*

ASAP

- Get set up: create **move file**, post calendar, and so on.
- Choose a **moving company**. Get multiple bids and references.
- Research **schools** at destination. Public? Independent?
- Start to gather children's essential **records** in a secure folder that travels with you.
- Choose a **real estate agent** at destination.
- Make arrangements to sell or rent your **current home**.
- Make **travel** arrangements for family and pets.
- Research **temporary housing** options in case they become necessary.
- Look hard at your **possessions** for things to give away or sell.
- Start a log of **moving expenses** for employer or taxes.
- Start to gather information about resources in **destination city**.

ONE MONTH BEFORE MOVING DAY

- Fill out change of address forms (for IRS, subscriptions and bills, etc.).
- Obtain medical and dental records, x-rays and prescription histories.
- Set up a checking account and safe deposit box in your new city.
- Take inventory of your belongings before they are packed, ideally with pictures.
- Arrange for help on moving day, especially looking after children.

TWO WEEKS BEFORE MOVING DAY

- Confirm travel reservations.
- Clean rugs and clothing and have them wrapped for moving.

---

*Copyright © PrimeGenesis® LLC. To customize this document, download Tool 6.4 from www.onboardingtools.com. The document can then be opened, edited, and printed.

TOOL 6.4 (continued)

- Close bank accounts and have your funds wired to your new bank.

- Check with your insurance agent to ensure coverage through your homeowner's or renter's policy during the move.

- Give a close friend or relative your travel route and schedule.

ONE WEEK BEFORE MOVING DAY

- Switch utility services to new address.

- Prearrange for important services—such as a working phone.

- Collect valuables (important documents, jewelry, etc.) from safe-deposit boxes, and so on.

ON MOVE-OUT DAY

- Be sure valuables are secure and ready to go with you. Carry important documents, currency, and jewelry yourself, or use registered mail.

- If customary, have cash on hand to tip movers.

- Have water, drinks, and snacks available for movers in appropriate place.

ON MOVE-IN DAY

- Have camera on hand to record damages.

- Have people ready to (1) check in items, (2) direct items to right place.

- Have water, drinks, and snacks available for movers in appropriate place.

CHAPTER 7

Take Control of *Day One*

MAKE A POWERFUL FIRST IMPRESSION

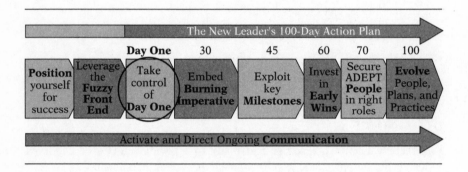

The New Leader's 100-Day Action Plan

| | | Day One | 30 | 45 | 60 | 70 | 100 |

Position yourself for success | Leverage the **Fuzzy Front End** | Take control of **Day One** | Embed **Burning Imperative** | Exploit key **Milestones** | Invest in **Early Wins** | Secure **ADEPT People** in right roles | **Evolve** People, Plans, and Practices

Activate and Direct Ongoing **Communication**

Our brains remember information "presented first and last, and have an inclination to forget the middle items."[1] People will remember vividly their first impressions of you and their last interaction with you. Although you can update their last interaction constantly, you are going to be stuck with those first impressions. So, be careful when choosing them. Be careful about the messages you send with your words, with your actions, with the order of your actions, with the signs and symbols you deploy. This is why Day One is the pivot point for onboarding. Many people who are important to your new role will form their first, indelible impression of you on this day. As with the Fuzzy Front End, we encourage you to reconnect with your own BRAVE preferences and orientation, and

---

[1]Hilton, Elizabeth, "Differences in Visual and Auditory Short-Term Memory," *Indiana University South Bend Journal*, 4 (2001).

think carefully about who you are encountering, and already starting to influence.

There is no one right way to do this, but there are many wrong ways to do this. It is all about the first impression received. Different people will have different impressions of the same thing depending on their perspective and filters. The problem is that prior to your first interactions with them, you can't understand their perspective and filters. So not only is there no one right answer, it will be difficult to figure out the best answer for your particular situation. This is another reason it is so valuable to get a jump start on relationships and learnings during the Fuzzy Front End. One of the powerful things about embracing the Fuzzy Front End is that it enables you to manage the initial impressions you make on those key people outside the noise of Day One. Managed well, it will also help you make better choices about your early days.

What Are You Going to Do on Day One?

That question, more than any other, stumps our clients. Most leaders fail to think about and plan Day One as thoroughly as it deserves. In fact, even those leaders who do a phenomenal job throughout the Fuzzy Front End find themselves stumbling on their first day. For some reason, leaders are often lulled into complacency when deciding what to do on Day One. Often they passively accept a schedule that someone else has planned out for them. Or they plan to do what seems to be the traditional Day One activities of meeting those people "around" their office or filling out the required forms, unpacking, and setting up their office.

Not you. What you say and do on Day One is going to inspire others. Not with cheesy motivational tactics, but through meaningful words and actions that create excitement about the things to come. Do not underestimate Day One's importance. Plan it with great care and make sure it communicates your message, exactly as you want it, to the people you most want to reach.

No two leaders' first days will ever be the same because the combination of variables in every situation begs for different Day One plans.

However, when planning your Day One, here are some general guidelines and principles to consider:

- *It is personal*. As a leader, you impact people's lives. These people will try hard to figure out you and your potential impact as soon as they can. They may even rush to judgment. Keep that in mind at all times.

- *Order counts.* Be circumspect about the order in which you meet with people and the timing of when you do what throughout Day One and your early days.

- *Messages matter.* Have a message per Chapter 1. Know what you are going to say and not say. Have a bias toward listening. Know that strong opinions, long-winded introductions and efforts to prove yourself immediately are rarely, if ever, good Day One tactics. People will be looking to form opinions early. Keep that in mind while deciding when to listen, when to share, what to ask, who to ask, and how you answer. When you speak, keep it brief, on point, and meaningful.

- *Location counts.* Think about where you will show up for work on Day One. Do not just show up at your designated office by default.

- *Signs and symbols count.* Be aware of all the ways in which you communicate, well beyond just words. Think BRAVE!

- *Timing counts.* Day One does not have to match the first day you get paid. Decide which day you want to communicate as Day One to facilitate other choices about order and location.

Tool 7.1 at the end of the chapter provides a convenient checklist for thinking about these things.

Make Careful Choices about Your Day One Plan

Using the preceding guidelines and your knowledge gained during your Fuzzy Front End, you should be well positioned to start planning how your Day One should take shape. Look for indications of what actions might be especially effective and powerful and work those items into your agenda, if possible.

Many of our clients have found value in holding early meetings with as many of the people in their reporting line as they can muster—in person, by videoconference, by teleconference, or the like. These early meetings give everyone a chance to lay their eyes on the new leader. It does not really matter what you say in this meeting because no one will remember much beyond hello unless you make a mistake. If they do remember, they'll probably remember the things you wish you'd never said. So, we advise new leaders to say: "Hello, nice to be here," and not much else at this point.

Another tool our clients have found valuable is the New Manager Assimilation Session. We have included a template for this at the end of this chapter (Tool 7.2). It is easy to deploy and is an effective tool that allows all the questions that everyone really wants to ask you to be brought forward in a forum where a critical mass can hear what you have to say, all at the same time. This prevents person A from filtering the message to person B who filters it again and so on. There will always be rumors. But this process, originally created by Lynn Ulrich of the Jarvis Institute and deployed in great depth at GE, goes a long way toward squelching most of the rumors, innuendos, and misinformation.

Don't Reinvent the Wheel: Start with Our Prototypical Agenda

Although no two executives' Day Ones are ever the same, it's often easier to start with a model.

You can use the following sample agenda as a guideline for crafting your own Day One:

- Early-morning meeting with your boss to reconfirm and update.
- Breakfast meeting with broad group to say hello (and not much more).
- One-on-one meetings as appropriate.
- New Manager's Assimilation (Tool 7.2) over lunch with direct reports and their direct reports.
- Afternoon activity/meetings/walkabout to reinforce key message.
- End-of-day cocktails/coffee/social for more informal greetings.
- Courtesy notes, voicemail for thank-you's or follow-up, where needed and appropriate.

We have used many variations of this agenda and ones that don't look anything like it. This format is a good fit for the straightforward, vanilla, most-likely scenarios. Use it as a guideline and if you alter it, know why you are deleting something and why you are adding something else.

Perhaps the best way to get across the power of a well-planned Day One is through examples of some of our clients' Day One experiences.

Leverage Your Agenda
as a Symbol of What's Important

Edgar was joining a company as CEO. He told us that the most important thing he had to do was to change the mind-set of the organization to become more customer focused.

"What are you doing Day One?"

"I've got this planned. I'm showing up, introducing myself to the team and launching five committees to tackle the five most important priorities."

"What happened to being more customer-focused?"

"What do you mean?"

"How does your planned Day One demonstrate that your main goal is to become more customer-focused?"

"I guess it doesn't."

"What does it say to your customers?"

"Well, nothing, they won't know about it."

"Exactly."

Edgar changed his plans. He did introduce himself to the team, but then explained, "I'm leaving now. Because, before I'm prepared to talk to any of you about anything, I want to get out and spend some time with our customers."

Edgar then proceeded to talk to customers . . . for the next 10 days. On the third day, the chairman called him to express his concern. "What are you doing traipsing around the country? I hired you to run the business."

"I can't do that until I've learned a little about our customers."

By the end of the first week, customers started calling the chairman to tell him how impressed they were with the new CEO. "He listens. We're excited about him."

Finally, Edgar came back into the company with a comprehensive understanding of what the customers wanted and knowledge of where his company was falling short. He shared that knowledge with his new team. He met with his direct reports one-on-one to get their perspective on the customers and then used all that information to craft a Burning Imperative around a customer-centric vision.

He took the message forward by calling the top 50 managers together to tell them how the new company Burning Imperative was crafted with their input as well as the customers. He explained how the Burning Imperative drove the priorities. He said, "Based on our jointly developed Burning Imperative, I'm happy to announce the formation of five committees to work on our top five priorities."

Although the top five priorities were essentially the same as he'd originally planned, they contained powerful nuances that better fit the customers' needs, and his initiative had significantly more credibility because he involved the customers and his staff. His early actions sent a strong communication about the customer's role in the company going forward.

Choose Location, Signs, and Symbols with Care: People Will Notice

Thomas lived in Singapore and joined a large bank as head of their Asia group. He was going to work out of the Singapore office for a few months and then move to their Asia headquarters in Tokyo.

"What are you going to do on Day One?"

"I thought I'd go into the office, do paperwork, and start meeting people."

"Which office?"

"Singapore."

"Why?"

"Because I'm here. Why not?"

"Because you're the head of Asia and the Asian headquarters is Tokyo. If you start in Singapore, you'll be perceived as the head of the Singapore branch until you show up in Tokyo in January."

So, instead of starting in Singapore and doing paperwork, Thomas and his wife flew up to Tokyo and took his direct reports and their spouses out to dinner the night before he started. Then, at 9:00 AM Tokyo time, Thomas arranged a videoconference and introduced himself to his 256 regional employees while standing in the middle of the Tokyo trading floor. Then he met with direct reports during the day. Finally, to cap off his first day, he took the bank's largest customer in Japan out for dinner.

Do you see how these actions represent a big difference in terms of location, signs, and symbols? Everything communicates. Showing up to do paperwork in Singapore sends a different message from showing up and taking charge at the headquarters.

Understand the Culture

Buell was moving into a company as head of marketing. We were on the phone with him and the company's director of human resources. Fresh from Thomas's success in Asia, we suggested a similar dinner with spouses for Buell's team. When the director of human resources explained that her company never did anything with spouses, Buell modified it to be dinner without spouses. Deploy different tools for different situations.

Don't Necessarily Go to Where Your Boss Is

Gerry was starting work in London, but most of his direct reports were in a newly acquired company in Birmingham. During his Fuzzy Front End, Gerry learned that the Birmingham folks were concerned that they would be required to move to London as a result of the merger. That wasn't the case, but Gerry realized that it could become a crippling fear. So he chose to spend Day One in Birmingham to ease people's fears and to address the rumors up front. He used the New Manager's Assimilation tool to extract the common fears of the Birmingham group and went in with a strong and credible message that their jobs and their location were safe. To further underscore the message, he set up an office that was complete and functional and hired a secretary at the Birmingham office before his Day One meetings.

On the other hand, Khalil was coming in to run three divisions of a different company. The largest was in Odessa near where he lived. The second largest was in Omaha, and the smallest was in Lawrence. His boss's office was in Lawrence. Khalil chose to spend Day One in Lawrence, attending his boss's staff meeting in the morning and then spending the afternoon with the division that reported to him. For Khalil, it was important to signal to his boss that, even though he was living in Odessa, he was going to be available to be part of his boss's team.

Leverage Your Message on Day One

Karen was coming into a bank to merge three divisions into one. "How are you going to get to know the people at each division?"

"I'm in luck. Each division manager has an off-site meeting already planned for my first two weeks. I'm going to use those as a chance to meet the key players and get to know them."

"Will that be the first time you meet them?"

"Sure, why not?"

"Because it doesn't match with your main objective or your message."

The problem was that Karen's individual divisional meetings perpetuated the culture of three different divisions as opposed to one combined group. Each of the divisions was in close proximity to each other, so to set a new course, Karen rented a theater for Day One and invited the entire staff of each division. Then she introduced herself to the entire staff of the new division at the same time. She followed this with a social event designed to get the three divisions mingling.

She eventually went to the old divisions' off-sites, but only after setting the stage for the new, combined division.

Be Present

Kim was coming into a new company as CEO. The old CEO and founder was going to stay on as chief innovation officer.

"Tell me about Day One."

"Oh, I'm all set. I am going to get in early to get my office set up. Then I am meeting with the old CEO from 9 to 11. Then meeting with the CFO from 11 to 12. After lunch I'm going to take care of some logistics and work on my messaging for my first official communication with the company.

"Are you a hermit?"

"What a silly question. Of course not."

"Well, if I work for you and if I haven't seen you by noon of your first day I'm pretty convinced you're either a hermit, or shy, or are not too concerned about 'us' since all you've done is lock yourself in your office."

Instead, Kim called a meeting of the company's top 100 managers at 8:30. She introduced herself, told everyone how glad she was to be there. She then had meetings with the old CEO and CFO. But, at this point, it was okay because she'd made an initial connection with her team.

Be Mindful of the Unintended Consequences

Arthur was moving from California to Montana to head up human resources at a large corporation. When asked what he was doing Day One he suggested he was going to spend it in a human resources orientation. We get this answer often from leaders, and we generally strongly suggest that they do otherwise. We love enlightened human resource leaders and we work with many of them, but the fact remains that most company's human resource orientations are not something a senior executive should be allocating his time to on Day One. Almost always, that is best done during the Fuzzy Front End. But since Arthur was the head of human resources, we did feel that there was some value in his experiencing the human resource orientation. We still suggested he redefine his approach to Day One.

In the end, Arthur pushed back his official Day One so that he could go up to Montana a week early. He used that created time to meet with most of his key stakeholders. On his official Day One, he sat through every minute of the HR orientation, allowing no interruptions. It sent a message to his team that human resources was indeed important; and it allowed him to have an informed opinion of the orientation process and how it needed to change.

At the end of his Day One, Arthur bumped into the CEO who asked him how things were going so far. So Arthur told him about the premeetings with peers and his teams as well as his positive impressions of the HR orientation. The CEO could not figure out how Arthur had gotten all that done in just one day.

Dress to Fit In

Jeb got invited to a meeting at a golf club on a Saturday morning. He was told that the dress was business casual. But he was in Japan, so he suspected that might mean something a little different. He wore gray flannels, a formal shirt and blazer. As it turned out, he was the only one not in a suit and tie.

Conversely, Dave joined a company where people dressed casually—jeans, shorts, flip-flops, T-shirts—even to the most formal meetings. He noticed the casual clothes during his Fuzzy Front End, but still decided to show up in a suit on Day One because he thought it signified leadership. After two months, he was still wearing a suit to work. No tie, but the suit trousers and jacket. People thought he was clinging to the armor of his old ways and that he was turned off or disapproving of the new culture. His direct reports even referred to him as "The Suit." He should have lost the suit before Day One.

Think carefully about Day One. Think about how you want to learn and communicate. Do you want to start by meeting your team in the office or off-site? Should your meetings be structured as one-on-ones or as a group? Do you want to start with a full-company meeting? Do you want to start with casual meetings? Do you want to start by telling them about you or learning about them? Do you want to start with the team or with customers? From the preceding examples, you can deduce that there is no one right answer. But just by asking yourself the questions and answering thoughtfully, you will be miles ahead of the game.

What Not to Do on Day One

You probably would not believe some of the stories that we could tell you about silly things leaders have done on Day One. Some actions have boggled our minds, but we'll leave the really bizarre stories aside and just list a few common mistakes on Day One. Please:

- Don't leave to look for an apartment or home.
- Don't show up late.
- Don't have lunch meetings with former colleagues.
- Don't consume alcohol at lunch.
- Don't tell anything but the mildest joke.
- Don't spend excessive time on the phone setting up logistics for your move.
- Don't dress inappropriately.
- Don't decorate your office.
- Don't say anything (good or bad) about your former company.
- Don't say anything negative about anybody in your new company.
- Don't use a PowerPoint presentation to introduce yourself.
- Don't schedule a doctor's appointment.
- Don't tell too much information about your personal life.
- Don't panic if things go awry.
- Don't mention that you read our book if you do any of the things that are on our don't do list.

HOT TIP

Manage Day One: Even though everything communicates, some communication is more important than others. How you spend Day One leaves an indelible impression. Control the agenda, even if you have to redefine which day is Day One.

Day One: Summary and Implications

At the start of a new role, everything is magnified. Thus it is critical to be particularly careful about everything you do and say and don't do and don't say—and what order you do or say them in.

QUESTIONS YOU SHOULD ASK YOURSELF

- What am I doing on Day One? What does it communicate?
- Am I being careful about all the ways I am communicating on Day One?
- Am I making the impression I want to make on the people I choose to make it on?
- What might people want to know and how will I answer the questions should I be asked?
- What is my message and does my Day One agenda support it?

TOOL 7.1

Day One Checklist*

OFFICIAL DAY ONE

_____

_____

EFFECTIVE DAY ONE

_____

_____

YOUR MESSAGE

_____

_____

YOUR ENTRY PLAN

INITIAL LARGE GROUP MEETINGS

_____

_____

INITIAL SMALL GROUP MEETINGS

_____

_____

NEW LEADER ASSIMILATION DATE?

_____

_____

OTHER INTERNAL STAKEHOLDER MEETINGS

_____

_____

EXTERNAL STAKEHOLDER MEETINGS

_____

_____

EXTERNAL STAKEHOLDER PHONE CALLS

_____

_____

New Manager's Assimilation Session*

The Ulrich/GE new manager assimilation process gets questions on the table and resolved immediately that would fester without it. This is a useful session to conduct in the first days or weeks of a new leadership role.

STEP 1: **Provide a brief introduction and an overview of the objectives of the session and review the process to all involved** (team and new manager).

STEP 2: **Team members, without the new leader present generate questions about:**

1. The new leader (you).
   (Questions may concern professional profile, or personal hopes, dreams, rumors, preconceptions, concerns, etc.)
2. The new leader as a team manager.
   (Questions may concern what the leader knows about the team, priorities, work style, norms, communication, rumors, etc.)
3. The new manager as a member of the broader organization.
   (Questions may concern what the leader knows about the organization, how they fit, priorities, assumptions, expectations, rumors, etc.)

The team should also answer the following questions that they'll present to the new leader:

1. What does the new manager need to know to be successful in their new role?
   What are the top three issues?
   What are the secrets to being effective?
   Are there any ideas for the new leader?
2. What significant issues need to be addressed immediately?
   Are there any quick fixes that are needed now?
   Are there any difficult areas of the business that the new leader should know about?
3. Other questions and ideas?
   What is the one question that you are afraid to ask?
   What additional messages do you have?

STEP 3: **New manager rejoins teams to answer questions, listen, and learn.**

---

*Copyright © PrimeGenesis® LLC. To customize this document, download Tool 7.2 from www.onboardingtools.com. The document can then be opened, edited, and printed.

CHAPTER 8

Motivate and Focus Your Team with Ongoing Communications (Including Social Media)

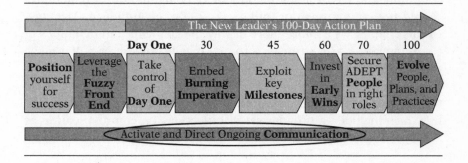

The New Leader's 100-Day Action Plan

| Day One | 30 | 45 | 60 | 70 | 100 |

Position yourself for success | Leverage the **Fuzzy Front End** | Take control of Day One | Embed **Burning Imperative** | Exploit key **Milestones** | Invest in **Early Wins** | Secure **ADEPT People** in right roles | **Evolve** People, Plans, and Practices

Activate and Direct Ongoing **Communication**

Everything communicates—everything you say and do, and everything you don't say and don't do. Furthermore, everything great leaders say and do flows directly from their own core values, beliefs, and intentions. Be, Say, Do. Once again, we go back to BRAVE as the foundation of your 100-Day Plan. We believe it's helpful to consider Say and Do as a communication plan. Leaders live their message. Their message lives beyond them. This is why your 100-day action plan can actually be seen as an element of your overall communication approach and why you need to think through this approach before you say or do anything. What's really important to you? What's important to the people you're communicating with? What do you want to communicate? How? When?

We started this book with a strong statement about what our fundamental, underlying concept is:

> Leadership is about inspiring and enabling others to do their absolute best together to realize a meaningful and rewarding shared purpose.

The starting point for your communication approach should be that shared purpose. Communication is about moving your target audience from its current reality toward a reality newly shaped by that purpose.

In Chapter 1 we introduced the underlying ethic of Be, Do, Say, communication as an integrated mode of being in the world, and presented the communication pillars: You, Target Audience, Message. In this chapter we explore more deeply the elements and dynamics of communication as a strategy, a tool, a means, and an end. We make this exploration useful and practical for you—a set of things you can plan and do—so we lay it out in a linear form, even though we know that in reality a communication is often not especially linear. (We have also included a broader set of reflections on communication as an appendix.)

Where to Start and What You Need to Know

Before launching your ongoing communication efforts after Day One, you'll need to address several key components, each of which is essential. As a foundation to your approach, per Chapter 1, and prior to launch you will want to do the following:

- Identify Your *Target Audience.*
- Craft an *Overarching Message.*
- Determine the *Key Communication Points.*

Identify Your Target Audience

As you'll recall from Chapter 1, you will want to start with your target audience. Now is the time to define your target both specifically and broadly, taking into account what you learned during your Fuzzy Front End. You will want to answer the following questions about your audience as you fill in the broader stakeholder map included as Tool 8.1:

- With whom are you communicating? Be as specific as you can and include everyone and all groups that can have an impact, including your target, their primary influencers, and other influencers. Answer each of the following questions with people in your entire target audience in mind.

- What are they currently thinking and doing? What's most important to them?
- What do they need to stop doing, keep doing, or change how they are doing it?
- What do they need to know to move them from their current state to the desired state?

Craft an Overarching Message

Now is the time to lock in the central message that works for you at this moment in time. This is the pivotal tool that connects you and your target and guides all your communication points. Make sure that your message and voice are in sync and that they are authentically yours. In this context, be sure to consider:

- Why do the audiences need to change?
- What will things look like after they change?
- What should they do next?
- When should they do it? How?

Determine Your Key Communication Points

As you start your new role, recall that you can't get audiences to do anything different unless they believe that there is a reason for them to do that (platform for change), they can picture themselves in a better place (vision), and they know what their part is (call to action). Your communication points flow from your message, the platform for change, the vision, and the call to action. Leverage what you learned in the Fuzzy Front End and in the context of your new role. You'll want to be clear on each of these three foundational points:

1. *Platform for change.* The things that will make your audiences realize that they need to do something different than what they have been doing.
2. *Vision.* Picture of a brighter future—that your audiences can picture themselves in.
3. *Call to action.* Actions the audiences can take to get there.

Once you have thought through these foundational points, distill them down to one driving message and your main communication points. Don't ever forget that your audience is always asking, "What does this mean for me?" Although the communication points that answer that question will certainly evolve over time, get clear on where you're starting.

With these points determined, the foundation of your communication approach is in place. Now you'll want to move to develop and implement the communication elements that flow from these. Five elements to consider are:

1. Signs and symbols
2. Media
3. Touch points
4. Stories
5. Monitor and adjust

Signs and Symbols

Often, signs and symbols can speak louder than words.

Some of the most compelling and telling signs and symbols (think: Be, Do, and Say) include:

- How time is allocated and spent.
- The chosen control point metrics and processes.
- The way decisions are made.
- How communication norms are set around mode, manner, frequency, or disagreements.
- If, how, and when evidence of changes in behaviors and attitudes are recognized.
- If, how, and when early wins are celebrated.
- If, how, and when appropriate role changes are made.
- If, how, and when those that won't make the change are addressed.
- Acquisitions or divestiture of companies, divisions, services, functions, and talent.

It is not uncommon for less experienced leaders to disdain "high ceremony" in favor of "just get it done." Although "getting it done" is certainly a crucial mind-set for a leader, the ceremonial—that is to say that the nonverbal component of communication is truly important—and underestimating it not only deprives you of a crucial tool, being unaware of it can get you into serious trouble.

Media

The media you select are the methods or vehicles you choose to deliver your message. It is more common to distribute your message through multiple media. The options have exploded in quantity and kind, each one with slightly different effects on how the message is perceived. What people often fail to consider is that the same medium will have different effects on different messages. There is great opportunity here, and great danger. The same message sent via a press release will be perceived differently than the exact same message sent via Twitter or Facebook. A creative or fun free-for-all with a listserv can be great for some communication efforts (a friendly rivalry) and disastrous for others (communicating a change in organizational structure). It's worth slowing down and thinking through the message, the medium, and your goals carefully.

Media will fall into one of three main types: Two-Way, Alternating, and One-Way:

Simultaneous two-way media

Face-to-face, one-on-one: This is still the most powerful medium. When it really matters, when the personal stakes are high, when you really need to deploy words, tone, and body language to their fullest potential, and when you really need to soak in the other's words, tone, and body language, this is the required medium. The ease and seeming intimacy of certain new media—e-mail, texts—can lead to a fateful error of judgment about not using face-to-face, one-on-one communication when it should be used. A recent campaign for smart phones spoofs on such errors when a woman breaks up with her romantic partner by texting him while he sits across the table from her. Almost no one ever regrets lifting his or her fingers off the keyboard, getting out of his or her office and walking over, driving over, or flying over to have a face-to-face, one-on-one conversation. Choosing this correctly is a matter of leadership.

Small group meetings: Particularly useful for pulling together diverse groups to solve problems, explore issues, and have multiplayer conversations.

Medium- and large-group meetings and events: Useful media for disseminating knowledge and answering some questions live.

Videoconferences: Good for two-way communication of words, tone, and body language without traveling.

Videochat: Good for two-way communication of words, tone, and some body language without traveling.

Phone: Good for two-way communication of words and tone (no body language), without traveling.

Alternating two-way media

These are one-way media that allow for *almost* instantaneous response. Indeed, they are so fast that they often feel like simultaneous two-way media:

Online chat: The closest thing to a written phone call. Although it does not directly communicate tone, the instant back-and-forth and emoticons come close to replicating a conversation.

Text messages: Good for very quick, targeted communication of words and small pictures and graphics. Lots of emoticons and back-and-forth as well.

One-way media

Mass and social media: Useful for disseminating information broadly, quickly.

Some examples:
- Facebook: Broad, general market, consumers.
- LinkedIn: Useful for business-to-business communication.
- Blogs: Broad dissemination of information and ideas.
- Twitter: Broad, quick dissemination of messages up to 140 characters.
- Network sites: Multiple uses, critical for most participants.
- News feeds: Broad dissemination of information.
- Bulletin boards: Dissemination of ideas to a subscribed group.
- Posters.
- Television, radio, print, and so on.

Video: Good for one-way communication of words, tone, and body language.

Voicemail: Good for one-way communication of words and tone.

FIGURE 8.1 Media by Interactivity and Appeal

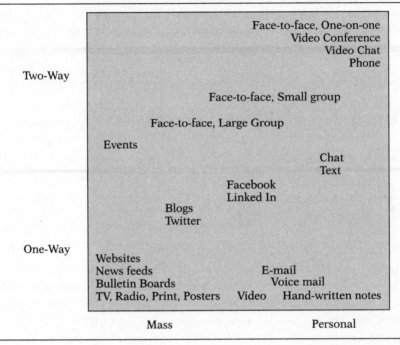

E-mail: Good for one-way communication of words. Given the amount of e-mail bouncing around the world these days, it's ever more important to make your subject lines work for you, use headlines, and ensure readability.

Hand-written notes: Once so ubiquitous, now so rare that they make a bigger impact when used.

In Figure 8.1 we have mapped media against their type and their personal versus mass appeal.

Touch Points

Touch points are points at which those "target audiences" are *touched* or reached by your message. Effective communication must include multiple touch points in multiple venues. You'll need to determine both the number of people you reach and the frequency in which you touch them. For the key individuals and groups that you want to touch, map out a series of media methods to do so, including face-to-face conversations, phone calls, videoconferences, notes, e-mail, and more general mass- and social media communications.

Stories

Storytelling is one of the most powerful communication tools. As Peter Guber describes in his article on "The Four Truths of the Storyteller,"[1] the most impactful stories embody:

- **Truth to the teller:** Sharing and conveying the deepest values with openness and candor.

- **Truth to the audiences:** Tapping into what's important and delivering on what is emotionally fulfilling for them.

- **Truth to the mission:** Driving toward a purpose that is meaningful and rewarding for the teller and for the audience.

- **Truth in the moment:** Fitting into the appropriate context for each audience, each time.

Take note that the core element is truth.

Keep in mind that the story itself is not enough. You must live the story. Your followers won't really believe what you show or say; they will believe only what you actually do. This is why storytelling is necessary, but not sufficient. This is why it's so important to live your message. You must model the attitudes and behaviors you want others to follow so that others can share your understanding and your dreams, feelings, and commitment.

Monitor and Adjust

You are going to lose control of the communication as soon as you start. People relate to others what they've heard, so they will apply their own filters and biases. Shame on you if you're not ready for that. Have a system in place to monitor how your message is translated. Be ready to capitalize on opportunities and head off issues. You can't prepare for any eventuality, so if you can think through a range of possible scenarios you're more likely to be able to use those contingency plans as a starting point for your response.[2] Know how you will measure the success of the message. Just getting it out to the audience does not mean that you've been successful. Know, too, how often you will measure if your message is being received as intended.

---

[1]Guber, Peter, "The Four Truths of the Storyteller," *Harvard Business Review*, January 2008.
[2]Shannon Stucky of Financial Dynamics explained the importance of this to me. As she and her colleagues in FD's Special Situations group work across the whole range of stakeholders, they've learned the importance of preparing in advance for the surprises that will have the most impact.

Think deeply about communication. This can lead you to some surprising places.

Peter was brought in to head the telemarketing group for an insurance products company. He had done his diligence and recognized that there were some severe risks the company faced. New competitors had sprung up and were seizing market share on their most successful products. Unlike his company, which was 80 percent field reps and 20 percent telemarketers, the competitors were all telemarketing. Peter's new company had a higher cost structure, but historically had a better closing ratio because of the face-to-face selling proposition.

To fend off the increased competition and declining market share, the previous head of telemarketing had implemented several much needed changes simultaneously: a new phone software system, a new structure for processing inbound versus outbound calls, and a new way of prioritizing call prospects. Although the changes were needed, the former manager failed to get buy-in from key stakeholders and compounded the problem by failing to adequately communicate the significance of the changes. As a result, he created a disaster rather than a cure and he was asked to leave.

Before his Day One, Peter had done comprehensive due diligence and leveraged his Fuzzy Front End to get a better sense of what was behind his predecessor's disastrous departure. During the process, he picked up that one of the well-intentioned new changes had unwittingly pitted the telemarketers against the field reps. Tempers were high. Both groups were blaming each other and were angry at senior management for allowing this to happen. Sales, profitability, and customer satisfaction had been plummeting and no one was taking the lead to solve the problem. Peter realized that he had to have a coherent message on Day One about how he and his team were going to work with the field reps, their managers, and their peers, to develop a truly shared purpose. He knew that it had to be a team effort oriented around a clearly articulated goal. It was going to take persistence and commitment to overcome frayed nerves and to get both sides to bury the hatchet and really start working as a team again.

Peter's message on Day One was:

> As a unified team we are going to immediately focus on increasing high-quality leads and assure an excellent hand-off with genuine responsiveness going back and forth between the teams to increase sales, profitability, and customer satisfaction.

Peter then set about deploying a multipoint communication plan—most of which he had developed during his Fuzzy Front End. He deployed standard but rock-solid messaging actions:

- One-on-one meetings with key stakeholders.
- Special interteam calls.
- Company-wide e-mail about the competitive challenge and the response.
- A leaders group to review progress and report on it.

He then deployed less traditional elements, which were already in place with the new system, but had never even been rolled out. He felt that this was a good way to demonstrate the many benefits that the new system had yet to offer. Specifically he:

- Leveraged the website to attract customers and better channel leads.
- Targeted prospects via e-mail: This had only been done in a haphazard way before, but Peter launched a comprehensive campaign and used it to get the message out about the face-to-face advantage his company offered.
- Kept the team abreast of market news about major industry events through the website, the e-mail, the callers, and the supporting materials for the field reps.
- Launched a new caller software system that allowed the field reps to actually hear recorded conversations with the prospects, which helped them develop a better understanding of the telemarketer's challenges and enabled them to be better positioned to speak with prospects.
- Integrated e-mail into the existing customer relationship management (CRM) system, which allowed for a much more efficient and natural way of communicating between the two groups.
- Activated an instant messaging system between the telemarketers and the field reps that turned out to be a game changer as it allowed for almost instant responsiveness and created a feeling of camaraderie between the two groups.

He simultaneously seeded his campaign with key leaders in both groups by way of the "leaders group." He took his time with each group, meeting individually with members and then with the whole group several times to break down the mistrust. With his team, Peter co-created a Burning Imperative that focused on achieving two benchmarks: a historic rate of high-quality leads and closed deals in a record time frame. He leveraged a network of media to get the Burning Imperative out to all the key stakeholders. Then he created a public scorecard for results and celebrated "early adopter" teams with strong results via congratulatory e-mail and a company-sponsored dinner. To keep up the momentum and energy, he encouraged "chatter" about the results and other ways to improve.

In short order, the two teams rallied around a common goal. What had been two demoralized groups of people showing up for work turned into one fiery team with the will to win, with results that matched the will. They reached both benchmarks 30 days early.

HOT TIP

Think in terms of a network of communication: Discover your core message. Then use that to guide key communication points in an iterative set of concurrent conversations across a network of multiple stakeholders and a wide variety of media all built on a foundation of trustworthy authenticity. Effective communication is hard work. But it will be one of the most important and most enduring things you do.

A Logical, Sequential Approach to a Communication Plan

Now that you understand the foundations and the secondary elements, you're probably wondering where to start. Our title to this section might be a bit misleading. Although it would be nice to have a communication plan that is entirely logical, sequential, and entirely manageable, the truth is that your network of communications will be a living network full of constant feedback, interactions, and adjustments. At times you may feel like you're supervising grade school recess instead of conducting the Berlin Philharmonic. That's okay. That's the world we now live in. Media savvy means media effective. Media effective means business effective. As companies too numerous to count can tell you, missteps in media can be very, very costly.

Manage your communication plan as an iterative set of concurrent conversations around a set of topics that you propose and guide. We want you to shape it as best you can, but know that in most cases some element of your communication network will always be taking on a direction of its own, including ones you didn't anticipate or possibly may not like. You need to be acutely aware of how different media strategies get different results. If you really aren't interested in people airing their opinions about the newly announced merger, don't invite it. If you feel that you have a culture that can embrace this and can convert it to a positive energy-building activity, then you might want to consider it.

That being said, you do have to start somewhere, and we think it's useful to map out a sequence of communication actions, knowing that you may want to, or have to, adapt to a communication process that is not linear.

These basic steps of a communication campaign can help you keep a calendar of actions in mind:

Plan by taking the pieces we discussed earlier, including both the foundational and the secondary elements (the overarching message, key communication points, signs and symbols, media and touch points, etc.) and then planning how to deploy them over the next steps.

Seed the message before you start on Day One and throughout your early days.

Launch by leveraging work on the Burning Imperative as appropriate.

Roll out by leveraging Milestones and celebrating Early Wins.

Reinforce when doubters inevitably raise their heads—by implementing your Role Sort.

Institutionalize by embedding key routines and processes.

Graphically a campaign looks like Figure 8.2.

Plan

Your plan is the sum of the elements we discussed earlier, plus the elements detailed below.

FIGURE 8.2   Communication Campaign

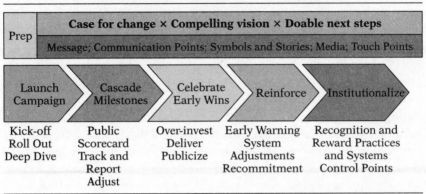

Seed

You generally do not want to start with a big launch that catches everyone by surprise. Instead, seed your message with an ever-growing set of stakeholders before your launch. The seeding process gives you an excellent opportunity to test your message and delivery, observe individual reactions, and subsequently sharpen your message. Do not underestimate the power of seeding. If you follow the steps of our prototypical 100-day plan (not that anyone does exactly), this seeding phase runs from well before your start right through to your Burning Imperative workshop.

Seed Your Message—Even If You Do Not Actually Say the Words

Deborah had grown up in her firm over the past two decades. When the head of the 5,000-person manufacturing organization was recruited away seven months earlier, she had been named interim head. Now, after a thorough internal and external search, the CEO and board had just named her to the job on a permanent basis. Her plan was to spend her first two months just listening and learning. She didn't want to come out with any formal pronouncements, visions, or the like. She wanted everyone to think she was open to new ideas and new ways of doing things—especially since she became an insider.

The trouble with that approach would be its unintended consequence of making some people think that she was randomly fishing without a clue, or, worse, was simply indecisive. She had just been named as one of the top five officers of the firm. People looked to her for leadership and direction. When she spoke, people thought she was speaking for the CEO and board.

A friendly ally from a surprising corner—the international sales group—took her aside at a meeting. Fortunately, Deborah listened to the feedback. So, she modified her intended approach. She thought things through and crafted a first, tentative, hypothetical message to help focus her first two months of conversations. She still didn't come out with any formal pronouncements, visions, or the like, but her message guided her choice of what people to talk to in what order, what questions to ask, and what hints to drop. Instead of turning her mind into a blank slate, she used those two months to test and seed her message.

Deborah's company had been a star performer based on its leading-edge manufacturing technologies. Deborah knew that the company had to continue to invest in the technologies to stay on that leading edge. So her going-in mantra was "Top Tech."

With that in mind, she started her learning tour by visiting the organization's technology-innovation centers and meeting with its Top-Tech performers. She probed them about what had made the company successful so far and what resources they'd need to continue to be rated Top Tech. She visited the company's key outside partners on the technology side and asked them the same questions. She visited customers and asked them about their future needs and how the company's Top Tech approach could help them over time.

Then she pulled her direct reports together to craft a shared Burning Imperative, starting the day by sharing what she'd learned on her Top Tech tour. Then, they cascaded that shared Top Tech Burning Imperative down to the next layer of management to craft a set of plans to keep the company top in tech.

Then, and only then, at the end of her first two months, did Deborah send a note to the 5,000 people who talked about all the great things they had done on the technology front to give the company a competitive advantage in manufacturing and how the top management team in manufacturing was committed to investing in them to ensure that the company stayed at the leading edge of technology-based manufacturing.

Launch

Launches can be big, subtle, or somewhere in between, and the style of the launch should match what you and your team are comfortable with.

You need to be in genuine agreement with the method of launch, or it will show. It also needs to be in keeping with the culture of the organization, unless you are trying to shock the existing culture.

The way you launch the campaign could be one of its most powerful signs and symbols. Look at the presidential party conventions. For the most part these days, conventions are shows. But convention planners know that everything communicates and they are careful about who speaks when, saying what, against what backdrop. You should do no less.

Many of the people we work with use the Burning Imperative workshop to transition from seed phase to launch phase. They use the workshop to get their core team aligned around the Burning Imperative and then use it as the basis of their communication campaign launch.

Whether you use that as the point of inflection, you will likely want to kick off the full-blown campaign with some sort of launch and follow that up with some sort of broader roll out—either through subgroup meetings or mass communication.

Your follow-up to the launch can include:

- Meetings or calls with key individuals.
- Subteam workshops/meetings to gain buy-in.
- Regrouping with the core team to gather input and adjust to what you learn as appropriate and practical.
- "All-hands" meetings, videos, or calls.
- "All-hands" e-mail confirming the direction.
- Deep-dive meetings with selected individuals to drive the message.

Cascade Milestones

However you choose to do it, launching is a major step. But you've just begun. Now you have to make it real by proving that you are going to deliver those achievable next steps. This is where you will likely want to deploy some sort of public scorecard where everyone can see results against key milestones.

Make sure that you are clear on what you are going to track. Make sure that you actually do track it and report it. Make sure that you're driving your key communication points at every touch point having to do with milestones: with your core team, their direct reports and deep-dive meetings throughout the organization. Then, adjust what is going on to drive the milestones that are on track even faster and get caught up on the ones that are falling behind.

Repeat the Message

In this effort, repetition is not just good, it's essential. We'll say it again—repetition is not just good, it's essential. In other words, you're going to have to create different ways and times to repeat the same message over and over again. You do that with a combination of Be, Do, Say. You'll get bored with your own message well before the critical mass has internalized it, but don't shy away from repeating it. Do not ever let your boredom show—make sure that your energy and excitement levels are "felt" about the message. When you're done, do it again, fitting it into the right context for each audience each time.

Celebrate Early Wins

Somewhere along the way, you will have identified an early win for your first six months. As part of this campaign, you will have overinvested to deliver that win. When it is complete, celebrate it, and celebrate it publicly. This is all about giving the team confidence in itself. So invest your time to make the team members feel great.

Reinforce

There is going to be a crisis of confidence at some point. At that point the team will question whether you're really serious about these changes and whether the changes you are making are going to stick. Jeannie Daniel Duck describes this in her book, "The Change Monster."[3] Be ready for the crisis and use that moment to reinforce your efforts.

The first thing you have to do is to have an early-warning system in place to see the crisis developing. By this time you should be able to tap other "eyes and ears" throughout the organization to get an "on the street" read of the situation. These are going to be people who feel safe telling you what's really going on. They might be administrative staff, those outside your direct line of reports or they might be people far enough removed from you that they don't feel threatened by telling you the truth. Whoever they are, you need to identify them and cultivate them.

---

[3]Duck, Jeannie Daniel. 2001. *The Change Monster*. New York: Three Rivers Press.

The main sign of the impending crisis will be the naysayers or detractors raising their heads and their objections again or more boldly. It is likely they will go quiet during the period of initial enthusiasm after the launch of the Burning Imperative. But they will usually find it impossible to stay quiet forever. Their return to naysaying will be the first signs of the crisis and their point of view will spread if you don't cut it off.

So hit the restart button fast. Make it clear that you are committed to the changes. Regroup your core team members to confirm their commitment. Take action against the blocking coalitions. This is a good time to shine the spotlight publicly on some people who are still in the way or to move some people out.

Some good steps at this point may include:

- Regroup with your core team to gather input and adjust as appropriate.
- "All-hands" meetings, videoconferences, or calls to highlight progress and reinforce the Burning Imperative.
- Follow-up note confirming the commitment to the Burning Imperative.
- Follow-up phone calls with each individual on the core team.
- Reinforce Burning Imperative at each key milestone with core team, their teams, and so on.
- Meetings or one-on-ones with key people or groups at a level below your direct reports.
- Field or plant visits.
- Implementing a structured monitoring plan.

Institutionalize the Change

Next, you'll want to put in place practices that will ensure that the changes you made so far become part of the core fabric of how you do business.

Some of the ways that you can do that include:

Recognition and rewards: This is a great place to start. Make sure that your recognition and reward system is built or modified to recognize the behaviors and attitudes that are important to—and show support of—the new way of doing business. Make sure that they reward the results you want and do not reward the results you do not want.

Mode, manner, frequency, and disagreement: You must modify all four of these aspects of communication to fit the new business directives. This step is often overlooked, but it is important and, once implemented, it works on its own to reinforce how and when you want things communicated.

Decision points: Be sure to modify how decisions are made; push them as close to the customer/client as you can.

Control points: Modify the control points so you are measuring the right thing with the right reporting processes.

Beyond these three, there is a whole host of other supporting systems and practices that you can line up to reinforce the new way of doing business.

Communication: Summary and Implications

Not surprisingly, because we live in the midst of a communication revolution, the guidelines for communicating are changing dramatically. As much as we would like to treat communication as a logical, sequential, ongoing communication campaign, in many cases, it's more essential to manage it as an iterative set of concurrent conversations.

- Take into account the network of multiple stakeholders as you specifically identify your target audiences.
- Discover and leverage your overarching message as the foundation for guiding iterative concurrent conversations by seeding and reinforcing communication points through a wide variety of media with no compromises on trustworthiness and authenticity.
- Monitor and adjust as appropriate on an ongoing basis.

Don't hesitate to deploy an old school logical, sequential communication campaign when appropriate—though we expect that to be the case less and less over time.

QUESTIONS YOU SHOULD ASK YOURSELF

- What is the message?
- Is the message compelling?
- Do I know how I'm going to get people to embrace that message?

TOOL 8.1
Broader Stakeholder Map*

		NAME	POSITION	INTERACTION PLAN
UP	MANAGEMENT, BOARD			
ACROSS	KEY PEERS, INTERNAL ALLIES			
	CUSTOMERS, SUPPLIERS			
DOWN	DIRECT REPORTS			
	INDIRECT			
OTHER				
GOVERNMENT				
REGULATORS				
MEDIA				
ACTIVISTS				
ALLIES				

TOOL 8.2

Communication Guide*

Target Audience

Core target

_____

Primary influencers

_____

Other influencers

_____

Core Message

_____

_____

_____

_____

_____

Communication Points

_____

_____

_____

_____

Promise

_____

Reason to believe

_____

Supporting examples

_____

_____

_____

_____

Media

Offline/live

_____

Online

_____

Social

_____

Tracking

How to measure success?

_____

How often to measure?

_____

Contingency plans?

_____

TOOL 8.3

Communication Campaign Milestones*

	How	Who	When
Plan Ready			
Message/communication points			
Signs, symbols, stories identified			
Media and touch points set			
Seed Message			
Early testers			
Early adapters			
Other seeding			
Launch Campaign			
Kick off			
Roll out			
Deep dive			
Cascade Milestones			
Public scorecard			
Track and report			
Adjust			
Reinforce			
Early warnings			
Adjustments			
Recommit			
Institutionalize			
Recognition and reward			
Practices			
Control points			

PART IV

IMPLEMENT YOUR 100-DAY ACTION PLAN

CHAPTER 9

Embed a *Burning Imperative* by Day 30

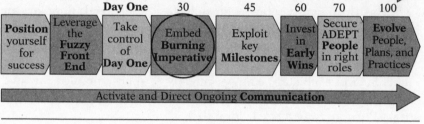

You can control your schedule during the Fuzzy Front End—mostly because no one expects you to do anything. You can probably control your schedule on Day One or, at least, have a big influence on it—mostly because no one expects you to have thought it through as much as you will have after reading this book. Your control will be far less over the rest of your first 100 days—because all sorts of people will be putting all sorts of demands on your time. Carving out team-building time is going to be tough. But building a high-performing team is essential. So make the time.

Creating the Burning Imperative

On top of everything else you have to do, and all the other demands on your schedule, make the time to implement the building blocks of tactical capacity. The starting point, and indeed the foundation, is the

Burning Imperative with its components of headline, mission, vision, objectives, goals, strategies, and values. Experienced, successful leaders inevitably say that getting people aligned around a vision and values is the most important thing they have to do—and often the most difficult. The foundation of success is ultimately you, your Be, Do, Say, your BRAVE orientation, which works as the pivot for galvanizing those of the group.

The Burning Imperative is a clear, sharply defined, intensely shared, and purposefully urgent understanding from each of the team members of what they are "supposed to do, now" and how this Burning Imperative works with the larger aspirations of the team and the organization.

The Burning Imperative must have a shorthand summary or headline—most likely containing a strong, action-oriented verb. This is a brief statement, or tagline, that reminds team members of the entire range of work—from mission through strategy and the statements behind each step—and specifically of their commitments and responsibilities in relation to that work. For example, "Embed a strong Burning Imperative by day 30."

To be clear, a Burning Imperative is different from a shared purpose. The difference between the two is timing, intensity, and duration. The shared purpose drives the long term while your Burning Imperative drives the next phase of activity, now on the way to the long term.

Remember the Apollo 13 example of "get these men home alive." Clear. Sharply defined. Intensely shared. Purposefully urgent. It trumps all petty concerns. It didn't replace the overall shared purpose of exploring the universe to increase man's knowledge. The Burning Imperative moves the team forward to that longer-term shared purpose. That's what you're aiming for.

We all saw the same thing in northern Chile in 2010 when 33 miners were trapped for 69 days 2,230 feet below the ground. Almost no one thought that rescuers would ever retrieve the bodies, let alone pull them out alive. But after 17 days of being trapped underground without contact with anyone, the miners sent a message to the surface that they were all alive! Instantly, the Burning Imperative was set: "Get these men out alive!" No one had a plan on how to get it done when the Burning Imperative was set, but the rescue team, with help from people around the world, invented a way to get those men home safe. Now that is a Burning Imperative at work!

Perhaps equally impressive, the rescue workers achieved their Burning Imperative to "get these men out alive" by navigating an environment even more treacherous than deep space or a deep mine shaft—the conflict between wives and mistresses! (Keeping some of those men safe once they got home was a different task.)

Don't Hesitate to Burn Rubber on the Way to a Burning Imperative

The Burning Imperative drives everything everyone does every day. More than any single other factor, this is what distinguishes highly successful teams from teams that flounder and fail. More than any other single factor, this is the key to surviving and thriving in a complex transition. This is the heart of tactical capacity. Teams with a clear Burning Imperative can be more flexible in their actions and reactions because each individual team member can be confident that his or her team members are heading in the same direction.

Not everyone agrees on how fast you should move to get this in place. The argument for stretching out this process is that the risks of picking the wrong Burning Imperative are greater than the risks of moving too slowly. There have certainly been cases where this has been true. If things are going well, there's less urgency to change things.

However, failing to track and build momentum early can create problems of its own. If some negative external factor intervenes before you have started to track and move (e.g., you lose a key customer or a vital team member), you may have a debacle to deal with. We all have seen that the pace of change is accelerating as information flows more and more freely. In that environment, even if things are going well, competitors are going to converge rapidly on your position.

You need to move quickly. Today, it is better to get moving and adapt as appropriate. How fast should you move on this? Fast. Give it good thought, but get this in place by the end of your first 30 days.

Harold was 100 days into his new role as VP of marketing for a $1 billion manufacturing company when his boss asked him to pick up business development as well. (Harold had handled the initial steps of his complex transition well indeed.) So Harold hit a restart button with the new team, pulling them together for one of our Burning Imperative workshops.

The company had experienced serious problems from an unbalanced pipeline in the past but had been unable to frame the problem and the solution. The team members agreed that their Burning

Imperative had to be one that drove them to "create opportunities beyond the current horizon." After robust discussion, they determined that to achieve their goals they needed 10 new high-level prospect meetings, 10 new contracts, and 10 final deliverables accomplished within the year. The team created a tagline for the Burning Imperative: 10-10-10! They also gained agreement on the underlying mission statement, vision, objectives, and goals as well as the strategies, and plans that flowed from those. Everybody walked away from the workshop with an absolutely clear and precise sense of the role they were to play in driving the mission, vision, objectives, goals, strategies, and values of the company. "10, 10, and 10!" was the rallying cry.

What emerged from this Burning Imperative was a much clearer understanding by all three main parties—business development, senior management, and delivery team. Each group had to ensure all parts of the pipeline, with delivery helping business development with new prospect meetings, and business development helping the delivery team lock down actual delivery (managing expectations and time table), and senior management paying close attention to the balance and rhythm of resources and pitching in directly as needed.

What is extraordinary is not so much what they did, but how fast they got it done. From the moment this team first came together until the time the CEO approved the plans only 30 hours had elapsed. To achieve this, the team followed the outline as detailed in the Burning Imperative Workshop (Tool 10.1) at the end of this chapter. On its completion, one member of the team said, "I've been here six years. It's the first time I've known what I was supposed to do."

HOT TIP

The Burning Imperative: This is the centerpiece of tactical capacity. When people talk about getting everyone on the same page, this is that page. Use whatever methodology you would like to get it in place. But get it in place and get buy-in early. In a hot landing when there is an acute need for the team members to act, it's imperative that they do so quickly. It is not that there are just diminishing returns to doing this after day 30, there is an actual cliff. After day 30, the sense of urgency dissipates almost immediately and things start slipping precariously. So you really need to do whatever it takes to get this done by day 30. This is a big deal. We feel strongly about this.

The components of the Burning Imperative are headline, mission, vision, values, objectives, goals, strategies, and plans. These drive the team's actual plans and actions. If you are unclear about the differences between all these things and how they work together, stop. Go to Appendix IV for a more detailed explanation. It will be well worth your time to get familiar with these basic building blocks of leadership.

Burning Imperative

The components of the Burning Imperative are headline, mission, vision, values, objectives, goals, strategies, and plans.

Headline: The all-encapsulating phrase or tagline that defines your Burning Imperative.

Mission: Why here, why exist, what business are we in?

Vision: Future picture—what we want to become; where we are going.

Values: Beliefs and moral principles that guide attitudes, decisions, and actions.

Objectives: Broadly defined, qualitative performance requirements.

Goals: The quantitative measures of the objectives that define success.

Strategies: Broad choices around how the team will achieve its objectives.

Plans: The most important projects and initiatives that will bring each strategy to fruition.

People often confuse the difference between a mission and a vision. Sometimes people just combine the two. But they are different. A mission guides what people do every day. It informs what roles need to exist in the organization. A vision is the picture of future success. It helps define areas where the organization needs to be best in class and helps keep everyone aware of the essence of the company.

Similarly, people confuse objectives and goals. Objectives connect qualitatively with the vision. Goals must be quantitative. They must be SMART: Specific, Measurable, Achievable, Realistic, and Time-bound. (Teams will often resort to a tagline referring to a goal such as 10, 10, and 10!) But as the leader, you need to make sure that you keep connecting this goal with the objective. (Ensure a stable pipeline of new business and deliver reliably against it!)

Sometimes the mission works as a headline. Sometimes the vision or priorities work. It doesn't matter. All that matters is getting everyone on the same page.

Make It Happen

How do you build the individual elements—mission, vision, values, and so on—and roll them up into a Burning Imperative? You and your core team need to invest time and work into conceiving, shaping, articulating, and communicating each element and then helping translate these into a unified Burning Imperative that works as a headline for the entire plan and that focuses individuals on their particular roles and responsibilities. It may seem daunting, but once it gets going and the team connects with the project, it develops a momentum and urgency of its own. The light clicking on for the team is one of the most exciting and memorable feelings that you and your team will ever have.

There are different ways to do this. If the leader does not have confidence in his or her team, a consultative approach tends to work best. In this case, the leader will draft a first-cut Burning Imperative and then get everyone else's input one at a time. This way the leader never loses control of the conversation.

We have used workshops with great success. The workshop tool in this chapter (Tool 9.1) is designed to help you and your team reach consensus on your mission, vision, objectives, strategies and values. We have done these workshops in marathon single daylong sessions, but often it works best when two or three days are dedicated to the cause.

The operative word is consensus. You probably already have a mission, vision, objectives, strategies, and values in your head. They may even be down on paper. Your team members may have told you that they agree. But, do they know them off the top of their heads? Do they (did they ever) really believe them? Do they really mean anything? Are they current? Inspiring? Do the mission, vision, objectives, strategies, and values really drive their actions? Do they really see what they're doing as a Burning Imperative or just something nice to do to pass the time of day? Your job as a leader is to make sure that everyone on the team can genuinely answer yes to those questions.

Bryan Smith lays out different ways of rolling out ideas: telling, selling, testing, consulting, and co-creating.[1] In most cases we

---

[1]Smith, Bryan, *The Fifth Discipline Field Book* (Boston: Nicholas Brealey, 1994).

recommend the concept of co-creating. The rewards of "creating together" are so immense and so memorable that the process alone is the strongest antidote to forgetfulness and indifference. You don't want the team members thinking that their mission is just a slew of buzz words that you threw at them. Sadly, that is the destiny of many so-called Burning Imperatives.

The premise behind the Burning Imperative workshop is to co-create the Burning Imperative with your core team so that it is shared by all. After the meeting, you should test the Burning Imperative by letting others in the organization consult with your core team. They may have perspectives that will lead to slight tweaks. You should be open to wording changes and some new ideas during the test but be careful to preserve the meaning of the Burning Imperative that you and your team co-created.

Do not make the mistake of attempting to let an entire organization co-create its Burning Imperative. There is a limit to the size of effectively creative teams, just as there is probably a limit to an effective college seminar size. Everybody needs to participate and when it would take two hours just to have everybody speak for two minutes (e.g., to introduce themselves) you know you're in trouble. If the co-creating team is too large, you're likely to end up with something that is acceptable to most and inspirational to none. By co-creating with just your core team, you can lead the team toward more inspirational ideas. A good target size for the group is 5 to 12 people.

Done right, a Burning Imperative workshop is an intensive session with a lot of personal sharing and dialogue. Expect to learn a lot about your team members. Expect them to learn a lot about you. It is possible that you'll end up with a Burning Imperative very close to what you came in with. It is more likely that you won't. Even if you do, there's power for all in the learning. As T. S. Eliot says in "Little Gidding":

> *We shall not cease from exploration.*
> *And the end of all our exploring*
> *Will be to arrive where we started*
> *And know the place for the first time.*[2]

---

[2] Eliot, T. S., "Little Gidding," in *Four Quartets* (New York: Harcourt Brace Jovanovich, 1943)

Workshop Attendance and Timing

In the real world, you'll be taking over an existing team with existing priorities and existing schedules. It is unlikely that your team members will have planned to take out a day from their current work to sit around, hold hands, and sing folk songs. First point, this is real work and the Burning Imperative workshop tool is focused on real business issues. It ends up being a strong team-building exercise, but as a by-product of the work. Even so, there will be some team members who are reluctant to adjust their existing schedules to accommodate this workshop, particularly if you push to hold it sometime in your first 30 days.

Stick with the plan. Find the date in your first 30 days that works best for most people and then give the others the option to change their schedules or not. This approach has two advantages:

1. It keeps things moving forward in line with the 80 percent rule. Not everything is going to be perfect. Not everyone can be at every meeting. You and your team will move forward as best you can, helping others catch up and adjusting along the way.

2. It gives you early data about different team members' attitudes and commitment. Everything communicates; and everything communicates both ways. By inviting people to a Burning Imperative workshop, you are sending a powerful message. Their turning it down because they have something more important to do returns a different message. How you handle overt resistance will be an important early test of your ACES model.

Follow Through Consistently

Follow through and then follow through again. Pulling people together, investing the time in this, and then not living by it, is worse than not doing it at all. A strong Burning Imperative is a covenant of honor. Once you put it in place, you must live it if you expect people to follow your lead. You must follow through on your commitments. You must support people who flex standard procedures in pursuit of the Burning Imperative.

Gerry was a volunteer with his local life squad/ambulance service. One day he heard an accident while raking leaves in his front lawn. He ran down to the end of the street and started treating the victims, enrolling bystanders to summon the police, life squad, and help in other ways. Two of the victims walked away and two had to be taken to the hospital.

After the run to the hospital, Gerry was at the station helping to clean out the ambulance for the next call when the life squad captain walked in.

"Gerry, I noticed you were on the scene of this accident without your red life squad coat on."

Gerry explained why he had gone straight to the scene without putting his coat on, going to the station, and riding with the ambulance even though he had been on call.

"But wearing your coat is important so people can identify you as a life squad member."

"Good point. I'll be careful the next time. . . . Wait a minute. How did you notice I wasn't wearing my coat?"

"I drove by."

"Are you telling me you drove by the scene of a two-car accident, saw that I was the only life squad member there and you chose to come by here and remind me to wear my coat the next time? How about stopping to help!"

It doesn't matter what words they actually used. The underlying Burning Imperative of every life squad, ambulance team, or first responder of any sort must be "help people in need." This life squad captain was not living the message. You must. Be. Do. Say.

Burning Imperative: Summary and Implications

The Burning Imperative is the cornerstone building block of tactical capacity.

Everything pivots off a business's headline, mission, vision, values, objectives, goals, strategies, and plans:

Headline: The all-encapsulating phrase or tagline that defines your Burning Imperative.

Mission: Why here, why exist, what business are you in?

Vision: Future picture—what you want to become; where are you going?

Values: Beliefs and moral principles that guide attitudes, decisions, and actions.

Objectives: Broadly defined, qualitative performance requirements.

Goals: The quantitative measures of the objectives that define success.

Strategies: Broad choices around how the team will achieve its objectives.

Plans: The most important projects and initiatives that will bring each strategy to fruition.

For the Burning Imperative to drive everything everyone actually does every day, it must be truly embraced by all. Thus, you should strive to get it in place and shared early on—within your first 30 days at the latest.

HOT TIP

In most cases, to establish an environment of co-creation it is best if you, as the leader, do not facilitate the Burning Imperative workshop. By being a participant as opposed to the facilitator it puts you in a better position to listen and understand your team's input and perspective, which will help you craft a truly co-created Burning Imperative. The dynamics alone of you sitting with the team as opposed to leading in front of the room tends to foster a richer and more honest dialogue from the team. It's about the team, not about you. You want to emerge with a team's Burning Imperative, not the leader's.

QUESTIONS YOU SHOULD ASK YOURSELF

- Have we laid the right foundation on which to build a high-performing team?
- Have we identified a Burning Imperative?
- Is it compelling enough to the key stakeholders?
- Do we have the strategies and defined goals to make it real?

TOOL 9.1

Burning Imperative Workshop Tool*

This is a one-day, off-site workshop to drive consensus around headline, mission, vision, values, objectives, goals, strategies, and plans. All members of core team must attend. This workshop will determine the team's Burning Imperative.

Preparation:

• In premeeting communications, set a clear destination for the meeting (headline, mission, vision, values, objectives, goals, strategies, and plans).

• Set context—current reality—broader group's purpose.

• Send invitations, set logistics.

• Prepare to present your current vision (leader); prepare to explain your role (team members).

Delivery:

• Detail the destination: headline, mission, vision, values (facilitator), objectives, goals, strategies, and plans.

• Present the current vision (team leader).

• Present the current subgroup roles (team members).

• Set up what's important.

• Review the corporate/larger group purpose (team leader).

• Revise the team's mission, vision, objectives, goals, strategies, and plans in turn by encouraging an open, but focused discussion to expand ideas, group them into similar categories, select the ones that resonate with current vision,

(continued)

rank them in order of importance, solicit individual drafts, collect common thoughts, create a group draft based on input that includes the Burning Imperative headline (facilitator).

- Discuss how the new Burning Imperative is different from the old situation (facilitator).

- Summarize what it will take to achieve the Burning Imperative (facilitator).

- Wrap up and tie the results back to the destination and communicate the next steps.

Follow up:

- Share with broader team for their input.

- Make refinements if required.

- Communicate the final results to all key stakeholders.

CHAPTER 10

Exploit Key *Milestones* to Drive Team Performance by Day 45

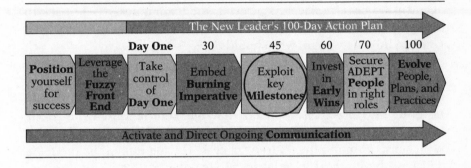

Milestones are the building blocks of tactical capacity that turn a Burning Imperative into a manageable action plan. Your team's milestone management practice, if done right, will be a powerful team reinforcer. This is all about follow-through. Burning Imperative meetings tend to produce many ideas and choices on flip charts. They are all completely useless unless someone takes action to make them happen. This chapter is about ensuring that they do. In brief, to help ensure that the team delivers the desired results, in the time frame specified, you should strive for absolute clarity around:

- Decision rights
- Accountabilities
- Linkages across groups

- Information flows
- Collaboration

Once this is done, move the focus from the individuals to the team.

Follow Through—Or Don't Even Start

Sam's team put a lot of time and energy into creating a Burning Imperative during a two-day workshop. They left excited and ready to move forward. Then Sam got busy and never put the milestone management process in place. As a result, the team quickly went back to doing things the way they'd been doing them before. If Sam wasn't going to follow through, why should they?

The real test of moving from strategy to tactical capacity lies in the actual practices that are set up among team members. Tactical capacity implies, by definition, that significant leeway should be built into practices. A team that has internalized its Burning Imperative, mission, values, and objectives will have developed a keen sense of mutually assured success. Having done this, the team will have built a real foundation for true tactical capacity, and will do what it takes to succeed, even if that means adapting and modifying aspects of the initial plans that were laid out. There should be nothing mechanical about this aspect of preparing for and executing a complex transition. It requires nuance, insight, close monitoring, and collaboration.

Practices are the things that enable people to implement the plans. They need to be coupled with systems of metrics and rewards that reinforce the desired behaviors. There is an old saying: "Show me how they are paid and I'll tell you what they really do."

John Michael Loh, United States Air Force Air Combat Commander during the first Gulf War said: "I used to believe that if it doesn't get measured, it doesn't get done. Now I say if it doesn't get measured it doesn't get approved . . . you need to manage by facts, not gut feelings." As Michael Bloomberg the mayor of New York City puts it, "You're entitled to your own opinions, but not your own facts."[1]

Specific performance measurements, accountabilities, and decision rights free people and teams to do their jobs without undue interference and provide the basis for nonjudgmental discussion of performance versus expectations and how to make improvements.

---

[1] Michael Bloomberg, University of Pennsylvania Commencement Address, May 2008.

It is essential that people know what is expected of them. When the expectations are clear, people also must have the time and resources needed to deliver those expectations. The milestone management process is focused on clarifying decision rights and making sure that information and resources flow to where they need to go.

Milestones Are Checkpoints along the Way to a Defined Goal

Recall these definitions from Chapter 9:

Objectives: Broadly defined, qualitative performance requirements.

Goals: The quantitative measures of the objectives that define success.

Strategies: Broad choices around how the team will achieve its objectives.

Now add:

Milestones: Checkpoints along the way to achieving objectives and goals.

NASA and the Apollo 13 ground team provide a useful example of this. The objective of getting the astronauts back home alive after the explosion in space was not only compelling, but overwhelming.

It was easier to work through milestones one-by-one:

- Turn the ship around so it would get back to earth.
- Manage the remaining power so it would last until they were back.
- Fix the carbon monoxide problem so the air remained breathable.
- Manage reentry into the atmosphere so the ship didn't burn up.

The power of milestones is that they let you know how you're doing along the way and give you the opportunity to make adjustments. They also give you the comfort to let your team run toward the goal without your involvement, as long as the milestones are being reached as planned.

You might evaluate your team's journey to a goal like this:

Worst case	The team misses a goal and doesn't know why.
Bad	The team misses a goal and knows why.
Okay	The team misses a milestone but adjusts to make the overall goal.
Good	The team anticipates risk as it goes along to make key milestones.
Best	The team hits all milestones on the way to goal . . . (in your dreams).

Imagine that you set a goal of getting from London to Paris in 5½ hours. Now imagine that you choose to drive.

You set off on your journey.

It takes you 45 minutes to get from Central London to the outskirts of London.

Thirty minutes after that, you wonder: "How's the trip going so far?"

You have no clue.

You might be on track. You might be behind schedule. But it's early in the trip so you probably think that you can make up time later if you need to. So you're not worried.

If, on the other hand, you had set the following milestones, you would be thinking differently:

- Central London to outskirts of London: 30 minutes.
- Outskirts of London to Folkestone: 70 minutes.
- Channel Crossing: load: 20 minutes; cross: 20 minutes; unload: 20 minutes.
- Calais to Paris: 3 hours.

If you had set a milestone of getting to the outskirts of London in 30 minutes and it took you 45 minutes, you would know you were behind schedule. Knowing that you were behind schedule, you could then take action on alternative options. The milestone would make you immediately aware of the need to adjust to still reach your overall goal.

You and your team are going to miss milestones. It is not necessary to hit all your milestones. What is essential is that you and your team have put in place a mechanism to identify reasonable milestones so that you have checkpoints that allow you to anticipate and adjust along the way.

Manage Milestone Updates with a Three-Step Process

Deploying a mutually supportive team-based follow-up system helps everyone improve performance versus goals. Organizations that have deployed this process in their team meetings have seen dramatic improvements in team performance. Follow these three steps as well as the prep and postinstructions laid out here and in Tool 10.1 and you'll be well on your way to ensuring that the team achieves their desired results on time.

Prep: Circulate individual milestone updates to the team to read before each meeting so you can take update sharing and reporting off the agenda, while still deploying a disciplined process to make sure that information flows where it needs to go. Executives often skip this step much to the team's detriment. It seems like an easy process to put in place, but we've heard every reason in the book as to why it has not been implemented. Usually there are some logistic protocols that need to be established, tracking method choices and time frames established for submitting and distribution of information before the process can begin. If at all possible make these choices before the Burning Imperative meeting takes place and announce them at the end of the meeting or shortly after. Make these choices immediately. You must require that everyone complete the update and premeeting review on time. If you allow excuses here, the rest of the process takes a hit. Yes, it can be a pain to get it started, but once it is embedded as a team expectation and value, you'll be thankful that you endured the brief period of pain. Just do it. Trust us.

Step 1. Use the first half of each meeting for each team member to headline wins, learning, and areas in which the person needs help from other team members, but do not work through items at this point. Discussing items here reinforces a first-come, first-served mentality where the people who share later in the order tend to get squeezed for time. The "help from other team members" is often the most important part of the meeting. Each of these items should be captured. It's a good idea to keep a set time limit for each individual update. Those who tend to be long-winded might not like it, but the rest of the participants will appreciate it. A tight and controlled limit goes a long way to making the meetings more dynamic.

Step 2. Pause at the meeting's halfway point to prioritize items for discussion so the team can discuss items in the right priority instead of first-come, first-served. These won't necessarily be the universally most important items because some items should be worked with a different group or subset of the team. You should make note of those items in the meeting, but defer them to another meeting where the full and proper group can address them. Instead, give priority to the most important items for *this team* to work on *as a team, at this time*. Tend to give priority to items that are off-target, in danger, or areas where help is needed. Develop a list in descending order of priority.

Step 3. Use the second part of the meeting to discuss, in order, the priority list you determined to be the overall team's most important issues and opportunities. The expectation is that the team won't get through all the items. That's okay because you're working the most important items first. (Which is why you paused to prioritize items.) This is the time to figure out how to adjust as a team to make the most important goals, all the while reinforcing predetermined decision rights.

Post: Defer other items to the next meeting or to a separate meeting. Update the tracking reports with any changes or new directions. Communicate major shifts to those key stakeholders who need to know.

HOT TIP 1

Anticipation is the key: At first, milestones will go from "on track" to "oops we missed" with no steps in between. You'll know the process is working well when people are surfacing areas they "might miss" if they don't get help from others. Focus your love and attention on these "might miss" items to get the team to help. It will make people feel good about surfacing issues and will encourage them to bring future issues to the group for help.

HOT TIP 2

Banish the first-come, first-served mentality. This milestone process is easy to deploy for disciplined people and teams. It is hard for less disciplined people because they want to work items first-come, first-served. Resist that. Follow the process. You'll learn to love it. (Well, maybe not love it, but you will appreciate it. It will strengthen your team.)

HOT TIP 3

Integrate across instead of managing down: The milestone meetings are great forums for making connections across groups. The further you rise in the organization, the more time you'll spend integrating across and the less time you'll spend managing down. Senior managers don't like to be managed from above or have their decision rights compromised, but everyone appreciates improved information flows and linking projects and priorities across groups.

Use Milestone Management at the Board Level

Garr's board meetings were out of control. Individual board members kept taking the meetings' agendas off-track in order to emphasize their own favorite issues.

To combat this, Garr put in place a milestone management process.

Each board member submitted his or her updates to the board secretary ahead of the board meeting. The secretary then compiled them and sent them back to everyone at least 48 hours in advance of the board meetings.

At the two-hour board meetings, the first hour was spent with the 24 board members giving a two-minute recap of their updates, emphasizing the areas where they needed help or thought more discussion was warranted.

At the halfway point, the board president looked at all the outstanding issues and ordered them from highest priority to lowest priority.

The board spent the next hour working through the issues in priority order, not worrying about time. They never got through the entire list in the meetings. But that was okay because the issues they got to were more important than the issues that had to be discussed later.

This schedule revolutionized the board meetings. Everyone got two minutes in the spotlight. Everyone got a chance to raise issues. But the agenda was no longer managed on a first-come, first-served basis. As a result, the board could spend more time on the more important issues.

Milestones: Summary and Implications

Tracking milestones is not a revolutionary idea. However, the idea of using them as a management tool and as a team-building tool is a new idea to most leaders and their teams.

Compiling milestones is a waste of time if you do not have an efficient, effective, and clear process in place to track them.

Define them and begin tracking and managing them immediately. Use the process to establish and reinforce expected team norms in three steps.

1. Get milestones in place.
2. Track them and manage them as a team on a frequent and regular basis.
3. Implement a milestone management meeting that includes:

    Prep: Gather and circulate updates in advance of meetings.

    Share wins, learning, and areas for help (might miss) in first half of meeting.

    Prioritize items.

    Work items in priority order.

    Post: Defer other items to next meeting or separate meeting. Update and communicate.

QUESTIONS YOU SHOULD ASK YOURSELF

- Is everyone clear on who (roles) is doing what (goals), when (milestones), with what resources and decision rights?
- Are we doing all we can to make sure that information and resources flow to where they need to go?
- Is there a system in place to manage milestone achievement so I do not have to do it myself on an ad hoc basis?
- Am I effectively using milestone management as a team-building tool?
- Am I certain that all my milestones are on track? If so, how can I be sure? If not, why not?

TOOL 10.1

Team Milestones*

MILESTONES MANAGEMENT PROCESS

- Leader conducts a weekly or bi-weekly Milestones Management meeting with his or her team.

- Prior to Milestones Management meetings:

  Each team member submits his or her updates.

  Designated person compiles and circulates updated milestones in advance of the meeting.

- At Milestones Management meetings

First part of the meeting:

Each team member gives a five-minute update in the following format: most important wins, most important learnings, areas where he or she needs help.

Midpoint of the meeting:

The leader orders topics for discussion in order of priority.

Second part of the meeting:

Group discusses priority topics in order, spending as much time as necessary on each topic.

The remaining topics are deferred to the next Milestones Management meeting or a separate meeting. Key items are updated and communicated.

(continued)

---

*Copyright © PrimeGenesis® LLC. To customize this document, download Tool 10.1 from www.onboardingtools.com. The document can then be opened, edited, and printed.

TOOL 10.1   (continued)

MILESTONES TRACKING

MILESTONES	WHEN	WHO	STATUS*	DISCUSSION/ HELP NEEDED
PRIORITY PROGRAMS				

*Useful to color code:
  Green: On track.
  Yellow: Lagging, but will be made up.
  Red: Heading for a miss.

CHAPTER 11

Overinvest in *Early Wins* to Build Team Confidence by Day 60

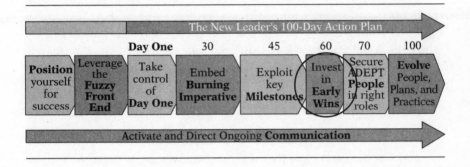

T here is often a conversation about six months after a leader has started a new role. Someone will ask the new leader's boss how the new leader is doing. You have probably taken part in these conversations before.

"By the way, how's that new leader Rhonda doing?"

"Rhonda? She's fabulous. Love the intelligence. Love the attitude. She may be off to a slow start. But what a great hire! Really like her."

Result: Rhonda's probably on the way out; or, at the very least, in real trouble. Rhonda may not find out about it for another 6 to 12 months but her boss's "off to a slow start" planted a seed of doubt that could eventually lead to an unhappy ending for Rhonda.

After all, senior leaders are hired to deliver results first and foremost, and it is assumed that the required intelligence, personality, and attitude come along with the package. So when that question is asked about your transition, you want the answer to be about specific results, or early wins.

Compare the previous answer with "Rhonda? Let me tell you about all the things she's gotten done."

In that scenario, Rhonda's made. Of course, she has not done it all herself. Her team has. But Rhonda got the team focused on delivering early wins and by doing so gave her boss something concrete to talk about.

Early wins give the leader credibility and provide the team confidence and momentum—three very good things. For NASA and Apollo 13, fixing the oxygen problem was the early win that made the entire team believe they could succeed and gave them the confidence to deal with the rest of their challenges and the momentum to push forward despite incredible odds.

Our early win prescription is relatively simple:

1. Select one or two early wins from your milestones list:
   - Choose early wins that will make a meaningful external impact.
   - Select early wins that your boss will want to talk about.
   - Pick early wins that you are sure you can deliver.
   - Choose early wins that will model important behaviors.
   - Pick early wins that would not have happened if you had not been there.

2. Establish early wins by day 60 and deliver by your sixth month:
   - Early means early. Make sure that you select early wins in your first 60 days that you and the team can deliver by the end of your sixth month. Select them early. Communicate them early. Deliver them early.
   - Make sure that the team understands the early wins and has bought in to delivering them on time.
   - This will give your bosses the concrete results they need when someone asks how you are doing.

3. Overinvest resources to ensure that early wins are achieved on time:
   - Do not skimp on your early wins. Allocate resources in a manner that will ensure timely delivery. Put more resources than you think you should need against these early opportunities so that your team is certain to deliver them better and faster than anyone thought was possible.

- Stay alert. Adjust quickly. As the leader, stay close and stay involved on the progress of your early wins and react immediately if they start to fall even slightly off track or behind schedule.

4. Celebrate and communicate early wins:

   - As your first early wins are achieved, celebrate the accomplishment with the entire team. This is important and should not be overlooked.

   - In conjunction with your communication campaign, make sure that your early wins are communicated as appropriate.

In general, "early wins" are not synonymous with "big wins." They are the early, sometimes small, yet meaningful wins that start the momentum of a winning team. They are the blasting caps, not the dynamite. They are the opening singles, not the grand slam home run. They are the first successful test market, not the global expansion. They are found generally by accelerating something that is already in progress instead of starting something new. They are sure to generate credibility, confidence, momentum, and excitement.

Don't Wait Too Long to Build Momentum

Rudy Giuliani went into the 2007–2008 campaign for the Republican nomination for president of the United States as the early favorite, leading the national polls by a substantial margin. He put virtually all his effort into winning the first big primary in Florida to build momentum going into "super Tuesday" when half the states would hold primaries. In doing this, he chose to skip the earlier, smaller states like Iowa and New Hampshire.

Before the Florida primary, when the political pundits were asked about Rudy Giuliani, his strategy left them with nothing to say, while several of the other candidates had tangible results to speak to. Rudy took himself out of the debate precisely because he had no results to talk about. The other candidates positioned themselves at the top of the headlines for weeks and developed confidence and momentum that rose to counteract Giuliani's early lead. His "win big" strategy backfired because it took too long to deliver tangible results and it led to a disastrous third-place finish in Florida that forced him out of the race.

Focus on the Results with the Most Impact

Pamela came into lead sales and marketing for a struggling software provider. Pamela knew that the product was very strong and well priced, but the company had little market penetration because of its less than stellar marketing efforts. Immediately on joining, Pamela co-created with her team a compelling Burning Imperative and the resulting strategies, plans, and milestones. Her team's important milestones included redoing the marketing strategy, positioning, branding, brochures, and a new trade show booth.

As an early win, she and the team picked redesigning the trade show booth and the trade show's strategy. Her logic was that there was a major trade show coming up in a few months and this was a great chance to make a powerful impact on the market. She knew that if the team was successful, the end result would be a significant increase in client interest and inquiries. If she could increase client requests for proposals, she knew fortunes would turn around because the sales team had an excellent close ratio once it got on a client's radar. By generating more client requests, she knew she would gain credibility for the marketing group, gain confidence for her team, and give senior management some meaningful results to talk about.

She closely managed the project while effectively engaging her team along the way and she delivered a superior product in record time. Pam's team came up with a concept that attracted key clients and then blew them away once they were there. The sales team gave more presentations during the trade show than they had in the previous eight months. Her team's early win generated tangible, effective, and exciting results. It was far better than what they had achieved before and it was clearly something they never would have accomplished without Pamela. It was a great early win!

HOT TIP

To qualify as an early win, the result must be something that would not have been accomplished without you taking the leadership role. If it would have been accomplished without you in the role, it is not significant enough to be considered an early win. The early win should signify to the team and the other stakeholders that something has changed for the better. However, it must be seen and felt as the team's win and not your personal win alone.

Champion the Champions

Oscar decided to focus his efforts on four projects. He reached into his organization to pick four "champions" to drive the projects and then gave them extra support and resources to ensure that they could deliver in their new roles.

Three of the projects produced early tangible results. One did not do so well.

But the three that did well were enough to turn the whole business around. The division that Oscar had been brought in to run had experienced declining sales for 24 months, and continued its downward trend during Oscar's first two months. However, as the early win projects started to deliver results, the downward trend stopped in month three with a 1 percent uptick. By month four, it was up 4 percent and in month five, it was up 10 percent. It was clear to all that the successful delivery of the three early wins was behind the overwhelming jump in sales. That success bought Oscar more time to achieve a win on the fourth plan.

No one even bothered asking how Oscar was doing in month six. Everybody knew because the numbers told the story.

Redefine Success

When we presented the idea to Quincy, he did not like the early win concept at all. He had just become the new head of the music division of a major entertainment company that was looking to make a dramatic impact on the music industry and turn around years of declining sales. Quincy knew that the existing pipeline of artists could not deliver the sales punch that his bosses were looking for, and he was certain that it would take 12 to 18 months to deliver anything tangible. To him, delivering a meaningful early win in his first six months seemed impossible.

So, we helped him rethink how he defined early wins. He borrowed the pipeline concept from pharmaceutical companies and created a recording pipeline. On Day One, the pipeline was near empty. But, by month six he had an exciting array of new artists signed and viable projects in the pipeline and could show senior management the new face of the music division as his measure of success. His early win was showing tangible momentum toward a longer-term goal.

Charter the Team for the Win

It is essential that the early win create a sense of confidence and momentum in the team that can only happen when the team drives the win. You, as the leader, can inspire and enable by directing, supporting, and encouraging the team in the process; but it can't be your win. It must be the team's win. Therefore, your role as leader is to set the team up for success and support its efforts. The team charter and its five core components are useful in doing that. They are laid out here and in Tool 11.1.

1. Objective—What?
    - Clearly and specifically define the early win.
    - Use the SMART goal format to define specifically the early win and the required goals along the way.
    - The goals must generate tangible results.

2. Context—Why?
    - Provide the information that led to the desired results of the early win. (Be sure to include customer requirements if they exist.)
    - Explain the intent of the early win to ensure that team members understand the collective purpose of their individual tasks. Monitor and adjust along the way to achieve that purpose while minimizing unintended consequences.
    - Clarify what happens next. Make sure that the team understands the follow-on actions to ensure that momentum is sustained after the win is delivered.

3. Resources—With what help?
    - Ensure that the team has and can access all the human, financial, and operational resources needed to deliver the objective. (Remember, for an early win, you're going to over-invest in resources to ensure delivery.)
    - Clarify what other teams, groups, and units are involved and what their roles are.
    - Allocate resources in a timely manner to ensure delivery.

4. Guidelines—How?
    - Clarify what the team can and cannot do with regard to roles and decisions.

- Lay out the interdependencies between the team being chartered and the other teams involved.
- Decide what essential data is needed to measure results.
- Provide frequent and easy access to required data.

5. Accountability—Track and monitor.

- Clarify what is going to get done by when by whom and how the team and you are going to track milestones so that you can know about risks in advance and can intervene well before milestones are missed.
- Clarify command, communication, and support arrangements so that everyone knows how they are going to work together.
- Schedule regular updates.
- Know the signs when course corrections or reevaluations are necessary.

Overinvest in Early Wins:
Summary and Implications

Early wins are all about credibility, confidence, and momentum. People have more faith in people who have delivered. You want your boss to have confidence in you. You want the team to have confidence in you and in themselves. Early wins will provide that confidence.

QUESTIONS YOU SHOULD ASK YOURSELF

- Have I identified an early win that will accomplish all that it needs to in terms of securing my job and giving the team confidence?
- Do I have confidence in the team's strategy and tactical capacity to deliver this win?
- Am I certain that I have invested enough resources to accomplish the win?
- Do I have a comprehensive plan to monitor and adjust to ensure an early win victory.

TOOL 11.1

Team Charter Tool*

Useful for getting teams off to the best start on their way to an early win.

OBJECTIVES/GOALS Charge the team with delivering specific, measurable results (SMART)

_____

_____

CONTEXT Information that led to objectives:

_____

_____

Intent behind the objectives:

_____

_____

What's going to happen after the objective is achieved:

_____

_____

RESOURCES Human, financial, and operational resources available to the team. Other teams, groups, units working in parallel, supporting or interdependent areas.

_____

_____

GUIDELINES Clarify what the team can and cannot do with regard to _roles_ and _decisions_. Lay out the _interdependencies_ between the team being chartered and the other teams involved.

_____

_____

ACCOUNTABILITY Be clear on accountability structure, update timing, completion timing.

_____

_____

Secure *ADEPT* People in the Right Roles and Deal with Inevitable Resistance by Day 70

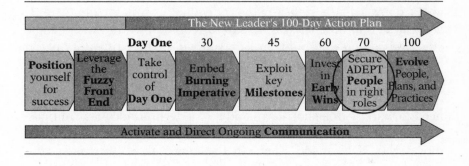

Of all the tools in your toolbox, putting people in the right roles is one of the most powerful. It is also the most explosive. As you seek to evolve (or shock!) the culture, these moves will be the most decisive and will have the greatest impact.

Often, team members of a culture or organization that is beginning to evolve will watch and wait to see if there are any consequences for not evolving with the new culture. They will pay particular attention to the team members who say things like, "All that meeting and report stuff is fine, but if it means I have to change what I do, forget it!" The moment somebody is terminated or moved or promoted, those who have been resisting the change often develop a completely different view of things. There is no single way to impact BRAVE more quickly than changes to the organization chart.

Everybody on the team feels it when people moves are made. Everyone will have an opinion (usually strong) on the moves and how they affect them. Personnel moves spark emotions, fears, and egos, so you need to be careful and thoughtful about who, what, and especially when you move people. Recognize that moving people should actually be seen as your most potent communication tool: this woman means business and she means it now!

As a leader, you can help your team and the people you're working with to see their roles in a more comprehensive light if you make an effort to link it directly to their career development. Many people are not in the right role for the team's mission or even for their own professional development. Moving roles is often as much about doing what is right for the individual as it is for the team. If you can develop the leadership skill of communicating with people effectively about roles and careers, you will be investing not only in the success of your 100 days, but in your own long-term success as a leader.

When it comes to sorting people and roles on your team, you need to work with a short-term and a long-term framework. Initially, you must look at your team to determine what if any short-term moves should be made. Then, in the longer term, you must continue to monitor your team. This chapter deals with the short time frame. We use a process called ADEPT to develop the team over time. Appendix V gives you a context for this and the ideas you can apply over time.

The headlines are:

Acquire	Scope roles.
	ID prospects.
	Recruit and select the right people for the right roles.
	Attract those people.
	Onboard them so that they can deliver better results faster.
Develop	Assess performance drivers.
	Develop skills and knowledge for current and future roles.
Encourage	Provide clear direction, objectives, measures, and so on.
	Support with resources and the time required for success.
	Reinforce desired behaviors with recognition and rewards.
Plan	Monitor people's performance over time.
	Assess their situation and potential.
	Plan career moves/succession planning over time.
Transition	Migrate people to different roles to fit their needs/life stage, and company needs.

Start by making sure that you've got the right people in the right roles. It's unlikely that you'll acquire a team that is perfectly set up to deliver against your Burning Imperative. If you're lucky, with a couple of small tweaks you'll be on your way to a world-class team. However, depending on the amount of change that you are trying to drive, you may need to do a major overhaul. If so, be prepared for a lot of work and a lot of disruption. The earlier you make that assessment the better. Don't make the mistake of delaying or avoiding the people changes that need to be made while hoping that some magical transformation will occur. It won't.

We push hard on this issue. Often we make our clients feel uncomfortable by suggesting that they make people moves faster than they've been used to doing. For some reason, it is human nature to put off such decisions. We have a strong bias for figuring them out as early as possible and making the moves quickly. It is hard medicine for most people to swallow, but it's much like a child's fear of pulling off a bandage quickly. Once it is removed, the child realizes that the process was not so painful after all. Get this process done quickly—you'll be happy you did. You certainly do not have to follow our advice on timing, but we strongly suggest that you do. Getting the right people in the right roles with the right support is a fundamental, essential building block of a high-performing team. Without the right people in the right roles, there is no team.

Getting ADEPT people in the right roles is guided by the team's mission, vision, and values, as well as by individuals' strengths. The mission determines the make-up of the ideal organization over the long run. The resulting strategies and plans help determine what roles are required to do the things that need to be done on a daily basis. This gives you a map of the roles you need to have—and the roles you do not need.

Southwest Airlines is in the business of transporting people by airplane. The organization needs to include people to maintain the planes, fly the planes, sell tickets, and service its passengers. It needs these roles. It does not need chefs, bartenders, or masseuses—even though some other airlines do have people in those roles.

With a picture of required roles in hand, you can now look at which roles will have the greatest impact on achieving your vision. The roles responsible for these tasks are the critical ones. The other roles encompass tasks that can be done merely "good enough." This is where strategy and people overlap—determining which roles need to be best in class and invested in, and which roles can be just maintained or outsourced.

The airline industry, as an industry, loses buckets of money over the long term. (This is true for most industries centered on transporting people.) Yet, Southwest makes money every year. Part of why it does is that it has figured out which are its critical roles. Southwest overinvests in maintenance roles so it can turn its planes around faster. It overinvests in training its stewardesses and stewards so passengers' in-air experience is fun. Conversely, it underinvests in food service and on-the-ground waiting spaces.

The NASA team members on Apollo 13 were aligned around a clear Burning Imperative, had clear milestones, and got an early win by fixing the oxygen/carbon monoxide problem. Although everyone was willing to do whatever it took to get the astronauts home safely, they stayed in their roles. One group of physicists figured out how to wrap the spacecraft around the moon and get it going in the right direction. Another group of engineers fixed the oxygen problem. Another group dealt with the reentry calculations. The spare crew members truly did whatever it took to try things out. They were all working together without getting in each other's way.

Strengths are necessary for success. But they are not sufficient. People must want to do well and they must fit in. It is helpful to think in terms of strengths, motivation, and fit.

Strengths

Now, you are ready to match the right people with the right roles. Marcus Buckingham and Don Clifton's[1] core premise is that people do better when they capitalize on their own, individual strengths—talent, knowledge, and skills.

Motivation

You did your own work on your values and goals as part of the Five-Step Career Plan (Tool 1.2). As a leader, you need to do a similar kind of work with your team members. If you understand their values, their goals, and how they see what they are currently doing in light of those goals, you have a terrific advantage in helping them find or live up to the right role for themselves and for the organization.

---

[1] Buckingham, Marcus, and Clifton, Donald, *Now Discover Your Strengths* (New York: Free Press, 2001).

Fit

Fit is about the match of an individual's BRAVE preferences with the Behaviors, Relationships, Attitudes, Values, and Environment of your culture. Take a hard look at attitudinal perspective, values, and biases.

Perspective is an attitude born out of how people have been trained to view and solve business problems. This is the accumulation of people's business experience as manifested in their mental models. People with a classic sales perspective may feel that they can sell any product to customers. Conversely, people with a more marketing perspective may feel the organization should modify its products and services to meet customers' needs. We are not suggesting that one perspective is better than the other, just that they are different.

We talked about values in Chapter 9, when discussing the Burning Imperative. It is rare for all of any individual's values to match all of the organization's values. However, it is important for most of the core values to match and for none of them to be in direct conflict with each other.

Different people behave at work in different ways. Some roles may require people with a greater sense of urgency. Some roles require people who think things through thoroughly before jumping in. If someone who tends to get a later start on the day is assigned the role of making morning coffee for the group before everyone else comes in, it would force the person to work in opposition to a natural bias and would most likely be a recipe for failure (and bad coffee).

Don't Wait

It is a classic tale. It was the Seventh Game of the 2003 American League Baseball Championship Series. The winner moved on to the World Series. The New York Yankees, perennial winners and its pitching ace Roger Clemens versus the Boston Red Sox with 86 years of disappointment and its pitching ace Pedro Martinez.

Fourth inning: Clemens is struggling. Yankee manager Joe Torre takes him out—early, decisively, without much discussion.

Eighth inning: Martinez is struggling. Red Sox manager Grady Little goes out to the pitcher's mound and asks if Martinez has "enough bullets in (his) tank." The response: "I have enough." Little leaves him in. "Pedro wanted to stay in there," Little said. "He wanted to get the job done, just as he has many times for us all season long." As Martinez put it, "I would never say no. I tried hard and I did whatever possible to win the ballgame."

Martinez and the Red Sox proceed to blow the lead and lose the game. Once again Clemens, Torre, and the Yankees go on to the World Series while two weeks later, Little loses his job.

As the sportswriters put it, Little's decision was "based more on loyalty and emotion than logic." From Torre's point of view, "In Game 7, you've got a short leash. I'd worry about his emotions after the game."

There is a lot in common between Game 7 and a complex transition. Everyone is on a short leash. So it's essential to move early, logically, and decisively.

Don't Let One Bad Apple Spoil the Batch

Charlie was the new head of the division. One of his direct reports, Jack, was deploying blatantly passive-aggressive tactics to undermine Charlie's authority.

On a regular basis, Jack would:

- Sit in the back of large meetings and carry on side conversations during Charlie's presentations.
- Refuse to work on the agreed divisional priorities until he and his team had completed their annual plans presentation.
- Refuse to do prework for Charlie's meetings because he didn't think the process was meaningful.

We had a tough conversation with Charlie about this: "You need to remove Jack from your team."

"Can't do it. My boss put Jack in place and I'm reluctant to make a move with someone he hired. I'll just work around him."

"If you remove Jack, there is a chance that your boss will think less of you as a manager because you didn't give Jack a chance. But, if you do not move on Jack, you will get fired within six months because Jack is going to make sure your team does not work."

Charlie removed Jack and filled the role with someone who was openly committed to the team's Burning Imperative. Six months later, Charlie's team had delivered on its early wins and was on schedule to deliver on its stated objectives. Charlie's boss commented on the high level of team unity, focus, and morale. He made no mention of Jack.

This story and the story of the Yankees beating the Red Sox in the American League Championship Series make the same point. You have to do what is right for the organization and what's right for the individuals. You have to find a way to get the right people in the right roles at the right time. You have to do it early and decisively. You should worry about their emotions—but never let them interfere with making the right decisions at the right time.

Keep People in the Right Roles

Iris was promoted from COO to president of her division. One of her first moves was to move someone into her old role. For that job, she selected Jamil, who had been doing an excellent job as the head of technology. Over the years of working with Jamil, Iris felt he was intelligent, possessed great people skills, and was completely reliable. She assumed he'd be a natural for the COO role.

After promoting Jamil to the COO position, she also asked Jamil's top technology person, Rita, to assume the now vacant head of technology role. Initially Iris was quite pleased with the new team composition and felt confident in her potential for success. However, within the first 30 days as she worked with her team to co-create a new Burning Imperative, she started to see that Jamil was failing miserably because he was totally unaccustomed to the more consensual decision making of senior management. He was struggling to adjust and causing friction among the other team members. Meanwhile, Rita had continued going about her job as if nothing had changed and was ill equipped to handle her new management responsibilities. As a result, the technology team made several costly mistakes, something that never happened under Jamil's leadership.

Iris was faced with a tough decision: admit that her first moves were a mistake, or try and live with the wrong people in the wrong roles. We strongly encouraged her to move quickly and correct the mistake. Living with the wrong people in such crucial roles would have been certain disaster. Convinced, Iris made the difficult choice to reorganize again. She quickly found a seasoned COO to run the division operations. She moved Jamil back into a technology role with a new title and added responsibilities that she knew he could handle and Rita was relieved of her management responsibilities. It was a painful retrenchment in the short term, but the realignment quickly produced benefits for the entire team. The team appreciated Iris's willingness to correct her own mistakes for the betterment of the team.

Once you have people in the right role, leave them there and support them in that role. Also, remember that just because someone is good in one role doesn't mean that the person will be good in another role that requires different strengths and motivations.

Cut the Pain Out Early
(Or, at Least, as Early as Practical)

Sherman had just taken over as general manager. He knew he had
to improve both the sales and marketing functions dramatically, as
soon as he could. To achieve that, he knew that he had to replace the
heads of both functions; but he also knew that both were extremely
valuable, respected, and valued employees who could make important contributions in other roles that would better leverage their
strengths, motivation, and fit.

So Sherman began searching for their replacements immediately, while being open with them about what he was doing. He
worked closely with them early on to build strong personal relationships with them and let them know that they were still a value to the
organization, but that their roles would change to better fit within
the changing organization.

Six months later, Sherman hired new heads of sales and marketing. He assigned the previous leaders as direct reports, but he put
them in new, more appropriate roles that enabled them to make an
important impact on the organization and actively help their replacements succeed.

How Fast Should You Move on the Team?

In general, we suggest having your plan in place to sort roles and
make people moves at the end of 70 days or 10 weeks. There will be
times when you need to move much faster, and there will be times
when it will take you longer to implement the plan but the 70th day is
a good target time frame to have it all figured out.

There is a risk in moving too fast. The risk is that you'll make
poor decisions and come across as too impulsive. By the 70th day,
you will have had a chance to see people in the Burning Imperative
workshop, in the milestone management process and, for some of
them, in the pursuit to deliver on an early win. By day 70, you should
have enough information to make those crucial decisions.

There's a larger risk in moving too slow. At about 100 days, you
own the team. Once you own the team, the problem children become
your problem children. You can't blame the team's failings or unre-
solved issues on your predecessor any more. Also, the other team
members know who the weak links are and they might have known
since before you took the helm. They will want you to have made

the tough moves. The number one thing high performers want is for management to act on low performers so the whole group can do better.[2] If you move too slowly, the other team members will wonder what took you so long.

To be clear, you may not be able to implement your decisions all at once. You may need to put in place transition plans that support weaker team members or keep strong team members in the wrong roles during the time it takes to get their replacements on board and up to speed. We're not suggesting that you make all your moves in your first 70 days, no matter what. We are suggesting that you have the plan in place and begin making moves as appropriate and that you do so with a bias to making the moves sooner rather than later.

A Pivotal Leadership Moment

Jeng-li knew he had a problem with his lead general counsel, Susanna. Her communication and management style along with her negative attitude and questionable values created a work environment that was far from what Jeng-li and the rest of his management team were trying to instill in the organization. However, he hesitated to do anything about it because he was worried how she might react and the resulting fallout. It turned out that everyone else on the management team was uneasy around Susanna, too. Eventually things got so bad that he could no longer avoid the problem. So he called in the corporate HR people and together they mapped out the plan to transition Susanna out of the organization.

Jeng-li scheduled a meeting with Susanna for 4:00 the next afternoon. At that meeting he and the corporate HR person presented the transition plan to Susanna and she was immediately escorted out of her office. Susanna had sensed the moment coming and left without incident.

Having successfully kept the transition plan under wraps until the last moment, Jeng-li knew that the news would get out quickly after the conversation with Susanna. He wanted to be the one to tell people what he had done and why. So, knowing that everything communicates (including the order in which people are communicated to) he thoughtfully planned whom he would communicate to,

---

[2]Thank you, Dave Kuhlman of Sibson Consulting for this insight.

when he would do it, and in what order. Immediately after his meeting with Susanna he told, in order:

1. His direct reports.
2. Susanna's direct reports.
3. Susanna's key contacts at the law firms that supported the division.

Then, the following Monday morning he sent an e-mail out to the broader organization.

In his messaging, he made a specific decision not to position Susanna's departure as being for "personal reasons" or the like. He made it clear that Susanna was being terminated because she was hurting the organizational culture. It was one of the strongest statements Jeng-li could make on the importance of organizational culture. He took action to preserve the desired culture, he was honest about why he did it, and he communicated quickly and clearly to everyone who needed to know. His approach was well received and greatly appreciated and it served to reinforce his personal values and the stated values of the team.

HOT TIP

Move faster on the team: Have a bias to move faster on your team than you think you should. The risks of moving too fast are nothing compared with the multiplier effect of leaving people in the wrong place too long. The number one thing that experienced leaders regret is not moving faster on their people.

Map Performance and Role

Putting the right people in the right roles is a key driver of success. The heart of Tool 12.1 is a grid that matches people with roles. The grid is based on two dimensions: performance and role appropriateness. Mapping people on this grid then helps inform decisions about which people are in the right roles and which are in the wrong so you can support some and move others. This is a simple but highly effective tool for thinking about a complex subject.[3]

---

[3]Note that this is different than Drotter's 9-box tool that crosses performance and potential. The 9-box helps you think about future promotions. This 4-box matrix of performance and fit with the role helps you think about whether people are in the right role now.

The Performance measure is drawn from an individual's last or current review/assessment in his or her current role. It is driven by results versus goals and supplemented with recently observed performance, behaviors, and communication.

The Role Match measure is a correlation of the strengths, motivations, and fit required for the role compared with the strengths, motivations, and fit of the person filling that role. The role's strengths, motivations, and fit should be drawn from position descriptions. The individual's strengths, motivations, and fit could be drawn from their latest review, Gallup's StrengthFinder, or another assessment questionnaire or tool.

Keep in mind that some people may be in the wrong role precisely because they have outgrown it and are ready for a promotion. If you leave these people in their roles you'll face a growing risk for decreased motivation. If there is indication that an individual is struggling to make up for a mismatch between their strengths and those required for the job it is also a sure sign of a wrong role for that person. The Evolve box is the appropriate place for these people. In either situation, the value of having a plan to move each candidate to a more appropriate role is clear. Delay those moves and you'll find yourself and your team in trouble.

In general, the suggested actions from Figure 12.1 are:

FIGURE 12.1 Performance versus Role Match

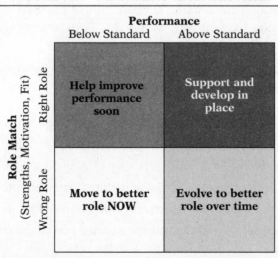

- **Support:** Right Role/Above Standard: Keep in current roles. Support and develop them. These people are helping and will continue to help. Make sure to push their ability to do good for others and for themselves as high as possible.

- **Improve:** Right Role/Below Standard: Invest to improve these people's performance. They can deliver with the right direction, training, and support.

- **Evolve:** Wrong Role/Above Standard: Actively look for better fit before performance drops. Resist the temptation to keep in current role. They are helping, but the potential exists for even more. There is also potential for flight as they become frustrated being in a role that is not right for them.

- **Move:** Wrong Role/Below Standard: Quickly move them to a better role inside or outside the team.

Mapping performance and role appropriateness facilitates a more urgent identification of who is in the right role and who is in the wrong role now. It is important not to confuse "role match" with "potential" because there is a significant difference between the two.

Potential gets at future promotions. What is required to help people move up the ladder? What is the appropriate timeline for those promotions?

Role match gets at the current position. What's the likelihood of their performing well in their current position?

Every organization has its own way of doing position profiles. The better profiles include the key elements of the mission, strengths, motivation, and fit. One way to do this is to answer the following questions in each of the following areas.

Mission

Mission gets at what you expect out of the position.

- What is the mission for this position? Why does it exist?
- What are the responsibilities associated with the role?
- What are the desired objectives or outcomes of the position?
- What impact should the role have on the rest of the organization?

Strengths

Strengths include the talents, knowledge and skills required to deliver the position's mission.

- What talents are required to achieve success in the role? (Consider talents to be a recurring pattern of thoughts, feelings, or behavior that can be productively applied.)
- What knowledge is required to achieve success in the role? (Consider what the role holder needs to be aware of or know. What are the required education, experience, and qualifications?)
- What skills are required to achieve success in the role? (Consider skills as the "how to's," or the steps of an activity. They can also be identified as capabilities that can be transferred such as technical, interpersonal, or business skills.)[4]

Motivation

Motivation is what will drive the person in the role to succeed.

- How do the activities of the role fit with the person's likes, dislikes, and ideal job criteria?
- How will the person progress toward the long-term goal? What will drive him or keep her focused?

Fit

Fit refers to the match between the person's character and the culture he or she will be operating in.

- Do the person's behaviors, way of relating to others, attitudes, values, and preferred working environment fit well with those of the *organization*?

---

[4]The strengths definitions are drawn from Buckingham and Clifton's *Now, Discover Your Strengths,* 2001.

- Do the person's behavior, way of relating to others, attitudes, values, and preferred working environment fit well with those of the *team*?

- Do the person's behavior, way of relating to others, attitudes, values, and preferred working environment fit well with those of the *leader*?

Secure ADEPT People in the Right Roles: Summary and Implications

Put in place ADEPT organizational processes to Acquire, Develop, Encourage, Plan, and Transition talent over time.

The mission informs the ideal organization and helps identify the required roles.

The vision helps identify which roles are required to be best in class.

Match performance, strengths, motivation, and fit of individuals and roles:

- Support and develop high performers in right roles.

- Improve performance of low performers in right roles.

- Evolve high performers in wrong role to better roles over time.

- Move low performers in wrong role to better role now.

Some of your most painful choices are going to be in this area. This is one of those areas where trying to please everybody will lead to pleasing nobody. Choosing to act on people who are in the wrong roles now or will soon be in the wrong roles is generally not the most enjoyable part of leadership. But it is an essential part.

QUESTIONS YOU SHOULD ASK YOURSELF

- Am I moving at the right speed to get the right people in the right roles?
- Do I have appropriate backup and contingency plans?
- Am I making the tough choices on people as soon as I have identified a mismatch?
- Do I have the right organizational processes in place for the longer term?

TOOL 12.1

Performance/Role Match*

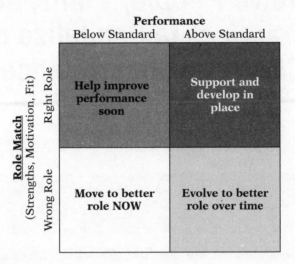

Performance

		Below Standard	Above Standard

Role Match (Strengths, Motivation, Fit)

Right Role: Help improve performance soon | Support and develop in place

Wrong Role: Move to better role NOW | Evolve to better role over time

People Actions:

Right Role/Above Standard:

Keep in current roles. Support and develop them. These people are helping and will continue to help. Make sure to push their compensation, employability, meaning in the work, and share in shaping of their maximum potential.

Right Role/Below Standard:

Invest to improve these people's performance. They can deliver with the right direction, training, and support.

Wrong Role/Above Standard:

Actively look for better fit before performance drops. Resist the temptation to keep in current role. They are helping, but the potential exists for even more.

Wrong Role/Below Standard:

Quickly move to a better role inside or outside the team.

CHAPTER 13

Evolve *People, Plans,* and *Practices* to Capitalize on Changing Circumstances

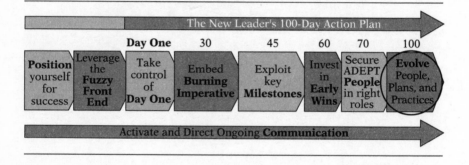

The New Leader's 100-Day Action Plan

		Day One	30	45	60	70	100
Position yourself for success	Leverage the **Fuzzy Front End**	Take control of **Day One**	Embed **Burning Imperative**	Exploit key **Milestones**	Invest in **Early Wins**	Secure ADEPT **People** in right roles	**Evolve** People, Plans, and Practices

Activate and Direct Ongoing **Communication**

The 100-day mark is a good moment to start thinking about how you are going to evolve your people, plans, and practices over time to capitalize on changing circumstances. It's useful to set up a predictable rhythm. This allows people to spend less time worrying about the process and more time figuring out how to react and capitalize on the inevitable changes around them. You probably won't be surprised to learn that we think that P³ (people, plans, and practices) is a good framework for doing just that. And you won't be surprised that BRAVE—Behaviors, Relationships, Attitudes, Values, and Environment—is foundation for assessing your progress and your opportunities.

Capitalizing on Inevitable Changes

The following are important elements to consider on a regular basis.

People

Succession Planning
- Align the longer-term organizational development plans with the longer-term (three-plus year) strategic plan.
- Do this on an annual basis.

Performance Management and Talent Review
- Track progress of the longer-term succession plan and the corresponding talent needs (one-year horizon).
- Do this on an annual basis.

Plans

Strategic Review, Refresh, and Plan
- Conduct a detailed long-term look at the business (three-year horizon), leading to choices around how to create and allocate resources over that longer-term horizon.
- Do this on an annual basis.

Operational Review, Refresh, and Plan
- Ensure that the right operational plans (one-year horizon) are in place that will enable you to deliver the next year's goals.
- Do this on an annual basis.

Practices

Business Reviews and Plan Updates
- Track progress in the context of the operational plan (one-year horizon) and make midcourse adjustments along the way.
- Do this quarterly.

Milestone Updates and Adjustment
- Track the monthly milestones to keep the team focused on the most important thing, as a team.
- Do this monthly, unless particular milestones are falling off target, in which case you should increase the frequency until the milestones are back on track.

Thinking about these things with these horizons allows you to have a good balance between long-term thinking and short-term execution. A number of our clients have blended these into an annual/quarterly/monthly meeting schedule. The idea is to have a meeting every month with time added once each quarter to deal with longer-term issues. It is a cycle with each piece feeding into the next. Use this calendar as a starting point and then adjust it to meet your organizational needs without dropping any key pieces:

Quarter	Month	Schedule
1	1	Milestone update and adjustment
1	2	Business review and adjustment/Talent reviews
1	3	Milestone update and adjustment
2	1	Milestone update and adjustment
2	2	Business review and adjustment/Strategic review and planning
2	3	Milestone update and adjustment
3	1	Milestone update and adjustment
3	2	Business review and adjustment/Succession planning
3	3	Milestone update and adjustment
4	1	Milestone update and adjustment
4	2	Business review and adjustment/Operational review and planning
4	3	Milestone update and adjustment

Adjust to the Inevitable Surprises

John Wooden, the legendary coach of UCLA basketball, whose teams won an astounding 10 U.S. College National Championships, said: "Things turn out the best for the people who make the best of the way things turn out."[1] As a leader, it is up to you to make the best of how things turn out. No matter how well you have planned your transition over the first 100 days, no matter how disciplined you are in your follow-up, some things will be different than you expected. Often your ability to keep moving forward while reacting to the

---

[1]Wooden, John and Jamison, Steve, 2005, *Wooden on Leadership*, New York: McGraw-Hill.

unexpected or the unplanned will be the determining factor whether your transition is deemed a success or failure.

One of the main advantages to starting early and deploying the building blocks of tactical capacity quickly is that you and your team will be ready that much sooner to adjust to changing circumstances and surprises. Remember, the ability to respond flexibly and fluidly is a hallmark of a team with tactical capacity. The preceding annual/quarterly/monthly meeting schedule will enable your team to recognize and react to the changes that might impact your team over time.

Not all surprises are equal. Your first job is to sort them out to guide your own and your team's response. If it is a temporary, minor blip, keep your team focused on its existing priorities. If it is minor but enduring, factor it into your ongoing P^3 (people, plans, and practices) evolution.

Major surprises are a different game. If they're temporary, you'll want to move into crisis or incident management. If they're enduring, you'll need to react and make some fundamental changes to deal with the new reality. When you're evaluating change, use Chart 13.1 to help guide you to an appropriate measured response.

CHART 13.1   Change Map

Type	Temporary Impact	Enduring Impact
Major change	Manage	Restart
	Deploy incident management response plan	Requires a fundamental redeployment of P^3
Minor change	Downplay	Evolve
	Control and stay focused on priorities	Factor into ongoing team evolution

Major but Temporary Surprises

Major but temporary surprises start out either good or bad. They don't necessarily stay that way. Just as a crisis handled well can turn into a good thing, a major event handled poorly can easily turn into a serious crisis. The difference comes down to preparing in advance, implementing the response, and learning and improving for the next time.

You may also want to look at Appendix IX for a variation on this that we developed with the American Red Cross. That specific variation and its iterative response approach is enabling the Red Cross's disaster response teams to start doing on day two what they previously weren't doing until day six of a disaster. That acceleration can be the difference between an incident becoming a minor crisis or a major event. The appendix also includes a 100-hour action plan tool for leading through a crisis.

1. *Prepare in advance.*

   As the team leader, it is on your shoulders to prepare in advance for potential surprises by anticipating potential events and crises and having procedures in place to follow if those things happen. Be assured that crisis events will never unfold exactly as you have planned for them. It is less important that you are exactly right in identifying the particular crisis that might come your way, but most important that you and the organization or team have a response in place for unexpected events.

   Think through the possible situations, your desired result, and basic approach to get there. Then map out what is going to get done by when and by whom, and how you are going to communicate with the stakeholders that are essential to implementing a successful response or those affected by the chosen response. Once your plans are in place, periodically review the response plan so you are ready to identify and react to surprises when they do hit. The better you have anticipated possible scenarios, the more prepared you are, the more confidence you will have when crises strike.

2. *Implement a response.*

   The reason you prepared is so that you all can react quickly and flexibility to the situation you face. Don't overthink or overmanage this. Do what you prepared to do and let others do what they prepared to do.

   When the inevitable surprise happens, put in place a specific plan for that particular event or crisis using your preplanned response as a starting point. Implement your response following the basic milestone management process. One important difference is that instead of running your milestone meetings on a monthly basis, you'll run them far more frequently. Depending on the crisis you may want to consider running them daily, if not even more frequently. Most likely, you will want to keep them relatively brief, laser-focused, and drive the team's time and efforts heavily toward the actual implementation of your crisis plan.

   Once you start to see results and the crisis starts to become stabilized do not make the mistake of pulling back your efforts too soon. Crises have a nasty habit of getting out of control because people take their eyes off the ball too soon. It is hard to know when the temporary event or crisis is completely over. So have a bias to stick with the follow-through longer than you might think is necessary.

3. *Learn and improve.*

Once the crisis is over it is essential to complete a comprehensive review of your organization's response across three key areas: Preparedness (precrisis), Response (crisis management), and Prevention (postcrisis). In each area, identify the gaps in your organization's performance and find ways to rectify them.

- **Preparedness:** Was the team adequately prepared to respond to the current crisis and implement the response?

- **Response:** Did the team respond well and how can it improve its capabilities to respond to future crises?

- **Prevention:** How can the organization reduce the risk of future crises happening in the first place?

Once your gap analysis is complete, take the steps to implement the changes required to improve your ability to deal with the next crisis. There will be a next one.

Major and Enduring

Major changes that are enduring require a fundamental restart. These can be material changes in things like customer needs, collaborators' direction, competitors' strategies, or the economic, political, or social environment in which you operate. They can be internal changes such as reorganizations, acquisitions, or spin-offs.

One major and enduring change that you are almost guaranteed to go through sometime is getting a new boss, or your boss getting a new boss. Take a look at the section on getting a new boss in Appendix VI and put those ideas into play immediately.

Whatever the change, if it's major and enduring, hit a restart button. Go right back to the beginning, do a full situation analysis, identify the key stakeholders, have a relook at your message, restart your communication plan, and get your P^3 realigned around the new purpose. Remember, the fittest adapt best.

Don't Forget Your Communication Efforts

One of the pillars of successful leadership is ongoing communication. These efforts must evolve to capitalize on changing circumstances as well. With minor changes, your message may remain the same. However, if the change is major, your message and touch points must be adjusted to match the new reality. In some cases, the change may be significant enough to warrant a complete revamping of the plan. Either way, make sure that you are controlling your own message and how it is communicated.

Finis origine pendet (the end depends on the beginning)— so says the Latin poet Manilius.[2] In a transition into a new leadership role, if you do not get the beginning right, the end will be ugly. If you follow this book's framework and take advantage of its tools, you will then be leading your team to the right place, in the right way, at the right time. If you do this, you will develop trust, loyalty, and commitment—and your team will follow. By using the proven onboarding methodologies presented in this book to enhance and synchronize your P^3 (people, plans, and practices), you will build the tactical capacity to inspire and enable others to do their absolute best together, to realize a meaningful and rewarding shared purpose that delivers better results faster than anyone thought possible.

---

[2] Attributed to First century Latin poet Marcus Manlius.

APPENDICES

Deploy Six Basic Elements of Leadership

In the Introduction, we quote Lao-tzu on the subtle art of great leadership:

> *The great leader speaks little. He never speaks carelessly. He works without self-interest and leaves no trace. When all is finished, the people say, "We did it ourselves."*[1]

In Chapter 1, inspired by Lao-tzu and the idea of the leader who speaks little and with great care, we break down the components of communicating leadership into a set of six basic elements that you should deploy deliberately and consistently to further develop your own leadership potential.

1. Listen and observe first.
2. Talk in order to listen and connect better.
3. Imagine the leaders' or key stakeholders' perspective.
4. Identify potential areas for leadership.
5. Lead through actions that communicate.
6. Carpe Diem.

---

[1] Paraphrasing the 17th verse of the *Tao Te Ching* by Lao-tzu.

In this appendix we return to those six basic elements to develop them further.

1. *Listen and observe first.*

Good leaders are good connectors. To establish strong connections, they listen and read situations effectively. Many new leaders land their new role on the strength of other more narrowly defined skills or accomplishments and may have had neither the natural tendency nor the opportunity to develop effective connecting skills.

Our position on this is adamant: you must cultivate listening skills and behavior, no matter where on the spectrum you fall naturally. As with most skills, you first recognize it as something you need to develop long term, and then you begin to practice it tactically. We recommend that you develop an ingrained habit of listening and observing first. Every time. Be sure to actively observe body language, facial expressions, tone of voice—all these communicate long before words are exchanged. Listen and observe as you go into meetings, conversations, and the like. Then, use that information to achieve a higher level of effectiveness.

2. *Talk in order to listen and connect better.*

Experienced communicators will talk *in order* to listen and to connect. They use a Socratic process, asking questions, or proposing possible ideas that create an environment in which key information or shifts in perspective will emerge. Connecting with the other person's likely point of view and/or emotional potential is the critical goal. This is especially important and effective in tense or potentially conflictive situations: "Okay, let me see if I hear correctly what you are saying." "Let me take a shot at capturing your position in my own terms. Let me know if I get this wrong." The simple gesture of signaling that you want to work with that person to achieve an understanding brings down antagonism or opposition while inducing cooperation and increasing trust.

People exercise leadership by speaking deftly with a goal of connecting and helping shape the common view.

3. *Imagine the leaders' or key stakeholders' perspective.*

To condition the path toward leadership, you need to see things from the leaders' broader perspective. Not just once, constantly. Work to understand, as well as possible, the team's or the organization's goals and objectives. These may be explicit, or they may not be. Actively frame your own work and the topics and issues that come up from that point of view. By connecting to the fundamental goals of the group, you are helping your team and key stakeholders accomplish their goals.

4. *Identify potential areas for leadership.*

   If you understand the group's and your leadership goals, you will find ample opportunities to help move things along in those directions. We encourage you also to remember that your actions communicate messages far beyond the surface. Take on more responsibility than asked. Help keep a colleague from going down a wrong path. In each case, take a good measure of the opportunity in terms of what you can do, whether there are risks involved, how it will shape your colleagues', subordinates', and superiors' perspective of you in the short term, and how this can build their perceptions of you as a leader for the long term.

5. *Lead through actions that communicate.*

   Here are a few ways of communicating leadership through action:

   ### Work

   If you can't do the work you're expected to be doing, it's going to be difficult to get to where you want to be. Do good work. Do the right work. Do timely work. Hey, do work ahead of time! Don't focus work on projects that don't matter to the team, or when they no longer matter to the team.

   It goes deeper than this though. Work has a stylistic, a social, yes a cultural dimension to it. Identify the organization's, your team's and your own cultural work values and be absolutely certain that your work is in sync with those values. In some environments creativity is at a premium. In others, speed and accuracy is. In others, consensus-based work sets the cultural standard. In others it's work done outside the group that rallies energy. Find the culture view of the organization's work and make sure that your career path is in alignment with it.

   ### Insight

   Leadership is often granted to those who show real insight (and display it in the appropriate way). There are many ways to show insight in ways that are important to the organization. Insight into any important aspect of the business will provide value. Teams constantly need leadership insight to help get past their challenges and to perform well. You will have opportunities on a daily basis to use your insight to help frame and to solve problems for your colleagues. But remember Lao-tzu: the great leader speaks little. Nobody appreciates a know-it-all.

Reliability

Reliability is a key feature for those who are promoted to leadership. But it comes in many forms and it's important to know which are likely to be important to the leadership and to the company as a whole. Shrewd leaders know how to shoulder a seemingly annoying or unpleasant responsibility simply to communicate that they are willing to do what needs to get done to help the team achieve their goals. The message should be clear; you are able and willing and can be relied on when it matters.

Judgment

Senior leadership usually uses this word in making decisions about important promotions and opportunities. Does this person have good judgment? Is this what would be said about you? Why? Why not? The important part of judgment is knowing the framework with which the organization values decision making and being thoughtful about how any given situation might fit in with that framework. Good judgment might be perceived differently in a small start-up than in a highly structured and conservative organization. All in all, being thoughtful about implications is the hallmark of good judgment. A calculated but big risk, that was well understood, may well be considered excellent judgment in some organizations, even if it fails. As Lao-tzu says, the great leader never speaks carelessly.

The word *judgment* often connects to relations with people. Leaders lead people, and have to make decisions and take actions with and about people. Even if you are not formally managing people, you are invariably involved in helping assess people and their work. Good judgment manifests itself in these informal ways long before anybody might ask you to be a manager.

Energy

People underestimate the importance of energy for leadership or for the health and success of a team or organization. The leadership is often tied in directly to the energy effects a person produces. Pay close attention to how you affect other people's energy. Pay attention to people who somehow generate energy in meetings and interactions. It is surprising how many talented people stumble in leadership roles because they fail the energy test. Take the test. Take it every day. Some tips:

Energize the group by talking up targets and goals.

Never spare kudos to individuals—praise everything good.

Be sparing of negative comments and pep talks, but use them as appropriate.

Make sure the team finds ways to celebrate successes.

Be attuned to negative moods in individuals or the group and seek to find what may be causing it.

Watch your own moods and find ways to turn them positive.

Humor

Look for ways to use humor to bond and energize the group. A common failing among leaders or potential leaders is a lack of self-deprecating humor. Done with care, this can help turn a hierarchically tense, guarded, and wary group of employees into a genuine team. The opposite—humor at others' expense—is counterproductive, and, sadly, common among people in leadership positions. If that's the way your humor runs, learn to redirect it. It will just get you in trouble. Since we're talking about getting in trouble, be careful about the humor that comes out in more informal situations, especially if drinking is involved. Steer yourself out of trouble, and help your colleagues do the same.

Conflict

Conflict is part of life, and certainly part of organizational life. Conflicts can freeze teams and cripple organizations. Groups almost inescapably have moments of internal conflict. A key sign of a leader is someone who can help the group handle its conflicts better. A leader helps people make sense of the conflict and see paths to resolution. Avoid taking sides but give the underlying causes their due, once a fair articulation of positions has taken place, create an atmosphere of respectful possibility. It is delicate work. As Lao-tzu says, the great leader works without self-interest and leaves no trace. If you've been doing your homework (listening, connecting, and understanding both the individual's and the group's goals) you will have the tools to help shift the group to a better place. The group will say, as Lao-tzu predicts, "we did it ourselves." Often without fully realizing why, the group will look to you for leadership as a result.

Avoid needless conflict yourself. A tendency to get into and mishandle conflict can absolutely collapse your career. However, there is such a thing as necessary conflict. Look for ways to allow all to keep (or regain) dignity and feel like what happened was fair and professional.

Inspiration

Successful leaders know how to tap into concepts and language that inspire people. Values and goals inspire people. Personal passion and commitment inspire people. Family, humanity, and personal connection inspire people. Inspiration is the difference between a team that comes in, does its work, and checks out versus a team where people derive significant personal satisfaction from their work and the success of their team. The building blocks are the individual relationships you have with your colleagues. You can begin to activate inspiration long before you're in a position to set goals for team members and challenge them to successes.

6. *Carpe diem.*

Sooner or later, a key leadership opportunity will emerge. You will need to act decisively. If you've been preparing for this, you are likely to recognize the opportunity. Think in advance about how you would respond to situations where there is a lot at stake.

When there is a lot at stake, many of us behave differently than we usually do, often to our detriment. Impulsive or panicky behavior is typical. A deep-seated fight-or-flight response can kick in. Generally speaking, neither one is best suited for the occasion. Consider carefully how you typically respond and what you can do to make sure that you respond the way you want to. Answering certain questions can help you get ready in advance. Are you prepared for a change in responsibilities? Are you willing to undertake a certain amount of risk or discomfort? How can you give yourself time for composure? Finally, how can you move from your own volatile feelings to the core elements of leadership—listening, connecting, understanding, and goal setting—and make sure that you are communicating these things even in the midst of this situation?

It's best to also end with Lao-tzu:

He works without self-interest and leaves no trace. When all is finished, the people say, "We did it ourselves."

Complete a Situation Assessment to Inform Your Plan

The fundamental purpose of this tool is to assess what's going on with your customers, collaborators, capabilities, competitors, and conditions (5Cs) and put that into a SWOT analysis so you can figure out your key leverage points and business issues.

The 5Cs

Customers: First line, customer chain, end users, influencers.

Collaborators: Suppliers, allies, government/community leaders.

Capabilities: Human, operational, financial, technical, key assets.

Competitors: Direct, indirect, potential.

Conditions: Social/demographic, political/government/regulatory, economic, market.

Customers

Customers include the people your business sells to—direct customers who actually give you money. It also includes their customers, their customers' customers, and so on down the line. Eventually, there are end users or consumers of whatever the output of that chain is. Finally, there are the people who influence your various customers' purchase decisions. Take all of these into account.

Federal Express sells overnight delivery services to corporate purchasing departments that contract those services on behalf of business managers. But the real decision makers are those managers' administrative assistants. So, Federal Express targets its marketing efforts not at the people who write the checks, not at the managers, but at the core influencers. They aim advertising and media at those influencers and have their drivers pick up the packages from the administrative assistants personally instead of going through an impersonal mailroom.

Collaborators

Collaborators include your suppliers, business allies, and people delivering complementary products and services. What links all these groups together is that they will do better if *you* do better so it's in their best interest, whether they know it or not, to help you succeed. Think Microsoft and Intel. Think hot dogs and mustard.

Just as these relationships are two-way, so must be your analysis. You need to understand the interdependencies and reciprocal commitments. Whenever these dependencies and commitments are out of balance, the nature of the relationships will inevitably change.

Capabilities

Capabilities are those abilities that can help you deliver a differentiated, better product or service to your customers. These abilities include everything from access to materials and capital to plants and equipment to people to patents. Pay particular attention to people, plans, and practices.

Competitors

Competitors are anyone that your customers could give their money or attention to instead of you. It is important to take a wide view of potential competitors. Amtrak's real competitors are other forms of transportation like automobiles and airplanes. The competition for consumer dollars may be as varied as a child's college education versus a Disney World vacation. In analyzing these competitors, it is important to think through their objectives, strategies, and situation,[1]

---

[1]This should likely include a look at profit pools as described by Gadiesh, Orit, and Gilbert, James L., 1998. "A Fresh Look at Strategy." *Harvard Business Review*, May.

as well as strengths and weaknesses to better understand and predict what they might do next.

Conditions

Conditions are a catchall for everything going on in the environment in which you do business. At a minimum, look at social and political, demographic, and economic trends and determine how those trends might impact the organization over the short-, mid-, and long-term.

TOOL A2.1
5Cs Situation Analysis Guidelines*

1. CUSTOMERS (First line, customer chain, end users, influencers)

Needs, hopes, preference, commitment, strategies, price/value perspective by segment.

First Line/Direct Customers
- Universe of opportunity—total market, volume by segment.
- Current situation—volume by customer; profit by customer.

Customer Chain
- Customers' customers—total market, volume by segment.
- Current customers' strategies, volume and profitability by segment.

End Users
- Preference, consumption, usage, loyalty, and price value data and perceptions for our products and competitors' products.

Influencers
- Key influencers of customer and end user purchase and usage decisions.

2. COLLABORATORS (Suppliers, business allies, partners, government/community leaders)

- Strategies, profit/value models for external and internal stakeholders (up, across, down).

3. CAPABILITIES

- Human (includes style and quality of management, strategy dissemination, culture values, norms, focus, discipline, innovation, teamwork, execution, urgency, politics).
- Operational (includes integrity of business processes, effectiveness of organization structure, links between measures and rewards and corporate governance).
- Financial (includes capital and asset utilization and investor management).
- Technical (includes core processes, IT systems, supporting skills).
- Key assets (includes brands and intellectual property).

(continued)

---

4. COMPETITORS (Direct, indirect, potential).

- Strategies, profit/value models, profit pools by segment, source of pride.

5. CONDITIONS

- Social/demographic—trends.
- Political/government/regulatory—trends.
- Economic—macro and micro—trends.
- Market definition, inflows, outflows, substitutes—trends.

Pulling it together:

SWOT analysis and thinking about
- Sources, drivers, hinderers of revenue, and value.
- Current strategy/resource deployment: Coherent? Adequate? Defacto strategy?
- Insights and scenarios (To set up: What/So what/Now what?)

SWOT

A SWOT (internal Strengths and Weaknesses versus external Opportunities and Threats) analysis is a good way to summarize this and lay out the current reality (see Tool A2.2).

Key leverage points are the internal strengths that can be brought to bear to take advantage of external opportunities. These are the corridors of ways to win. For example, if you have a strong beverage distribution system and the public water supply is contaminated, you could leverage your system to deliver safe bottled water to people.

Business issues are the areas of internal weakness that are particularly vulnerable to external threats. Fixing these are ways to avoid losing. If you have only marginally acceptable safety standards in your plants and there is pending legislation to increase legal safety standards well beyond those that you currently meet, that is a potential issue.

Finally, the sustainable competitive advantage is most likely one of the key leverage points that can be sustained in the face of business issues.

Use a SWOT to answer questions in three key areas:

1. What are the sources, drivers, and hinderers of revenue and value?

2. What is the current strategy? Are current resources properly deployment to support that strategy? Is the strategy coherent? Are the resources deployed adequate to deliver on the strategy? Is there a de facto strategy in play? (How does what you're actually doing match your stated strategy?)

3. What insights and scenarios can you develop? (What? So what? Now what?)

What are the facts and data? These are things you see and know. No judgment or bias is involved and anyone looking at the scenario would get the same facts or data.

So what should be done now that you know the facts and data? Draw conclusions based on your judgments and knowledge.

Now what actions should be taken given those conclusions?

TOOL A2.2

SWOT Form*

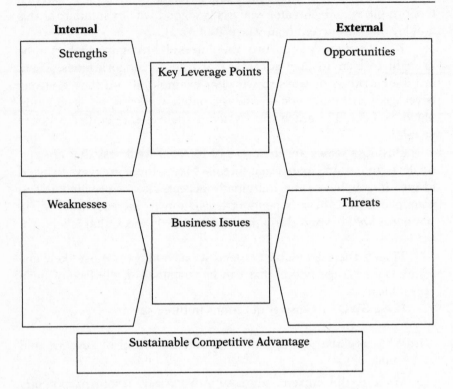

Internal

Strengths

Key Leverage Points

External

Opportunities

Weaknesses

Business Issues

Threats

Sustainable Competitive Advantage

STRENGTHS	**Internal to organization—things we do better**
WEAKNESSES	**Internal to organization—things we do worse**
OPPORTUNITIES	**External to organization—things to capitalize on**
THREATS	**External to organization—things to worry about**

KEY LEVERAGE POINTS

Opportunities we can leverage our strengths against (where to play to win)

---

*Copyright © PrimeGenesis® LLC. To customize this document, download Tool A2.2 from www.onboardingtools.com. The document can then be opened, edited, and printed.

TOOL A2.2   (continued)

BUSINESS IMPLICATIONS

Threats our weaknesses make us vulnerable to (where to play not to lose)

SUSTAINABLE COMPETITIVE ADVANTAGES

Key leverage points that can be sustained over extended period of time

Leverage These 15 Secrets to Become a Great Communicator

Much of what we have to say about communication you probably know already. But you may not know how to activate this knowledge into an effective overall communication plan and a concrete communication campaign in your first 100 days and beyond. You also may not realize just how important some of the more oblique aspects of communication really are. As you go through our general principles, consider them, and test them, you will be on a path to becoming a great communicator as well as to having a successful first 100 days.

Words Are Only a Small Part of the Game

It's not about the words. This may seem paradoxical or just wrong to you. Words are important. However, communication takes place on many nonverbal levels, and it's essential to develop skills in reading and using these nonverbal modes.

Context or Frame

Great communicators know how to choose or create the right context or frame for their messages. This can be choosing a large group versus a one-on-one situation, a casual circumstance versus a formal one. Or it can be the simple act of framing a message or a conversation: "I think this makes most sense if you look at it in the context of optimizing resources." Or alternatively, it can be setting the mood for a talk, conversation, or event by using humor, empathy, or other connective tactics. Large and small, literal circumstance or verbal context, we communicate in a context that is either chosen or created by us, or simply given.

The more you develop an awareness of how context or frame conditions the meaning and the reception of messages, the more effective your communications will be. It starts by observing carefully how context and frame are affecting communications in general, then noting carefully how masterful communicators manage it, and then by developing the skill.

Timing

Timing is everything. It's everything for jokes, for marriage proposals, in fact for every important communication.

Develop a keen awareness of how good your own timing is. Watch others who seem to get this right. Think carefully about the bigger picture—if I bring this up at this point, will it be more or less effective than holding it until x, y, or z happens? What if I say this other thing first?

A big part of timing is what others are expecting, what "is expected." Good communicators are very much in touch with expectations and play with and against those expectations to increase effect. It goes without saying that sometimes not saying anything or not saying what is expected can be just as effective as anything you might say.

Style

Leaders tend to have a different communication style from those who are not leaders. There are many styles of leadership, but the style is an important part of the message. Style can be completely nonverbal—posture, tone, and timbre of voice, eye contact, smiling or other facial expressions, and proximity to others. Verbal delivery is also a matter of style.

For the vast majority of us, this style is largely unconscious. It is just "who we are." Or—and this is important—it is a reflection of our mood or state of mind, or a reflection of the people you happen to be with. If your goal is to control your message and assure its effectiveness, you want to develop a more conscious and controlled feature. This is not the same, by the way, as having a highly self-conscious style. A winning style is often the opposite—natural and authentic.

These people know that this is how they come across and how they are. You can be aware and not stiffly self-conscious. Become aware of how style affects communication in yourself and others, and cultivate a style that suits your personality and your goals best.

Body Language (Especially Eye Contact)

Good communicators read body language very well and are good at using body language to good effect. To communicate, you need to connect. A sense of connection or the lack of it is strongly communicated and created through body language.

In face-to-face interaction, eye contact is the fundamental element. Strong, frank, and open eye contact is the sign of an engaged listener and speaker. Observe yourself. If you find that your eyes are sliding away from steady contact, you have serious work to do.

Body language is highly imitative, almost contagious. Part of context and timing is recognizing when and if the body language is propitious for your communication goal. We have seen many leaders highly hampered in their ability to lead effectively because of a sense of separation or disconnectedness that is readable in their own body language and those of their colleagues, superiors, and subordinates. We've also seen some remarkable turnarounds as they adopt a new sensitivity and approach.

A key area of opportunity is the whole realm of unofficial interaction. You need to learn how to use such interactions to create a sense of connection and engagement, and then how to transition to the more official or formal elements of the communication campaign.

Actions

Words and speech are actions, obviously. But a communication plan is greatly enhanced by an awareness of how certain kinds of actions shape, affect, support, or simply make the communication. A big area of nonverbal action revolves around what you choose to do and not do. What meetings do you attend or not attend? Are you present throughout? Are you on time, early, or late? How do you follow up on commitments? How and when do you make (or not make) decisions? Every action communicates.

Inaction and Silence

We have already called attention to this, but it's so important that it merits special attention. It can be easy to get caught in a kind of frenzy of action and communication. But if we think back to the basics of leadership and the idea that the leader is measured, thoughtful, and reliable, the lack of action or speaking can actually communicate this most effectively. It also suggests (and can help you achieve) an approach that is thought out and not simply reactive. This is all part of style, and we all have our own.

Rhythm and Repetition

In addition to speaking style, there is also frequency and duration. We have seen huge benefits occur almost immediately when people who tend to talk too much, or go on too long, learn how to interrupt themselves, thus creating more space for the people they interact with. Conversely, we have seen sharply positive reversals happen when people who tend to speak too little, or too formally, learn how to mix it up and volunteer more often.

Visuals

Many people simply respond better to visual information, either literally in printed form or on a computer screen, or in the form of visual imagery and analogies.

Less Is More

People complain about sound bites, but the fact is, the method works and it is nothing new. The great classical orators—from Cicero to Abraham Lincoln—knew a thing or two about sound biting. Brief sentences have more impact. Succinct explanations are understood better. Big concepts are remembered longer. Too much information stifles attention, bewilders the understanding, and saps the will. Keep it short. Keep it simple.

Once Is Never Enough

To get your message across, you need to repeat it. A lot. Don't underestimate the importance and value of repeating, repeating, repeating. Mix it up. But drill it home.

Test for Reception, Understanding, Agreement, Enthusiasm

People often speak and write to each other without any real communication taking place. The way to achieve effective communication is to test for effectiveness. This can be done directly—"What do you think? Does what I'm saying make sense to you?" or more indirectly, "I'd love to hear other people's thoughts on this topic. Maybe I'm missing something really important here that hasn't yet been brought out." Nonverbal cues can guide you to how directly you should test and whether you need to change course.

Emotion Communicates

Much of our education and professional work is based on argument, logic, and analysis. In certain environments, that really is the only way to communicate. But in the larger, fuzzier world of teamwork and team leadership, it's a huge mistake to rely on these hard-edged modes of communication. Communicate and connect through emotion. Acknowledge and show awareness of emotion—positive ones, negative ones. Connect your core message to emotional registers you know are important for you, your team, and your organization.

Framers Win

Communication is largely about framing. It is said that, "facts speak for themselves." But the truth is that people who help frame the facts are the most effective in communicating.

Sincerity and Passion Conquer All

It's important to begin and end with this point. Sincerity and passion are the core elements of effective communication and leadership. People do not follow insincere leaders, and they don't really listen to them. They also don't follow diffident leaders. This is why we have people use their core values as the foundation for their career plan. Stay in touch with your own values and your own passion, and much of the rest will simply follow suit. That foundation drives the momentum for success in the 100-Day Plan.

TOOL A3.1

Communication Planning Tool*

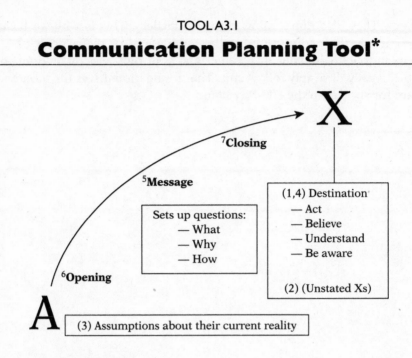

1. IDENTIFY YOUR **DESTINATION.**[1]

- What is the desired reaction and behavior you want from your audience/constituents?
- What specifically do you want, not want them to understand, believe, say about you, do?

2. BE EXPLICIT ABOUT **UNSTATED Xs.** What do you want listener to think about you?

3. ASSESS **CURRENT REALITY.**

- What does your audience/constituency currently understand, believe, say about you? Why?
- Develop a risk management plan including: potential obstacles, negative rumors, sabotage, legal requirements, unintended consequences and scenarios.

4. **REEVALUATE** DESTINATION IN LIGHT OF ASSUMPTIONS ABOUT AUDIENCE.

---

*Copyright © PrimeGenesis® LLC. To customize this document, download Tool A3.1 from www.onboardingtools.com. The document can then be opened, edited, and printed.

[1]Much of this is based on work by Sandy Linver and her company Speakeasy, also laid out in her book *Speak and Get Results*, Simon and Schuster, 1984.

TOOL A3.1   (continued)

5. **BRIDGE** THE GAP.

- What do people need to be aware of, understand, and believe to move from current reality to your destination?

6. **DEVELOP** CORE **MESSAGES** AND KEY COMMUNICATION POINTS (maximum five core messages).

7. **PACKAGE** THE MESSAGE.

- How should core messages be packaged for optimum effectiveness?
- What kind of supporting data do you need?
- What is your key opening message?
- What is your key closing message?

8. **DELIVER** THE MESSAGE.

- What are the best vehicles to reach your audience or constituents? What is the optimum combination? What is the best timing to release the message? Who and what influences whom?
- How do you best plant the follow-up seeds?

Press Interviews*

The key point is to take control of the interview. Time is on your side if you stay focused on what you want to communicate and you control the dialogue, just as it's on others' sides if they control the dialogue.

PREPARE

OBJECTIVE—What do you want out of the interaction?

ANTICIPATE QUESTIONS—Know interviewer, audience, and their interest factors (competition, conflict, controversy, consequences, familiar person, heartstrings, humor, problem, progress, success, unknown, unusual, wants/needs).

APPROACH—What way do you choose to go about achieving the objective? There are always different ways to get there. Consider them and choose one. This will lead to:

KEY COMMUNICATION POINTS—Key points you want to drive (three maximum). This will allow you to do more than just answer questions (questions are merely cues for your key points). These points need:

SUPPORT—Facts, personal experience, contrast/compare, analogy, expert opinion, analysis, definition, statistics, and examples.

DELIVER

BE clear, concise, complete (do one thing well), constructive, credible, controversial, captivating, correct (must correct significant errors on the part of interviewer or press).

BE yourself, liked, prepared, enthusiastic, specific, correct, anecdotal, listen, bridge, cool.

FOLLOW THROUGH

DELIVER on commitments.

Think through what worked particularly well and less well to IMPROVE for the future.

Bring More Discipline to Your Strategic Planning Process

T he strategic process is the first of the three critical ongoing processes required to run a business; the other two are operational process and organizational process. In the first part of this appendix we present the key underpinnings of strategy: mission, vision, values, objectives, goals, and strategies in broader detail. Following that is a suggested methodology for an effective strategic planning process.

Mission

Simply put, a mission statement informs the organization of what it is called to accomplish. The best mission statements are concise, clear, and motivating. They leave no question as to the "higher good" or the "ultimate focus" of the organization. The most common mistake that organizations make when crafting mission statements is that they are too complex and convoluted and as a result they do not provide meaning for anyone. Keep them pointed, accurate and inspiring. A few great mission statements:

> *Provide relief to victims of disasters and help people prevent, prepare for, and respond to emergencies.*
> —American Red Cross

> *Preserve and improve human life.*
> —Merck

To explore new worlds, discover new civilizations; seek out new life forms, and to boldly go where no one has gone before.
> —Starship Enterprise

Vision

A good vision is an appealing picture of future success, showing what the company will be like when the mission is accomplished. Some examples of clear and inspiring visions:

The world's premier engineering organization. Trained and ready to provide support anytime, anyplace.
> —U.S. Army Corps of Engineers

Create a world renowned, yet personable, showcase of maverick films, filmmakers and the technology that enables creativity.
> —Cinequest

A world in which every child, everywhere, has equal access to life-saving vaccines.
> —The Vaccine Fund

Values

Values are the beliefs and moral principles that guide the group's actions and decisions. They are important to them because they guide both individual's and team's behaviors and norms on a day-to-day basis. Value-driven teams do not believe that the end justifies the means and they will refuse to relinquish them in pursuit of its mission and vision.

Objectives

Objectives are the broadly defined, qualitative performance requirements of the business such as achieving market leadership or dominating a category. Objectives should be closely related to the company's vision. Objectives define what success looks like.

If the vision is "A world in which every child, everywhere, has equal access to life saving vaccines," the objectives might be: (1) creation of vaccines, (2) manufacture of vaccines, (3) awareness of vaccines, (4) funding for vaccines, and (5) distribution of vaccines.

Goals

Goals flow out of objectives. They are the metrics that will track progress against the objectives (profits, savings, top-line sales, etc.). Goals must be SMART (Specific, Measurable, Attainable, Relevant, and Time-Bound).

If the main objective is the creation of vaccines, the goal could be to develop three market-ready vaccines by June 30.

Strategies

At its core, strategy is simply generating and selecting options that will close the gaps between the objectives and current reality. It is about the creation and allocation of resources to the right place, in the right way, at the right time, over time that bring to fruition your mission, vision, objectives, and goals while maintaining values. A simple way to drive strategic choices is by asking two questions: Where are we going to play? How are we going to win? It is simple and focused. Strategy boils down to selecting which options to pursue and which options not to pursue.

Once your team members have established the mission, vision, objectives, goals, and values they can then create a set of strategic options and then choose which ones to pursue.

Your task as the leader is to select the most effective set of strategic options that will get you from your current reality to your desired destination. In addition to the gap between where you are and where you want to be there will most likely be some barriers that serve to keep that gap in place. Your strategy should guide the actions that your team takes to bridge that gap and eliminate those barriers.

The Six-Step Strategic Planning Process

The following six-step process will allow you to create a complete and robust strategic plan. We are not suggesting that this is the only way to do this. But it is a good way.

1. Set an aspirational destination (derived from the mission and vision).
2. Assess the facts of the current reality and develop potential future scenarios.

3. Identify options to bridge gaps between the current reality and the desired aspiration.

4. Evaluate options under different scenarios. Make choices.

5. Develop detailed plans that will deliver on selected strategies.

6. Act, measure, adjust, and repeat.

Set the Aspirational Destination

Strategic planning begins with the aspirational long-term destination, which should be derived directly from the mission and vision. It is important for this step to come before looking at the current reality. Starting with the current reality forces your team to build from the current existence, which results in a strategy that often falls short of an aspirational destination. Starting with the end in mind allows the team to build a clear and direct path toward the aspiration.

Assess the Facts of the Current Reality and Develop Future Scenarios

The next step is to analyze the current reality. This involves reviewing, once again, the 5Cs (Customers, Collaborators, Capabilities, Competitors, and Conditions) as well as performing a SWOT (Strengths, Weaknesses, Opportunities, Threats) analysis.

Developing scenarios is an exercise in trying to foresee potential changes in the environment (social, political, demographic, organizational, economic, etc.) that might impact your strategic choices. The changes are generally outside the control of the organization or the team. Given this, the organization cannot choose which one will happen, but it can determine the expected probabilities for each scenario happening. This information can then be used later to help determine the expected results of different strategic options.

Identify Options to Bridge Gaps between Reality and Aspiration

Next, determine what strategic options might create additional value (or in some cases, minimize its destruction). Be creative so you can come up with a range of options that could potentially address the issues and move the organization forward. For ideas, look at your key leverage points for offensive options and at your key business issues for defensive options.

This is a good time to get key stakeholder input. You are trying to generate ideas. So if your key stakeholders have good ideas, you want to know about them. Keep in mind that at this stage you are not looking for decisions yet, just input and options.

Evaluate Options under Different Scenarios

In this step you want to decide what strategic options create the most risk-adjusted value over time, under different scenarios. You want to evaluate options and scenarios leading to a range of forecasts based on transparent assumptions. At this point, the key stakeholders should become involved to understand and to help improve the components of the valuation assumptions.

Assume three scenarios for the future of the industry:

1. Industry consolidation: Number of customers shrinking.
2. Industry stagnation: Number of customers constant.
3. Industry expansion: Number of customers increasing.

To determine which of your strategic options has the highest expected value, you need to figure out what the payoff will be under each scenario and what the probabilities will be of each happening.

Eventually you will want to get the key stakeholders involved to agree on which options to pursue.

After a complete evaluation, you will want to decide on your core strategic choices that will clearly define where the organization will focus its efforts and how it will win versus its competition. Your goal should be to have three to five strategic choices that will deliver 75 percent of the goals.

Develop Detailed Business Plans

With your strategic choices in place, you'll want to develop a detailed business plan that addresses the strategic, operational, and organizational actions that are needed to implement each selected option. For each strategic choice you will want to consider: resource requirements and allocation, rules of engagement, critical business drivers, timetables, roles, responsibilities, capability enhancements, performance management plans, accountability, standards, measures, and goals.

Act, Measure, Adjust, and Repeat

Once the detailed business plan is in play you'll want to continually monitor its progress against your stated goals to ensure what you thought would happen is happening in a timely manner.

To ensure that the team members remain on target to get to their aspirational destination:

- Get milestones in place immediately.
- Track them and manage them as a team on a frequent and regular basis.
- Adjust as necessary.

This whole process is about you and your team together. Your team must feel like it's part of the process but so too must your key stakeholders.

Remember to include your stakeholders by:

- Obtaining their input to enhance scenarios and options. Be sure to engage with them and capture their ideas.
- Involving them to help understand and to improve valuation assumptions. Tap into their experience and context.
- Gaining their agreement on which options to pursue. (This should naturally occur as a result of the expected valuation of different options under different scenarios.)

Strategic Planning Summary

Strategic planning begins with the aspirational destination that is drawn from the vision and mission:

- Analyze the current reality by using the 5Cs approach.
- Complete a SWOT summary.
- Create strategy options to guide actions, overcome barriers, and bridge gaps.

- Get key stakeholder input into options and assumptions.
- Get key stakeholder agreement on which strategic options to pursue.
- Develop a business plan that addresses the strategic, operational, and organizational actions that are needed to implement each selected option.

Manage People and Practices with Standardized Processes that Are Public and Visual

An ADEPT Framework for Talent Management

Acquire

Scope roles

Identify prospects

Recruit and select the right people for the right roles

Attract those people

Onboard them so they can deliver better results faster

Develop

Assess performance drivers

Develop skills and knowledge for current and future roles

Encourage

Provide clear direction, objectives, measures, and so on.

Support with the resources and time required for success

Recognize and reward success

Plan

Monitor people's performance over time

Assess their situation and potential

Plan career moves/succession planning over time

Transition

Migrate people to different roles to fit their needs/life stage and company needs

Acquire

Scope Roles

It's critically important to get the role scope right, and to get others aligned around that scope. Be clear on the role's responsibilities, authority, and interactions with others. Know the required strengths, motivation, and fit. Make sure that all the key people who will interact with the new person in this role agree on these requirements. See Tool A5.1.

Identify Prospects

Look internally whenever you can. Promoting someone may be the ultimate form of recognition and sends a powerful signal to others in the organization. But, don't compromise. If you have to go outside to get the best people, so be it.

Recruit

Recruit and select by using a targeted selection system that works for you.

Attract

To maximize your chances of attracting candidates when you're recruiting, you must be selling them on how great your organization is even while evaluating them. There is no excuse for not making everyone who interviews with you want to join or refer others to you. (Candidates can sell themselves first and then do their risk assessment after they've been offered the job. Companies can't flip that switch in reverse.)

Onboard

Put your new recruits on the road to success even before they start. Make them feel welcome and valuable to an organization they can take pride in. Ensure that each new employee has a 100-day action plan in place. Encourage and enable relationships and provide new recruits with any help they may need along the way.

Prepare Your Own Message and Touch Point Plan

Start with your own message to new recruits. What do you want them to understand, believe, and do? These might include the context of their role, your vision of success for them, your ideas around their priorities, what resources they can tap to drive success, and a call to action.

Craft a plan to deliver that message. Manage the welcoming signs and symbols—especially your own time. Model the behaviors and attitudes that you want your new recruits to adopt. Preempt others' potentially counterproductive influences on the new recruits by telling them stories in advance about the organization that help them understand it.

Follow through with your own media/touch point plan. Think about things like prestart meetings, calls, notes, and packages. Just don't disappear until Day One. If possible, be there to welcome new recruits and introduce them on Day One. Investing time in your recruits will help them understand and believe how much you value them.

Encourage and Enable Relationships
As you know, one of the big things new recruits can do between acceptance and their first day on the job is to jump-start key relationships. You can and should help your recruits identify the most important stakeholders that they should connect with before their first day. Make the introductions. Then get out of the way.

If the position has been open for a long time, you've probably been doing at least part of your new recruit's job. Along the way, you've established relationships with people who are going to be working closely with the new recruit. There is a risk that the strength of your relationships with these people can get in the way of your new recruits' building their own relationships with them. So initially, take a step back as necessary so you don't undermine your new recruits' communication or decision flows with those key people. We're not in any way suggesting that you ignore or damage these key relationships but allow them to adjust to the new situation.

Provide Help
There's no doubt in our completely unbiased minds that giving this book to the people you hire is a great way to help them succeed. The question is when? Giving this book to them the day after they accept the job will allow them to take advantage of the Fuzzy Front End (between acceptance and Day One). It will even be better to give them a copy when they receive the offer to help them better assess the risks they are facing and prepare for their new roles. You really do want them to know and understand the risks. You and your organization will be far better off if your recruits turn down the job, than if they accept a bad match, show up, and fail.

Since we wrote the first edition of *The New Leader's 100-Day Action Plan*, an entire industry has grown up around executive onboarding. Most of the practitioners focus on assimilation coaching; helping new leaders assimilate into their new culture. This is a vital service, but it is not the only assistance that can benefit new leaders. Think in terms of helping your new recruits on three levels: accommodating, assimilating, and accelerating.

Accommodating is all about providing resources to help them get set up in their office and at home—particularly if they are moving. The office part would include desks, computers, phones, PDAs, passwords, and so on. This is relatively straightforward stuff. Just make sure someone is taking care of it.

Assimilating is the next level up. Here you can help them map their stakeholders and make sure that they have orientation and onboarding programs and meetings set up, and also have the time to follow through on them.

Accelerating is one more level up. Not every new recruit needs to accelerate his or her onboarding. Acceleration is not appropriate when the person you hire has a lot of time to learn and the risk of doing something wrong outweighs the risk of not doing something right. But when there is a need for a new person and their team to deliver better results faster, acceleration is essential. In that scenario help them follow the program in this book. Better yet, consider bringing in people with an expertise in this process (see www.PrimeGenesis.com) to give them extra leverage up front. It will all but guarantee that the new hire and their team deliver better results faster.

Develop

Identify the most important drivers of performance, assess how individuals are doing against them and then develop their skills and knowledge in those areas.

As a leader you will want to strengthen people's skills and knowledge to help them be more successful in their current role and prepare them for future roles.

We agree with Gallup's notion that a strength is a combination of talents, skills, and knowledge. Since talent is innate, you can't do anything to build that. So your focus should be on skills and knowledge. We also agree with Gallup that your focus should be on helping people get even stronger in areas of strength rather than trying to "develop" their weaknesses into a strength. That process will be

frustrating for everyone involved. It is far better to build on their
strengths, and help them mitigate their weaknesses in other ways.[1]

Encourage

Whoever taught you to say "please" and "thank you" was prescient.
This is the key to encouraging people on your team.

"Please" is all about clarity around expectations: objectives, goals,
and measures. It's about enabling people to succeed by making sure
they have the direction, resources, tools, and support they need and
then getting out of their way. (And getting others out of their way.)
Big chunks of what we discussed about milestones, in Chapter 10,
are applicable here.

"Thank you" is about providing the recognition and rewards
that encourage each individual. Multiple studies have shown that,
in general, people are positively motivated by things like the type of
work they are doing, challenge and achievement, promotion prospects, responsibility, and recognition or esteem. Things like salary,
relationship with colleagues, working conditions, and their supervisor's style are basic factors that don't motivate if they are in the
acceptable range, but can quickly demotivate if there is a problem.

So the general prescription isn't all that hard. Make sure the
basic factors are good enough and won't cause problems, and invest
in the real motivators. It is not about motivating people. It is about
enabling people to succeed so they can tap into their own inner motivations. Seek to enable your team. Don't forget it.

You can encourage people by:

Clarifying how their individual roles fit with the broader group.

Establishing individual SMART goals (Specific, Measurable,
Attainable, Relevant, Time Bound) for them.

Required Resources

Just as it is important for people to understand how their goals fit
with the rest of the organization, it is equally important to make sure
that people have the resources and support (internally and externally)
they need to achieve their goals. It would be silly to ask the sales
force to sell 100 widgets per day with plant capacity of 50 per day.

---

[1] Buckingham, Marcus and Clifton, Donald, *Now Discover Your Strengths*, Free Press, 2001.

You would end up with unhappy customers, furious salespeople, and nervous breakdowns throughout the plant.

To help reinforce the creation, deployment, and achievement of goals, you need assistance. That assistance comes in the form of seven reinforcements: skills, knowledge, tools, resources, guidelines, linking performance and consequences, and driving actions and milestones along the way.

1. *Skills:* These are the how-to's or capabilities. Your goals may be perfect, but you will not reach them without the necessary skills in place. Know what those skills are, and know which ones you have to develop.

2. *Knowledge:* This boils down to facts that you are aware of and your experiences. The greater your breadth and depth of knowledge, the higher your chance of reaching your goals.

3. *Tools:* Without the right equipment, you cannot reach your goals. You must know what equipment is needed, what you have, and how to fill the gap.

4. *Resources:* The three key resource needs are human, financial, and operational. Make sure that resources are available to support your established goals in each of these areas. If not, you either have to change your goals to make them more realistic, or increase your access to the needed resource.

5. *Guidelines:* Establish boundaries so that everyone knows how far they can run. Everyone should know the things that you cannot do because they are outside the clearly established guidelines.

6. *Link between performance and consequences:* Make the link between performance and consequences explicit. If that link is properly established, everyone should know how the results will be rated.

As many organizations get larger and more bureaucratic, they tend to bunch people's annual raises in a narrow range, doing things like giving those who meet expectations a 3 percent to 5 percent raise and those who exceed a 4 percent to 6 percent raise. Over time, this has a devastating effect on performance because people see that they are not going to be rewarded for putting in extra effort to overdeliver and won't get punished for marginal underdelivery.

7. *Actions and milestones along the way:* You cannot do midcourse corrections if you do not know where you're supposed to be at midcourse. It is far easier to spot a problem when someone says, "we produced 9 widgets last month versus a goal of 30" than when someone says, "we experienced normal start up issues but remain fully committed to producing 360 widgets this year." As we saw in Chapter 10, laying out milestones is critical for understanding how to redeploy resources over time to achieve the overall goals.

Plan

Good planning starts with a situational and opportunity assessment. Organizational planning is closely linked with strategic planning. Figure out where you're going and the choices you will implement to get there. Then map out the organization, starting with what it needs to look like in the future state. Armed with that, you can look at people's performance to assess where they are now, where they could get to, and how they can best fit into the future organization.

The organizational evolution curve is hard to stay ahead of. A little long-term planning can go a long way. Make the mental jump to the organization of the future. Then step back and figure out what you have to do to get there. Some people can grow into their new roles by doing what they're doing now. Some people can grow into their new roles with an investment in their skills and knowledge. Some people can't grow into the roles and will have to be guided in different directions with others slotted in from inside or acquired from outside.

An integral part of long-term organizational planning is individual motivation. Some people can get to the place you need them to get to, but they don't want to do so. A good tool for working this through is the "Five Step Career Plan" from Chapter 1. Have the people who work for you complete or update this on an annual basis. It is a useful tool to keep in touch with their own personal long-term goals.

Transition

As discussed in Chapter 12, there are some people moves that you must make quickly. Generally you can evolve people into new roles over time.

Not all transitions are up. Some are across, some are down, and some are out.

Some people need to move to different roles at the same level to broaden their knowledge or skills or because their existing strengths can make a bigger impact somewhere else.

Some people may want to move down to roles with less scope, responsibility, or stress as they move into different life stages: adding kids, spouse retiring, and so on.

Leadership is about enabling and inspiring others to do their absolute best, together, to realize a meaningful and rewarding shared purpose. If everything stayed constant, people wouldn't have to transition to new roles. Everything is constantly changing, so transitioning people to new roles is often a big part of inspiring and enabling them to do their absolute best.

TOOL A5.1

Role Scope*

Job Title _____

Department _____

MISSION/responsibilities

- Why position exists
- Objectives/goals/outcomes
- Impact on rest of organization
- Specific responsibilities
- Organizational relationships and interdependencies

VISION

- Picture of success

STRENGTHS

- **Talents** (A recurring pattern of thoughts, feelings, or behaviors that can be productively applied.)
- **Knowledge** (what you are aware of, facts, and lessons learned)
  - Required education and training
  - Required experience
  - Required qualifications
- **Skills** (How to's, or the steps of an activity. Capabilities that can be transferred)
  - Technical
  - Interpersonal
  - Business

MOTIVATION

- How activities fit with person's likes/dislikes/ideal job criteria
- How to progress toward long-term goal

TOOL A5.1   (continued)

FIT

- BRAVE: Behaviors, Relationships, Attitudes, Values, Environment

APPROVALS

Dept. Manager/Supervisor _____

Human Resources _____

Leading When You Were *Promoted from Within* or Internally Transferred

Τhe basics of (1) get a head start, (2) manage your message, and (3) build your team, apply in every case. What's different is what you need to get a head start on and the restrictions around that, the nature of your message and the context for that message, and the conditions and context of your team building.

Promoted from Within or Lateral Transfer

Consider the successful handoff in a running relay race. The new runner, who's already on the track, does three things: (1) prepares and starts moving in advance; (2) takes control of the transition by putting his hand where he wants the baton placed; and (3) accelerates decisively following the handoff. Those promoted from within or making a lateral transfer should follow the same model.

The basics of new leadership apply whether it's in a new company or the same company. The fundamental difference between moving to a new company and making an internal move, however, is that, like a relay runner preparing to receive the baton, you are already on the track. Unlike joining an organization for the first time, when you have to create a new positioning for yourself, when you're making an internal move, people already know you or know people that know you. Thus, to a large degree, this is an exercise in repositioning yourself within the organization.

When you make an internal move, keep in mind that:

You can't control the context.

Although you may not be able to influence the circumstances surrounding an open role, you often can influence
planned promotions and moves in advance. Under a planned
move, you will usually have time to do some due diligence
and transition planning before you are officially named.

However, when a move is unplanned, you must figure
out the real story before jumping in to the new role. Don't
be caught off guard by the surprise of the move and forget
to do your required due diligence. For you to be successful
it is important for you to have some level of understanding of the true backstory behind the unplanned move. The
story may be a positive one, or it may be ripe with controversy, but either way, you must know.

Finally, be sure to clarify and deliver expectations
whether it is a permanent role or an interim appointment.
Determining delivery expectations in a permanent role is
an easier process, but interim roles can be tricky because
delivery expectations can be all over the map and often
contradictory. If an interim transition is to be successful
there must be agreement across the key stakeholders on
expected results and timeframes.

It's hard to make a clean break.

In many ways, you are in the new job at the moment of the
announcement regardless of what may be announced as
your official start date. Unlike coming in from the outside,
people know you and can instantly start thinking or imagin-
ing you in that role. You may even start to get calls regarding issues and decisions related to the role. Even with these
new demands coming at you before you've officially started,
you are still accountable for results in your old job.

More often than not you will still be accountable for
your old job even after you start your new job. Going back
to the relay-runner analogy, you're really making two hand-
offs at the same time: the baton you're picking up from the

person who had your new job before you and the baton you're handing off to the person taking your old job. With regard to your old job, you don't want to be in a position where you hand the baton over too quickly, too roughly, or not in the "place" it was requested.

If you falter with the transition of your old job, the results can impinge on your success in your new role. As you reset your stakeholder list for your new role, also keep in mind that you now have an extra set of stakeholders—those that helped you along the way. They will not want to see you flub the transition after helping position you for your new role.

There is no honeymoon.

As an insider, you're expected to be fully up to speed the moment you start your new job. The good news is that you already have an internal network that you can begin to leverage immediately after your new role is announced. Although a promotion is certainly good news and lateral transfers may be as well, don't be blinded to the fact that in addition to your supporters, you'll most likely have detractors as well. You'll want to identify them early and keep them on your stakeholder list.

All this leads to three indicated actions for those promoted from within:

1. *Prepare in advance.* Work to understand the context and complexity of the new situation. Get yourself ready and exert whatever influence you can to shape your new role and set up success—as far in advance as possible.

2. *Take control of your own transition.* Be proactive and control the message and communication cascade—the timing of who hears what, in what order, in what medium—as well as clarifying what's changed and what has not changed. Protect your base by ensuring ongoing positive results in your old job and recognizing those who have helped you along the way.

3. *Accelerate team progress after the start.* This is where your knowledge of the organization can really help you. You and your new team can get a running start, leveraging positive momentum to accelerate the key strategic, operational, and organizational processes.

Prepare in Advance

The context of your move will impact the early leadership challenges you face. The smoothest and easiest transitions follow planned promotions or moves. When succession planning works and the right leader is in the right spot at the right time, most feel in control and few feel threatened. When this happens to you, be grateful and make the best of a good situation.

But it's not always like that. When there's a sudden leadership gap and you get an unexpected call to fill it, there's a significant challenge to regain control of the situation and of the rampant runaway emotions. Uncertainty and sudden change are scary for all.

Work to understand the thinking behind the decision and begin communicating with and understanding your new stakeholders. As discussed in earlier chapters, beware of writing people off as stakeholders or influences too quickly, only to find that they really can have an impact on how your organization sees (and evaluates) you. Look carefully at the number and quality of things changing in your own situation. You'll need far more help if you're getting moved to run a new function in a new industry in a new country than if you're taking over from the boss whose deputy you've been for the last decade.

An internal promotion suggests that senior management sees value in continuity, "insider knowledge," and a "known entity" (you) rather than the risk, hassle, and ramp-up time of an outsider. There may be an expectation of change, however, and insiders often lose grip of their opportunity by being afraid to "rock the boat" or by letting key collaborators assume that "nothing's really going to change." Get a clear sense of the expectations and deliver accordingly.

Manage Right through the Interim

Perhaps the most challenging case is when you have to fill a gap as the interim leader. Get clarity on whether *interim* means "holding the fort until we find the right person, which absolutely will not be you," "on probation with a good chance of becoming permanent," or "doing the job as a developmental opportunity on the way to something else." In either case, it's likely a good posture to engage fully with the work itself while eschewing the perks of the job—basically, focusing your efforts on the least prestigious, highest impact tasks and leaving the glory to others.

Patty had delivered in every job she'd had at the firm for 15 years. When her boss was moved to head a different division, senior management asked her to step in as interim division president while they did a thorough internal and external search for the new president. Patty kept doing exactly what she'd been doing. She finished the year's strategic planning and got senior management excited about her plans. She kept managing operations—and delivering her numbers. She kept moving ahead with the organizational evolution she and her previous boss had put in place, inspiring and enabling all. In the end, senior management would have looked silly picking anyone but her for the role.

Whatever the context, pause for a moment to craft a solid transition plan that includes the identification of key stakeholders and getting clear on your message. Then, get a head start before you start—jump-starting relationships with key stakeholders in particular.

Take Control of Your Own Transition

You will be perceived as starting your new job at the moment of the announcement, so try to control the timing of that announcement—particularly if you're moving into a vacant position. Remember that the announcement process includes far more than just the formal announcement itself. There are almost always leaks in advance and there are always people who should be told in advance, so you must be discerning about the cascade of information. In many cases you have to manage this down to a minute-by-minute level of detail to make sure that people hear about the promotion in the right order, in the right way, from the right person.

This is not a trivial issue. Be particularly sensitive to when, how, and from whom people hear.

Emotions will probably be running high and those hearing about the transition may include those who:

- Are being moved out of a job.
- Have allies or friends being moved out of a job.
- See someone else is getting a role they might have wanted.
- See this transition as particularly important to their own success—especially direct reports and peers of the new role.

If you're tempted to simply make one general and official announcement, think again. Trust and relationship building start with how people receive this kind of information. Anybody who gets a special advance notice will feel special, and as a new leader you want to use that capital wisely.

On the other hand, it's likely to be impossible for you to do all the one-on-one announcement meetings that you'd like. Even if you could, by the time you did your third or fourth the others on your list will probably have already heard. Also, in many cases, you want to have somebody else relay the information, helping frame the message in the context of that person's specific role or reporting situation. It's worth thinking all this through and then designing a communication campaign that simply and effectively reaches your key stakeholders.

Start by understanding that there are no secrets. It's not so much that the people you trust with secrets intentionally pass them on, but that they inadvertently slip. An HR executive's secretary was asked by one of us how people always seemed to find out about promotions in advance.

"It's easy. A senior HR person walks into our general manager's office carrying their big personnel ring binder. People take a guess and then go to that HR executive's assistant and say 'Great news about Larry. Isn't it?' Nine times out of 10, the HR assistant comes back with something along the lines of 'It is.' or 'Larry? Don't you mean Doug?' Either way, they will figure it out."

You can't possibly anticipate and prevent all the different ways information is going to leak. Just assume it will and guide the cascade of leaks as much as you can.

Expect Leaks and Manage Them—In Advance

Betty was going to be announcing a set of changes in her organization. She wanted to let people know in the right order, make sure that they all had the same understanding and not disenfranchise her managers all at the same time. The key pieces and schedule for her announcement cascade included:

Tuesday afternoon: Have one-on-one conversations with the individuals most emotionally impacted—including key peers, but not external stakeholders

Tuesday end of day: Place a conference call with all of her direct reports. Then allow the evening for them to leak the news to their direct reports.

Wednesday morning first thing: Place a conference call with her direct reports' direct reports. Then allow the morning for them to leak the news to their teams.

Wednesday at 11:55 AM: Send a formal e-mail announcement restating the key points that were discussed in the one-on-ones and conference calls.

Wednesday noon: Place an all-hands conference call to explain changes.

Betty's approach was particularly effective because she built in time for a few rounds of conversations to take place, but she didn't let more than a few hours pass without following up herself. By the time the official announcement happened, all the key parties had been briefed and therefore felt "in the know." For everybody involved, it felt like, "things were under control." They were and it allowed Betty to quickly move forward with the changes while minimizing the impact and maximizing her team's support.

Different Transitions Require Different Tactics

Gena was announcing a set of changes to her organization. She was promoting one person to lead manufacturing and announcing that the current head of quality control was leaving within the next six months and that his replacement was to be named later. Gena wanted to calm the direct reports of the exiting quality control leader preemptively without disempowering the newly named manufacturing leader. So, here's what she did:

- With regard to those people whose boss was going to be replaced within six months, she called each of them one-on-one just before the formal announcement to urge them to communicate any issues directly with her during the transition period.
- With regard to those people whose new boss was being named in the announcement, she did no preannouncement calls but left it to the new leader to call each of his direct reports individually immediately after the announcement (but not before).

Here again, Gena was tactically very shrewd. She helped channel potential disgruntlement to herself, while allowing the head of manufacturing to establish his authority.

"I'm Here to Listen" Is an Important Part
of Any Transition Announcement

Knowing that your message is also an invitation for communication is critical to achieving a successful transition. The anxiety that change triggers can be greatly allayed by inclusive communication.

Peter took over the New England region at a national mortgage company after the third successive regional director suddenly resigned within a short period of time. The team that Peter was about to lead was underperforming and not meeting its goals.

The first thing Peter did was to hold one-on-one meetings with each of his managers. They all had plenty of questions, opinions, and complaints about what was going wrong. Peter was ready to listen, but he wasn't ready to discuss anything during these meetings so he shut discussion down for "later." This was a mistake.

Peter didn't realize that the team was eager to make changes to solve the problems at hand and get their performance back on track. His unwillingness to enter into meaningful discussions immediately caused the team to see Peter as "just like the previous three managers who didn't last," and they quickly became disheartened. They immediately disengaged and it took Peter months of effort to get a sense of commitment from the team. Along the way, he lost two of the top producers.

He eventually discovered that the managers originally assumed that they would not be taken seriously and Peter's approach to the one-on-one meetings confirmed their suspicions. Their suspicions were not true, but Peter's actions made them seem as if they were. Peter missed the sense of urgency that his team had and did not pick up on the signs that they wanted an immediate and active discussion. He didn't get that they had been waiting for "later" through three previous managers and when Peter delivered the same message out of the gate, they quickly gave up hope. It was an avoidable mistake.

Announcement Cascade Timeline

Tool A6.1 at the end of this appendix is an announcement cascade checklist. Use this tool as a guideline to craft your transition communication cascade. Let's walk through the key components of stakeholders, message, preannouncement, formal announcement, and postannouncement:

Stakeholders
Start with mapping and prioritizing the internal and external stakeholders who may be impacted by the transition.

Internal stakeholders might include:

Former peers who helped you and your team get to the point where you deserve this new move.

New peers who are going to help you and your team be success-ful in advance.

Other people in your informal network inside the company—no matter what their level or official role—that can help you or your team learn and get things done (perhaps including the incumbent under the right circumstances).

Former and new team members.

External stakeholders might include:

Key customers—particularly those with close relationships with people involved in the changes.

Key suppliers and analysts.

Community leaders, government officials, regulators, and the like.

Message
The platforms for change, vision, and call to action in a transi-tion situation aren't any different than those you'd use when com-ing in from the outside. The point is to clarify them before you do anything else.

Preannouncement Timeline
Map the order in which you're going to tell people in advance, under-standing that the more people you tell, the further in advance, the greater the amount of leaks there will be.

Formal Announcement
This is the formal mass communication that goes out. Be clear on what it says, who says it, and exactly when it's distributed. This will influence your postannouncement timeline.

Postannouncement Timeline
Now that the cat's out of the bag, you don't have to worry about leaks anymore, but you do need to control the order of the commu-nications. You can do this by using a combination of mass, large group, small group, and one-on-one sessions to get your message out to the people you need to reach in a time frame that supports your announcement objectives.

"Presume Not That I Am the Thing I Was"[1]

After the announcement of your promotion or move, the clearer you can be about what's changed and what's the same. People are going to be trying to figure out the new you as quickly as they can. Everything you say and don't say, do and don't do will be interpreted and misinterpreted by someone.

"Everyone" includes those staying behind in your old world. In some cases, you'll be asked to continue to manage your old role during the transition. In others, someone else will pick it up. But in all cases, the positive or negative results in your old job will impact people's perceptions of you. This is why you must protect your base, ideally by making sure that you've got someone ready to fill your old role and working with them to support a smooth transition. Their success is your success.

Know That It's Hard to Make a Clean Break

Jean had recently taken over the company's operations in one country and had gotten off to a particularly fast start. Her management was so impressed that they quickly promoted her again to take on global operations. Unfortunately, the team in the country she had been running was not yet strong enough to continue to be successful without Jean's leadership presence. There was no replacement for Jean in sight. Jean had not prepared for another promotion that fast, and failed to control the transition. She kept getting dragged back to fix things in her "old" country and wasn't able to give her "new" role and team the attention they so desperately needed to accelerate progress. Not surprisingly, this story did not have a happy ending as people in both her "old" and new areas started doubting Jean's leadership.

Be Prepared to Enlist Support to Make a Fast Start

On the other hand, when Pat's management decided to merge another division in with hers, she immediately pulled together a group to help map out and implement the transition, including figuring out which people would best fill the new, combined roles. Pat and the group managed the timing of the communications so that people heard

---

[1]Shakespeare's newly crowned Henry V in Henry IV, Act V, Scene V: "Presume not that I am the thing I was; For God doth know, so shall the world perceive, That I have turn'd away my former self . . ."

about the changes in the way Pat chose through a combination of
e-mail, videos, large and small group meetings, and one-on-one phone
calls and live conversations. All this contributed to a smooth transition
for Pat and thus her team's success in the new combined division.

HOT TIP

Strive to shorten the time between announcement and start: One of the
biggest differences between joining from the outside and getting moved
from within is that more time between announcement and start is better
when joining from the outside—to give you time for preparation and preboarding conversations. On the other hand, when moved from within, less
time between announcement and start is better—to minimize the period
when you're doing two jobs.

Accelerate Progress after the Start

Many executives promoted from the inside underestimate how quickly
the organization will change their perception about them and how
quickly and naturally a new pecking order takes place. Most people are
simply practical about this kind of change. "Well, Ron's the boss now.
Let's figure out how he wants these things done and do it that way."
Be aware, however, that not everybody is so pragmatic and accepting.
Inside knowledge goes two ways. Your network includes supporters . . .
and detractors. Some of those detractors are people you rubbed the
wrong way in previous roles, others will be created during this transition. Watch out for those who wanted all or part of your new job and
be prepared for some people to work against your success. As Sun-Tzu
says, "Keep your friends close, and your enemies closer."[2]

Some of this is, perhaps, inevitable. Make sure that you've got
your supporters, scouts, and seconds are keeping you aware of the
mood of the larger group and what any detractors might be doing or
saying. You should try to counter negativity as much as practical. This
is important, but don't get overinvested in this. Your goal is to create
positive momentum quickly, and then turn your attention to accelerating progress by evolving the P^3 (People, Plans, and Processes).

---

[2]This was originally said by Sun-Tzu—400 BC, despite most of us remembering it as
one of the things Michael Corleone's father taught him "here in this room" in *The
Godfather II*.

Make it Real

Soon after Tom's promotion, he met with his key people for a day to dig into their thinking and recalibrate what was important. At the end of the day he told his team members that he agreed with their stated strategies but felt that they had not been given the resources they needed to make them real. Tom took the case to management to increase the group's budget to properly seed the new initiatives. The plan was so compelling that he won the additional resources. So he doubled the advertising spending against the existing campaign, quadrupled the funding for marketing efforts and quintupled the public relations budget. Over the next two years, Tom and his team grew the business a combined 50 percent.

Adjusting to a New Boss[3]

Sometimes in interim roles, you'll have an overlap with the person replacing you at the back end. Even though that's a relatively short period inside an interim assignment, take it seriously. It doesn't matter how successful you and your team have been. It doesn't matter what your previous results and ratings were. Whether it's interim or permanent, a new boss reshuffles the deck, just as you do when you're the new boss.

Given that, here are some tips for adjusting to a new boss under any circumstances:

Foundation

Treat your new boss decently as a human being; make the boss feel welcome, valued, and valuable. Enable the new boss to do good work. Do your job well—and not the boss's.

Attitude

Choose to be optimistic. Believe the best about your new boss. Focus on these positives at all times with all people, making sure that your spouse and closest confidants do the same. Avoid unguarded carping.

---

[3]This was adapted from Edward J. Coyne Sr. and Kevin P. Coyne's article on "Surviving Your New CEO" (*Harvard Business Review*, May 2007) and then expanded.

Approach

Proactively tell your new boss that you want to be part of the new team and follow up with actions that reinforce this.

Learning

Present a realistic and honest game plan to help the boss learn. This will likely pay important dividends.

- Clarify the situation and plans, offering objective options.
- Seek out the new boss's perspective early and often and be open to new directions.

Expectations

Understand and move on your new boss's agenda immediately.

- Know the boss's priorities.
- Know what the new boss thinks your priorities should be.
- Decide what resources you both agree to invest in your area.

Implementation

Adjust to your new boss's working style immediately. This is a hard shift, not an evolution.

- Control points: Give the boss requested information, in the format desired, at the frequency wanted.
- Decisions: Clarify decision-making choices. (When each of you decides. When each of you provides input.) Remember, the old rules are out. It's a new game.
- Communication: Clarify the boss's preferred mode, manner, frequency, and how disagreements are managed.
- Readjust your team's Burning Imperative, if necessary, to match your new boss's vision.

Delivery

Be on your "A" game.

- Be present and "on"—everything done by you and your team will be part of your new boss's evaluation of you.
- Deliver early wins that are important to your new boss and to the people he or she listens to. (In a restart, the score is reset. Your old wins and your team's old wins are history.)

You Deserve It

Perhaps the most important thing to keep in mind is that you got the promotion or move because key people were confident that you would be successful. Those key people together probably know more about the situation than you do. Furthermore, because you're getting promoted or moved from within, they know you. To paraphrase Virgil, if those key people think you can and you think you can, you certainly can. So, prepare in advance as much as you can. Take control of your own transition as much as you can and accelerate team progress after the start as much as you can. If you can manage that, then you and your teams can successfully transition the batons and do great things.

Leading When You Were *Promoted from Within* or Internally Transferred: Summary and Implications

You can't control the context—so prepare in advance and be ready to adjust as required.

- Understand the context (planned, unplanned, interim).
- Secure the resources and support you need—especially internationally.
- Go with the flow, regain control of the situation, or jump into the dirty work as appropriate.

It's hard to make a clean break—so take control of your own message and transition.

- Manage the announcement cascade.
- Secure your base, ensuring your "old" area's ongoing success.

- Recognize the people who helped you along the way.
- Use the time before you start to strengthen relationships and jump-start learning.
- Assess your predecessor's legacy and clarify what you'll keep and what you'll change.
- Manage first impressions in the new role—with all due respect.

There's no honeymoon—so accelerate team progress after the start:

- Evolve the stated and defacto strategies (Burning Imperatives).
- Improve operations and implement dramatic changes as needed (milestones, early wins).
- Strengthen your organization (role sort).

Note we have included a sample 100-day action plan for someone promoted from within from Comptroller to CFO as Tool A6.1c in Appendix XI—Sample 100-Day Plans.

TOOL A6.1

Announcement Cascade Checklist*

STAKEHOLDERS
INTERNAL

EXTERNAL

MESSAGE
PLATFORM FOR CHANGE

VISION

CALL TO ACTION

PREANNOUNCEMENT TIMELINE (ONE-ON-ONES, SMALL GROUPS, LARGE GROUPS)
PRIOR TO ANNOUNCEMENT DAY

ANNOUNCEMENT DAY

(continued)

TOOL A6.1 (continued)

FORMAL ANNOUNCEMENT

POSTANNOUNCEMENT TIMELINE (ONE-ON-ONES, SMALL GROUPS, LARGE GROUPS, MASS)
IMMEDIATE

FIRST WEEK

NEAR TERM

OVER TIME

Leading a Department/Team Merger, Reorganization, or Restart

The basics of (1) get a head start, (2) manage your message, and (3) build your team, apply in every case. What's different is what you need to get a head start on and the restrictions around that, the nature of your message and the context for that message, and the conditions and context of your team building.

Merging or Jump-Starting Teams

What's three plus three?

Six. Certainly. Sometimes. With some synergy it could be seven. With some loss along the way it could be five.

When you are transitioning to a role where you will be merging or jump-starting a team, it is not just about the new direction that you will chart, it is also about deciding how you will deal with the legacy issues of the past. Most likely there will be some aspects of the team's culture, norms, behaviors, and strategies that you will want to keep or leverage and others that you will want to wipe away immediately. The art of this transition is to determine what can stay, what must go, and how to blend those decisions into the new direction. By definition, these transitions require that a new course be charted quickly. Waiting to do so will allow any undesirable legacy issues of the past to quickly seed in the new group. To counter that you'll want to make decisions and communicate quickly and with absolute clarity.

To be successful in a merger or jump-start situation you have to start by knowing the:

- Objectives
- Boundaries
- Immediate Actions

Objectives

What is the organization trying to accomplish by merging or restarting the team? Is it a cost-savings move? Is it an efficiency play? Is it an effectiveness play? Is it an attempt to rethink, replan, and react so that you can accelerate progress with the same team? Whatever it is, get clear on the objective before you do anything else. As soon as you are clear, you'll want to make sure that everyone on the team is clear.

Boundaries

The boundaries are defined by what you can and cannot do with this new team. In a merger or jump-start situation, the boundaries always change. Sometimes they expand while at other times they are tightly shrunk. Often, boundary changes are assumed and are not stated. You can be certain that you will not receive the new boundaries nicely articulated in a PowerPoint presentation. It's your job to seek out and clarify the new boundaries and then clearly define them for your team. It is not until you have identified the new boundaries that you can begin to take action. So be clear on the boundaries you've been dealt. Know how those boundaries have limited or expanded your choices for action.

For example, when Procter & Gamble bought drinks company Sunny Delight they were confident they could improve the product formulation. But they had higher priorities for the first year of the acquisition (like integrating Sunny Delight's people into Procter & Gamble). So they put a boundary around product development, making any work on that off limits for the first year.

Immediate Actions

How are you going to win within those boundaries? Objectives and boundaries are essential to know but they have no value until you begin to take action. It is action that actually produces results and in a merger or jump-start situation, because there is always a great sense of urgency, you will want to take immediate actions. The objectives and boundaries will guide you to the immediate actions required. Initially, focus your attention on the immediate-term actions that will gain team alignment around the new call to action. Get that right and then you'll be well positioned to roll out the short- and long-term action plans. Proceed in this order: immediate actions, short-term actions, long-term planning.

Merging teams creates a new team. Restarting a team creates a new team. Begin building that team on Day One by being clear on the Objectives, Boundaries, and the Immediate Actions. Pay as much attention to building your new team over your first 100 days as you would if you were joining a new company. It's hard work—and worth it.

The International Manager

Adapting and Building Trust When You're a Foreigner

T he basics of (1) get a head start, (2) manage your message, and (3) build your team, apply in every case. What's different is what you need to get a head start on and the restrictions around that, the nature of your message and the context for that message, and the conditions and context of your team building.

International Moves

The nice thing about switching countries is that no one (including you) expects you to know anything. You are completely, certifiably, consciously incompetent. Don't laugh. It's a privileged state that you want to leverage while you can. But, while doing so you'll want to be making genuine efforts to adapt to the new culture.

As if transitioning were not hard enough, an international move adds an entire set of new variables. Some are obvious and others completely hidden. It would take an entire book, or series of books to address the many possible situations that could occur in an international move. After having made these transitions ourselves and worked with many clients who have done the same, we've built a framework that is adaptable to most situations and should go a long way to keep you out of trouble and expedite your international transition.

Get a Head Start—With the Move

Do not take a short cut in the personal setup time required for you and your family in an international move. Moves always take more time and energy than we think they will and that is doubly the case in an international relocation. It will take more time than you think it will. Plan on it.

Plan also to get help—certainly from your boss and local HR. But also from outside relocation experts, consulates, consultants, language teachers, tour guides, expat welcome committees, and so on. Remember, you are consciously incompetent. There is no shame in getting help. You and your family will need it.

When Lisa was being moved from Madrid to Paris, her employer let her know 24 months in advance to give her and her family an appropriate amount of time to learn the language and the customs. That gave her ample time to find a place to live, schools, doctors, stores, as well as get all the family's visas and documents in line. As a result, her transition was seamless.

HOT TIP

Moving almost always takes more time than anyone expects. Managing the logistics ahead of a move will make a huge difference in your transition.

Get a Head Start—With the Job

Craft your own onboarding plan (ideally in conjunction with your boss). By definition, your learning curve will be steeper internationally than in your home country. So your learning plan will be particularly important. Similarly, jump-starting relationships will involve more conscious effort than in your home country. Plan to invest that effort.

Manage Your Message

Managing your message is particularly tricky because of the dual translation issues. Translation Issue 1 is linguistic. Translation Issue 2 is cultural. What you say often does not match what they hear. What they hear often does not match what you mean and vice versa. Remember, it's about communication and intent, not the exact words. Just by being ever aware and conscious of these issues, you've made great strides already. If you are uncertain, seek advice.

Coca-Cola's CEO was giving a talk at a customer dinner in Japan. His English words were being simultaneously translated into

Japanese. At one point the translator stopped her literal translation and explained to her listeners that the CEO was telling a joke, which she was not going to translate. Instead, she would tell them when to laugh. After a few more seconds she counted down and told them to laugh. They did, preserving everyone's "face." ("Saving face" is a big concept internationally. Preserving it is what happens when you treat people with respect.)

Build the Team

Building a team is always challenging. In a different country, it is much more challenging. The key is building the team while respecting the individuals and their cultural heritage. Trying to impose your country's ways of behaving, relating, attitudes, values, and working environment on a different country's team members is almost certainly doomed to failure. Get a shared purpose in place and then form the team around that shared purpose in the context of its culture.

Jim, a U.S. citizen, had accepted a leadership role in a newly merged organization in Japan and his new team consisted of people from each of the previously separate organizations. He knew that cohesive team members were essential to his success and he wanted to make sure that they understood the blending of the two teams would lead to a stronger unit than what either team had previously experienced on its own. He wanted them to know that they would retain their individuality, but by working together they could produce great results. So, he used an analogy and suggested that the merged team was more like ingredients coming together in a gumbo than in a puree. Good analogy, right? What Jim didn't think about was that Cajun culinary analogies don't work in Japan. Rather than delivering a pointed message, he ended up trying to describe gumbo. He laughed about his mistake and for sometime afterwards Jim referred to himself as "Gumbo-san."

When Howard, a U.K. citizen, worked in Japan he never sat down in a meeting until someone told him where to sit. Seating in Japan was by rank and Howard was never sure what his relative rank was. His approach worked because he was unafraid to admit his ignorance and at the same time was respectful of the cultural norms. His colleagues took Howard's actions as a sign of respect and they were more than happy to help him learn and adjust.

HOT TIP

As long as you've shown respect for your host, cultural flubs are almost always overlooked and won't be damaging to you or the team. Sometimes, when handled properly they can help ease the transition or create a team bond. Be respectful, make an honest effort to learn the culture and apologize when you make a mistake.

Note that we have included a sample 100-day action plan for someone moving to France to take over as country manager for a large international company as Tool 6.1d in Appendix XI—Sample 100-Day Plans.

Leading through a Crisis

A 100-Hour Action Plan

The main body of this book lays out a sequential methodology for leaders and their teams to get done in *100 days* what normally takes 6 to 12 months. In a crisis or disaster, this time frame is woefully inadequate as teams need a way to get done in *100 hours* what normally takes weeks or months. This requires an iterative instead of sequential approach. That way follows.[1]

Start with the basic premise that leadership is about inspiring and enabling others. Enhance that with Leonard Lodish's idea that "It is better to be vaguely right than precisely wrong."[2] Then add Darwin's point that, "It is not the strongest of the species that survives, nor the most intelligent, but the one most responsive to change."[3] Add it all up and you get leading through a crisis being about inspiring and enabling others to get things vaguely right quickly, and then adapt along the way—with clarity around direction, leadership, and roles.

This plays out in three steps of a disciplined iteration in line with the overall purpose:

---

[1] This methodology was developed in conjunction with a number of people at the American Red Cross and especially Becky McCorry, disaster operations center director, Chris Saeger, director of performance improvement, and Armond Mascelli, VP disaster operations. It would be hard to find a group of people more closely aligned around a more meaningful shared purpose. It has been one of my life's great privileges to be able to work with them – George.

[2] Professor Leonard Lodish, lecture at the University of Pennsylvania, Wharton School, 1984.

[3] Attributed to Charles Darwin.

1. *Prepare in advance.* The better you have anticipated possible scenarios, the more prepared you are, the more confidence you will have when crises strike.

2. *React to events.* The reason you prepared is so that you all can react quickly and flexibly to the situation you face. Don't overthink this. Do what you prepared to do.

3. *Bridge the gaps.* In a crisis, there is inevitably a gap between the desired and current state of affairs. Rectify that by bridging those gaps in the:

   • Situation: Implementing a response to the current crisis.

   • Response: Improving capabilities to respond to future crises.

   • Prevention: Reducing the risk of future crises happening in the first place.

Along the way, keep the ultimate purpose in mind. It needs to inform and frame everything you do over the short-, mid, and long-term as you lead *through* a crisis instead of merely *out* of a crisis. Crises change your organization. Be sure that the choices you make during crises change you in ways that move you toward your purpose and not away from your core vision and values.

Prepare in Advance

One life squad ran a drill in conjunction with the fire and police departments. It involved a car running off the road and down an embankment. The squad had to get down the embankment, treat urgent trauma, and package the victims for the fire department to lift out of the ditch and load into ambulances. Twenty minutes into the drill was this exchange:

"Where's my baby?"

"Your daughters are in the other ambulance."

"But where's my *baby*?"

It turned out that in addition to the four adults and teenagers, there was another victim. Lesson learned: Make sure you account for all victims.

Preparing in advance is about building general capabilities and capacity—not specific situational knowledge. For the most part, there is a finite set of the most likely, most devastating *types* of crises and disasters that are worth preparing for. Think them through. Run the drills. Capture the general lessons so people can apply them flexibly to the specific situations they encounter.[4] Have resources ready to be deployed when those disasters strike.

React to Events

Our fight or flight instincts evolved to equip us for moments like this. If the team has the capabilities and capacity in place, turn it loose to respond to the events. This is where all the hard work of preparation pays off.

Bridge the Gaps

Although first responders should react in line with their training, keep in mind that random, instinctual, uncoordinated actions by multiple groups exacerbate chaos. Stopping everything until excruciatingly detailed situation assessments have been fed into excruciatingly detailed plans that get approved by excruciatingly excessive layers of management leads to things happening too late. The preferred methodology for what Harrald calls the *integration* phase is to pause to accelerate, get thinking and plans vaguely right quickly, and then get going to bridge the gaps.[5]

Situational Questions

Keep in mind the physical, political, and emotional context.

- What Do We Know, and Not Know, About What Happened and Its Impact (Facts)?
- What are the implications of what we know and don't know (conclusions)?

---

[4]John Harrald argues the need for both discipline (structure, doctrine, process) *and* agility (creativity, improvisation, adaptability) in "Agility and Discipline: Critical Success Factors for Disaster Response," *The ANNALS of the American Academy of Political and Social Science* 2006: 604, 256.

[5]Harrald ibid.

- What do we predict may happen (scenarios)?
- What resources and capabilities do we have at our disposal (assets)? Gaps?
- What aspects of the situation can we turn to our advantage?

Objectives and Intent

Armed with answers to those questions, think through and choose the situational objectives and intent. What are the desired outcomes of leading through the crisis? What is the desired end-state? This is a critical component of direction and a big deal.

For example, when a glass water bottle capper at a major beverage company went bad, grinding screw top threads into glass chips, the objective and intent were (1) stop the damage and (2) protect the brand.

Priorities

The American Red Cross provides relief to victims of disasters. In doing that, the prioritization of shelter, food, water, medicine, and emotional support varies by the type of disaster. If a fire destroys someone's home in the winter, shelter takes precedence. On the other hand, if a reservoir gets contaminated, the critical priority is getting people clean water.

These examples illustrate the importance of thinking through the priorities for each individual situation—and each stage of a developing crisis. The choices for isolating, containing, controlling, and stabilizing the immediate situation likely will be different than the priorities for the midterm response, getting resources in the right place and then delivering the required support over time. Those will be different from the priorities involved in repairing the damage from the crisis or disaster and preventing its reoccurrence.

Get the answer to the question, "Where do we focus our efforts first?" and the priority choices are clear.

Get priorities communicated to all, perhaps starting with a set of meetings to:

- Recap current situation and needs, and what has already been accomplished.
- Agree on objectives, intent, priorities, and phasing of priorities.
- Agree on action plans, milestones, role sort, communication points, plans, and protocols.

These are the same building blocks discussed in the main body of the book. However, a crisis is better managed by using an iterative approach than by using the more sequential approach laid out in Chapter 13. This is why we recommend early meetings to jump-start strategic, operational, and organizational processes all at the same time, getting things vaguely right quickly and then adapting to new information along the way.

Bridge the Gap between the Desired and Current State

Follow these steps in bridging the gaps between the desired and current state:

Support team members in implementing plans while gathering more information concurrently.

Complete situation assessment and midterm prioritization and plans.

Conduct milestone update sessions daily or more frequently as appropriate:
- Update progress on action plans with focus on wins, learning, areas needing help.
- Update situation assessment.
- Adjust plans iteratively, reinforcing the expectation of continuous adjustment.

Overcommunicate at every step of the way to all the main constituencies. Your message and main communication points will evolve as the situation and your information about the situation evolve. This makes the need that much greater for frequent communication updates within the organization, with partner organizations, and the public. Funneling as much as possible through one spokesperson will reduce misinformation. Do not underestimate the importance of this.

First officer Jeff Skiles was flying the airplane that took off, ran into a flock of birds, and lost both its engines. At that point, Captain Chesley Sullenberger chose to take over. With his "My aircraft" command, followed by Skiles's "Your aircraft" response, control was passed to "Sully" who safely landed the plane on the

Hudson River. Only one pilot can be actually flying a plane at one time. Two people trying to land the same plane at the same time simply does not work.

The same is true for crisis and disaster management. Only one person can be flying any effort or component at a time. A critical part of implementation is clarifying and reclarifying who is doing what, and who is making what decisions at what point—especially as changing conditions dictate changes in roles and decision-making authority within and across organizations. Make sure the hand-offs are as clean as the one on Sully and Skiles's flight.

Bridge the gaps between desired and current response and desired and most recent crisis prevention (improving things and reducing risks for the future).

At the end of the crisis, conduct an after-action review looking at:

- What actually happened? How did that compare with what we expected to happen?

- What impact did we have? How did that compare with our objectives?

- What did we do particularly effectively that we should do again?

- What can we do even better the next time in terms of risk mitigation and response?

Summary

Leading through a crisis is about inspiring and enabling others to get things vaguely right quickly and adapt iteratively along the way—with clear direction, leadership, and roles.

Follow these three steps:

1. *Prepare in advance.* Preparation breeds confidence. Think through your own crisis management protocols. Proposition resources. Identify and train crisis management teams.

2. *React to events.* Leverage that preparation to respond quickly and flexibly in the moment. This requires courage on the part of management to let people do what they are prepared to do without much oversupervision early on. However, it is important

to instill an "ask for help early," rather than a "wait until we are overwhelmed" attitude in the responders.[6]

3. *Bridge the gaps.* Do this between desired and current situations, response capabilities, and prevention, supporting team members in implementing purpose-driven, priority-focused plans while gathering more information concurrently.

---

[6]Chris Saeger, discussion at American Red Cross, May 2010.

TOOL A9.1

100-Hour Action Plan for
Crisis Management*

ORGANIZATION'S PURPOSE: _____

UPDATE:

Wins—Share and celebrate the good things that have already happened

_____

Learning—Share learning that can help others _____

Help—Highlight areas needing more support_____

PHYSICAL, POLITICAL, EMOTIONAL CONTEXT:

What do we know, and not know about what happened and its impact (facts)?

_____

What are the implications of what we know and don't know (conclusions)?

_____

What do we predict may happen (scenarios)? _____

What resources and capabilities do we have at our disposal (assets)? Gaps?

_____

What aspects of the situation can we turn to our advantage?

_____

SITUATIONAL OBJECTIVES AND INTENT:

_____

PRIORITY 1: _____ Leader: _____

ACTIONS: _____ When: _____ Who: _____

ACTIONS: _____ When: _____ Who: _____

ACTIONS: _____ When: _____ Who: _____

PRIORITY 2: _____ Leader: _____

ACTIONS: _____ When: _____ Who: _____

ACTIONS: _____ When: _____ Who: _____

ACTIONS: _____ When: _____ Who: _____

(*continued*)

---

*Copyright © PrimeGenesis® LLC. To customize this document, download Tool A9.1
from www.onboardingtools.com. The document can then be opened, edited, and printed.

TOOL A9.1 (continued)

PRIORITY 3: _____ Leader: _____

ACTIONS: _____ When: _____ Who: _____

ACTIONS: _____ When: _____ Who: _____

ACTIONS: _____ When: _____ Who: _____

COMMUNICATION:

PRIMARY SPOKESPERSON: _____ BACKUP: _____

MESSAGE: _____

COMMUNICATION POINTS:

1. _____

2. _____

3. _____

PROTOCOLS:

NEXT TEAM CALL/MEETING: _____

EXCEPTION GUIDELINES: _____

TOOL A9.1b

100-Hour Plan for Crisis Management Guide*

This section provides guidance on completing and using this tool.

Recall the three steps of crisis management:

1. Prepare in advance.
2. React to events.
3. Bridge the gaps.

This tool focuses on bridging the gaps between the desired and current state in the current crisis.

ORGANIZATION'S PURPOSE

Begin by recapping the organization's purpose to give everyone the same long-term view.

UPDATE

Start each meeting by "going around the table" with BRIEF updates from team members on wins, learning, and help they need.

PHYSICAL, POLITICAL, EMOTIONAL CONTEXT

Context is key. Complete as soon as practical and then update as things change—which they will.

What do we know, and *not* know about what happened and its impact? (These are facts, data, things everyone looking at sees the same way.)

What are the implications of what we know and don't know? (These conclusions are your opinions, drawn from the facts.)

What do we predict may happen? (Since you don't know what will happen, lay out a couple of possible scenarios.)

What resources and capabilities do we have at our disposal? Gaps? (These are your assets, both already deployed and available to be deployed, as well as holes you need to fill.)

(continued)

TOOL A9.1b   (continued)

What aspects of the situation can we turn to our advantage? (This gets at resources that can be reallocated from other parts of your organization or other organizations, or opportunities created by the crisis. Look back at the organization's purpose for guidance here.)

SITUATIONAL OBJECTIVES AND INTENT

This is about defining what is required to bridge the gap between the desired and current state in the current crisis. "Intent" gets at why that's important. For example, when a glass water bottle capper went bad, grinding screw top threads into glass chips, the objective and intent were (1) stop the damage and (2) protect the brand.

PRIORITIES

Be clear on whether your three priorities cut across all scenarios or whether they are options to pursue depending on which scenario unfolds. As you get new information, your priorities may change. Either way, each priority needs a single, accountable leader.

Then lay out the actions for each priority, with timing and a single, accountable leader for each action.

COMMUNICATION

Identify the primary spokesperson and back up, along with core message and three communication points.

PROTOCOLS

End each meeting with agreement on when you'll meet again and how people should deal with surprises between the meetings. There will be surprises.

Onboarding

HOW ORGANIZATIONS AND SUPERVISORS CAN DRAMATICALLY BOOST THE ODDS OF A NEW LEADER'S SUCCESS

The main body of this book is written for a leader moving into a new role. This appendix is written to that new leader's direct supervisor and is geared to helping him or her onboard that new leader (or any new team member). The following is adapted from the executive summary of *Onboarding: How to Get Your New Employees Up to Speed in Half the Time* by George Bradt and Mary Vonnegut.[1] Not surprisingly, we suggest that you read that book cover to cover if you really care about your new employees. Until you make time to do that, this appendix will get you started.

Onboarding is the process of acquiring, accommodating, assimilating, and accelerating new team members, whether they come from outside or inside the organization. The prerequisite to successful onboarding is getting your organization aligned around the need and the role.

Align: Make sure that your organization agrees on the need for a new team member and the delineation of the role you seek to fill.

Acquire: Identify, recruit, select, and get people to join the team.

Accommodate: Give new team members the tools they need to do the work.

---

[1]Bradt, George and Vonnegut, Mary, *Onboarding: How to Get Your New Employees Up to Speed in Half the Time* (Hoboken, NJ: John Wiley & Sons, 2009).

Assimilate: Help them join with others so they can do the work together.

Accelerate: Help them and their team deliver better results faster.

Effective onboarding of new team members is one of the most important contributions any hiring manager can make to the long-term success of his or her team or organization. Effective onboarding drives new employee productivity, accelerates delivery of results, and significantly improves talent retention. Yet few organizations manage the different pieces of onboarding well, so most people in new roles do not get clear messages about what the team and the organization want and expect from them. Even fewer organizations use a strategic, comprehensive, integrated, and consistent approach like the one described in the *Onboarding* book.

Why? Because onboarding is not something you do every day; it's hard to get good at it. With deliberate practice, however, you can accumulate onboarding expertise. This appendix lays out a framework that you can follow step-by-step.

In our work helping organizations get new leaders up to speed quickly, we have seen repeatedly that a primary cause of misalignment and disengagement of new employees is the way that most organizations split up their recruitment, orientation, training, and management efforts. In many cases, multiple uncoordinated players oversee discrete pieces of the onboarding process and make poor handoffs across those parts. Almost everybody has a story.

- People showing up to interview candidates without a clear picture of the position they're trying to fill, let alone what strengths they're looking for.
- High-pressure interviews that turn off exactly the sort of people the organization is looking to recruit.
- Closing the sale with a candidate who turns out to be wrong for the organizational culture.
- New employees showing up for the first day—and there's no one to greet them, no place for them to sit, no tools for them to work with, and no manager around to point them in the right direction.
- New employees getting off on the wrong foot with exactly the people they need to collaborate most closely with.

- New employees left to their own devices after Day One because the organization has a sink-or-swim mentality.

> *I have witnessed a lack of collaboration, cooperation, and coordination between the recruiting lead, the human resource generalist, and the hiring manager, that actually caused a new employee to show up for her first day on the job, without anyone knowing it. I reported to the hiring manager, and was asked to take care of "onboarding" this new employee. I was embarrassed for the company, myself, and her.*[2]

A new employee's failure to deliver usually stems from one or more of four things that you, the hiring manager, can influence:

1. A role failure due to unclear or misaligned expectations and resources (preparation miss). For example, a new global head of customer service who was hired before division heads had agreed to move customer service from their divisions to a central group.
2. A personal failure due to lack of strengths, motivation, or fit (recruiting/selecting miss). For example, a new head of marketing who was hired with direct marketing experience that was woefully out of date.
3. A relationship failure due to early missteps (head start/early days miss). For example, a new employee aggressively challenged a colleague before he or she fully understood the situation, making that colleague reluctant to share information with the new employee after that.
4. An engagement failure due to early days' experiences (management miss). For example, a new employee's manager who was not around during the employee's first month due to other priorities.

When any person takes on a new role, there is a risk that he or she will be misaligned with the organization. When you compound this with the disruption inherent in all organizational transitions, it's no wonder that so many new employees fail or decide to leave in the

---

[2]This is the first of several quotes from managers around the world who agreed to let us use their words just so long as we preserved their confidentiality.

first six months[3] and that as many as 50 percent of new employees fail to deliver what their organizations expect.[4] Often those failures or decisions aren't apparent early on. But the seeds have sprouted, and it's very hard to change the course down the road. A new job is a turbulent event for everyone.

Consider this case: A major consumer products company was experiencing high levels of new employee failure. It turned out that the organization had three distinct groups each working to improve its own area of responsibility without paying attention to the others. "Talent Acquisition" was focused on cutting expenses by increasing the use of contract recruiters. "Human Resources" was focused on improving the organization's orientation program. "Line Management" was implementing performance-based compensation to keep people more focused on the most important performance-driving activities.

We helped the organization get its hiring managers more involved in recruiting and orienting new employees throughout the process. The results were immediate and meaningful. Recruiting efforts became more closely aligned with hiring managers' expectations. Selection criteria became clearer. Hiring managers took a personal interest in their new employees' orientations and related activities. Candidates and new employees felt better about the organization at every step of the way, which resulted in increases in their effectiveness over time.

Because so many people have heard (or lived) these or similar stories, many organizations are looking for solutions. Many take recruiting, interviewing, and selecting more seriously. Many have utilized onboarding software or portals to manage hiring paperwork and tasks. Many hold managers accountable for the success of their employees. All these are good things. Do them. But you don't need this appendix to tell you that.

The ideas here can take your organization to a new level of effectiveness by improving and integrating the disconnected experiences and messages new employees get during the recruiting and on-the-job learning process. This is a powerful, vulnerable time in the life of an employee. It represents the most important teachable moment your organization will ever have with its employees. If you can plan and get each new employee and the organization in full alignment so that

---

[3]Martin, Kevin, presentation to the Human Capital Institute, Washington, D.C., April 16, 2008. Aberdeen's group 2007 study indicated that 86 percent of employees make a decision to stay or leave the firm in their first six months or less.

[4]Brad Smart, *Topgrading* (Upper Saddle River, NJ: Prentice Hall, 1999).

intelligent onboarding becomes part of your culture, you will make a material difference in your business results over time.

We are not reinventing the wheel. Most people understand or can quickly figure out the basics of acquiring, accommodating, assimilating, and accelerating new employees. The core premise is that things work better when all efforts point in the same direction, integrated into one Total Onboarding Program (TOP). Onboarding gets your new employees up to speed twice as fast as separate efforts to recruit, orient, and manage. It enables you to get more done in less time by:

- Compressing recruiting, hiring, and assimilation time.
- Reducing hiring mistakes by making everyone, including prospective hires, fully aware of what the job requires—from the employee and from the organization.
- Reducing new employee buyer's remorse and greatly improving retention.
- Aligning new employees with key business strategies.

The primary requirement is that you, the hiring manager, lead each new employee's onboarding experience all the way through. Start by creating the overall TOP plan. Get people aligned around that plan and its importance. Take primary responsibility for its execution and coordination across people and functions as you recruit. Give your new employee a big head start, and enable and inspire them. Figure A10.1 provides a rough chronology.

FIGURE A10.1 Total Onboarding Program

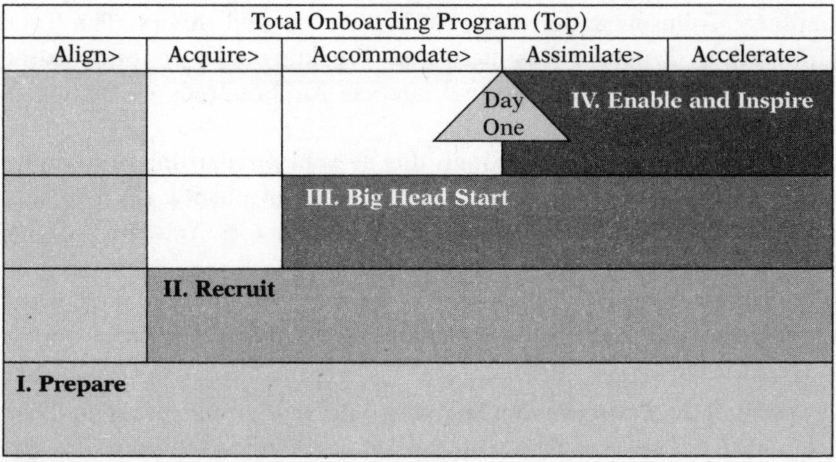

The main steps in onboarding new employees include preparation before starting to recruit, recruiting in a way that reinforces your message, giving your new employees a head start, and enabling and inspiring them.

1. *Prepare for your new employee's success before you start recruiting.* Understand the organization-wide benefits of a Total Onboarding Program. Clarify your destination by crafting your messages to the employee and the organization, and by creating a recruiting brief. Lay out your timeline, and align stakeholders.

2. *Recruit in a way that reinforces your messages about the position and the organization.* Create a powerful slate of potential candidates. Evaluate candidates against the recruiting brief while preselling and preboarding. Make the right offer, and close the right sale the right way.

3. *Give your new employee a big head start before Day One.* Co-create a personal onboarding plan with your new employee. Manage the announcement to set your new employee up for success. Do what it takes to make your new employee ready, eager, and able to do real work on Day One.

4. *Enable and inspire your new employee to deliver better results faster.* Make positive first impressions both ways. Speed the development of important working relationships. Provide resources, support, and follow-through.

We created this approach out of the best of what we've seen and developed in PrimeGenesis's onboarding work since 2002 with a wide range of organizations around the world like American Express, Cadbury, Johnson & Johnson, MTV, Playtex, and others. The Total Onboarding Program has delivered breakthroughs in onboarding effectiveness and organizational success for hundreds of managers and client organizations.

As you are working through the steps of onboarding, it's helpful to think about your role within the analogy of putting on a theater production in which your new employees are actors. You are:

The **Producer.** While preparing for success and recruiting, think of yourself as the show's producer, assembling resources for the show.

Then, the **Director.** While giving your new employees a big head start before Day One, think of yourself as the show's director.

You will co-create the plan, make introductions, announce the show, and generally get things ready.

Finally, the **Stage Manager.** After your new employees walk out on stage, you will continue to EASE (Encourage—Align—Solve—End) the way by managing context and the things happening around them.

The analogy is helpful because it gets you off the new employees' stage. You can't recite their lines for them. You can't hit their marks.

Your job is offstage. The balance of this appendix outlines the 12 steps of a Total Onboarding Program. Throughout, Total Onboarding Program plan and TOP plan refer to your plan as the hiring manager, integrating all the steps of onboarding. The personal onboarding plan is the plan you co-create with your new

FIGURE A10.2 Total Onboarding Program (With Details)

Total Onboarding Program (Top)				
Align>	Acquire>	Accommodate>	Assimilate>	Accelerate>
			Day One	**IV. Enable and Inspire** Resources, support, follow-through. (12) Speed important working relationships. (11) Make positive first impressions both ways. (10)
		III. Big Head Start Make your employee ready and able to do real work on Day One. (9) Manage the announcement to set new employee up for success. (8) Co-create a personal onboarding plan with your new employee. (7)		
	II. Recruit Make the right offer, and close the right sale the right way. (6) Evaluate candidates against the brief while pre-selling and pre-boarding (5) Create a powerful slate of potential candidates. (4)			
I. Prepare Craft your onboarding plan, and align your stakeholders. (3) Clarify your destination. Write a recruiting brief. And craft your messages. (2) Understand the organization-wide benefits of a Total Onboarding Program. (1)				

leader or employee regarding his or her own accommodation, assimilation and acceleration.

Prepare for your new employee's success before you start recruiting:

1. *Understand the organization-wide benefits of a total onboarding program.*

   Step 1 is to understand the importance of a single, integrated Total Onboarding Program by reading this appendix (or the Onboarding book).

2. *Clarify your destination and messages to the candidate and the organization.*

   This is where you move from theory to practice. Start by stopping to reconfirm your organization's purpose, priorities, and desired results. How will your new employee contribute? Think through what went well and less well when you and/or your organization onboarded new employees in the past. Map out clear, simple messages about this onboarding: your message to stakeholders, your message to candidates, and your message to your new employee.

   Reconfirm context. Determine your messages.

   Take this to the next level as an organization over time by looking at your overall messaging on an annual basis.

3. *Craft your timeline, write a recruiting brief, and align stakeholders.*

   This is about sharing your thinking with others, getting their input, and deciding together how to go forward. Start by crafting an onboarding plan that includes the work you did in Step 2, a recruiting brief, and a TOP timeline. Then get important players aligned around your plan. Investment of time here makes everything else more effective and efficient down the road.

   Create and get alignment around your TOP.

   Take this to the next level as an organization over time by embedding onboarding in your normal succession planning and talent management processes.

   Recruit in a way that reinforces your messages.

4. *Create a powerful slate of potential candidates.*

   Take charge of the employee acquisition process by laying out and implementing a comprehensive marketing plan that starts with your target and moves through where you are going to fish for new employees, the tools and resources you will use, and your timelines/milestones. Communicate, demonstrate, and live your employment brand every step of the way. Assemble a deep slate of strong candidates at the same time to give you options, so that you don't feel you have to close the sale with your lead candidate if it's not 100 percent right for everyone.

Inform and guide recruiting efforts.

Take this to the next level as an organization over time by creating a culture of continuous sourcing.

5. *Evaluate candidates against the recruiting brief while preselling and preboarding.*

While candidates can focus on getting you to offer them a job and then take a step back to evaluate the opportunity, you must buy and sell at the same time. Make sure that you are recruiting and interviewing in a way that communicates your employment brand. We use a strengths-focused, targeted selection/behavioral approach to interviewing with good success. We complete the interviewing process with formal postinterview debriefs, information gathering outside the interviews, and postinterview follow-ups with candidates to learn even more (and set up closing the sale later).

Make the hiring choice—while preselling and preboarding.

Take this to the next level as an organization over time by setting aside one day each month for interviews.

6. *Make the right offer, and close the right sale the right way.*

You know your organization is awesome. Just remember that a potential new employee may need to be convinced. So treat the offer as just one part of a strategic sale. The way you handle this and support your offerees due diligence efforts will impact the way he or she feels about you and your organization, with implications far beyond whether the answer is yes or no. You want offerees to say yes if taking the job is the right move for them, their supporters, and the organization over time. You want a "no, thanks" if it's not.

Close the sale. Support your new employee's due diligence efforts.

Take this to the next level as an organization over time by making training on strategic selling mandatory for all managers.

Give your new employee a big head start before Day One.

7. *Co-create a personal onboarding plan with your new employee.*

Co-creating a personal onboarding plan is the beginning of your working relationship. Listen, and demonstrate how much you value your new employee. Work together to think through the job and its deliverables, stakeholders, message, prestart, and Day One plans as well as personal and office setup needs. Clarify who is doing what next.

Co-create new employee personal onboarding plan.

Take this to the next level as an organization over time by creating an onboarding plan review board.

8. *Manage the announcement to set up your new employee for success.*

Making the announcement is one of the most important things you can do to help make your new employee feel welcome, valued by, and valuable to an organization he or she can take pride in. Think through and implement these steps:

1. Map the stakeholders.

2. Clarify the messages.

3. Lock in the timing and wording of the official announcement.

4. Map out whom to talk to before the announcement, when and how.

5. Map out whom to talk to after the announcement, but before the new employee starts.

6. Implement, track, and adjust as appropriate.

Clarify and deliver messages. Set up new employee's preboarding conversations.

Take this to the next level as an organization over time by running announcement cascade plans past the onboarding plan review board.

9. *Do what it takes to make your new employee ready, eager, and able to do real work on Day One.*

- Accommodate work needs (desk, phone, computer, ID, payroll, forms, etc.).

- Accommodate personal needs (family move, housing, schools, etc.).

Mind the details to give the new employee a first day that is in line with the opportunity/shared purpose and to put your new employee in a position to do real work starting Day One.

Ensure your organization produces a perfect Day One.

Take this to the next level as an organization over time by systematizing accommodation so you don't have to reinvent it every time.

Enable and inspire your new employee to deliver better results faster.

10. *Make positive first impressions both ways.*

Everything communicates. Pay attention to what people hear, see, and believe. Pay attention to the impact the organization is making on the new employee. Pay attention to the impact the new employee is making on the organization. Design the Day One experience as you would a customer experience. Don't leave first impressions to chance, because although people don't always remember what others did or said, they always remember how they made them feel.

Manage first impressions. Welcome. Introduce the new employee.

Take this to the next level as an organization over time by creating a prototypical Day One agenda that managers can adjust to fit each new employee's situation.

11. *Speed development of important working relationships.*

Assimilation is a big deal. Doing it well makes things far easier. Getting it wrong triggers relationship risks. There are a couple of things beyond basic orientation that can make a huge difference. We suggest that you set up onboarding conversations for your new employee with members of his or her formal and informal/shadow networks. Do periodic check-ins with those networks. If there are issues, you want to know about them early, so that you can help your new employee adjust.

Facilitate new employee assimilation initiatives. Be alert to challenges.

Take this to the next level as an organization over time by setting aside one day each month for group orientations and a newcomers' club with executive sponsors.

12. *Provide resources, support, and follow-through.*

The first step in giving your new employee the resources and support he or she needs is confirming your own requirement and appetite for change. If all you need is for your new employee to assimilate into the existing culture, you can probably mentor them yourself or with an internal coach. However, if achieving the desired results requires a new employee to assimilate into and transform the team at the same time, you will need to bring in external assistance. (If insiders could transform your culture, they would have done so already.)

Make sure that your new employee gains needed resources and establishes the building blocks of a high-performing team, as appropriate to his or her position:

1. What most needs to be accomplished (in place by day 30).
2. Clarity around what's getting done, when, by whom (by day 45).
3. One or two strongly symbolic early wins (identified by day 60, delivered by month six).
4. The right people in the right roles with the right support (by day 70).
5. A communication plan implemented on an ongoing basis.[5]

   Support. Mentor. EASE: Encourage-Align-Solve-End.

   Take this to the next level as an organization over time by creating a stable of internal and external mentors, coaches, and transition accelerators.

Follow-Through

Just as onboarding starts long before Day One, it ends long after the personal onboarding plan is executed. Follow through with your new employee to ensure ongoing adjustments and success or to redirect if things are not working. Check the process: audit, adjust, and plan improvements in anticipation of the next onboarding.

How you handle the acquisition, accommodation, assimilation, and acceleration of new employees communicates volumes to everyone. In many ways, this is one of the acid tests of leadership. If you follow the prescriptions in this book and stay focused on inspiring and enabling others to do their absolute best, together to realize a meaningful and rewarding shared purpose, then those others will happily follow you.

---

[5]See the main body of the "Onboarding" book or www.primegenesis.com for more on these building blocks.

Sample 100-Day Plans

When working with clients or interacting with our readers we are often asked for sample 100-day action plans. We usually don't provide sample plans because (1) every situation is different and (2) we have found that it often zaps some of the creativity and thinking that is required to come up with a comprehensive plan. Action items in samples somehow often seem to be great ideas for someone who is starting to develop their 100-day plan when in actuality they may not be as good of a fit as they initially seem. So, use these as a guideline, but realize that yours should look different, because every situation is different. Also these plans are summaries, so behind each pithy line item there lays detail, planning, and analysis. Finally, we suggest that you at least complete a first draft of your plan before you peruse the samples below. The last thing we would want to do is stifle your analysis or creativity with sample plans! We have included plans for three scenarios: (1) transitioning into a new company, (2) promoted from within, and (3) an international move.

TOOL A6.1b

100-Day Checklist—Sample: New Company—Head of Marketing*

To help you understand how this plays out, this sample new leader kept a weekly journal through his Fuzzy Front End and first 100 days. You can find it at www.primegenesis.com/blog/category/new-leaders-journal.

STAKEHOLDERS

UP: JACK (BOSS), SUSAN (BOSS'S BOSS)

ACROSS: ANDREW (HEAD OF SALES), BARNEY (HEAD OF PRODUCT DEVELOPMENT), CHESLEY (CFO), GERALD (AD AGENCY), HAL (PR AGENCY)

DOWN: DAVID (BRAND X DIRECTOR), ELLEN (BRAND Y DIRECTOR), FAITH (MEDIA DIRECTOR)

(FORMER*)

MESSAGE: OUR TIME!

PLATFORM FOR CHANGE INITIAL PUBLIC OFFERING HAS GIVEN US INCREMENTAL RESOURCES

VISION: MARKET LEADER IN OUR CATEGORIES

CALL TO ACTION: RESEARCH, DEVELOP, SELL, IMPLEMENT MARKETING INVESTMENT PLANS

FUZZY FRONT END

PERSONAL SETUP: GET FAMILY SETTLED IN RENTAL HOUSE, OFFICE, PHONE, COMPUTER, ETC.

JUMP START LEARNING: CONSUMER RESEARCH, CUSTOMER USAGE AND ATTITUDE, BASE PLANS

MEET LIVE IN ADVANCE: DAVID, ELLEN, ANDREW, BARNEY

---

*Copyright © PrimeGenesis® LLC. To customize this document, download Tool A6.1b from www.onboardingtools.com. The document can then be opened, edited, and printed.

TOOL A6.1b   (continued)

PHONE IN ADVANCE: GERALD, HAL, CHESLEY, FAITH

(ANNOUNCEMENT CASCADE*)

DAY ONE: (JUL 1) ORANGE JUICE WITH FULL TEAM, NEW MANAGER ASSIMILATION, IN-STORE VISITS

FIRST WEEK: REVIEW BASE PLANS, 1:1S WITH ALL MARKETING PEOPLE, AGENCY ORIENTATIONS

TACTICAL CAPACITY BUILDING BLOCKS

BURNING IMPERATIVE (BY DAY 30 – JUL 31)—WORKSHOP WITH MARKETERS, AGENCIES, SALES, PDD

MILESTONES (BY DAY 45 – AUG 15)—SET DAY II OF WORKSHOP

EARLY WINS PLANS (BY DAY 60 – AUG 31)—TBD (LIKELY NEW ADVERTISING CAMPAIGN)

TEAM ROLES (BY DAY 70 – SEP 10)—TBD (LIKELY SHIFTING RESOURCES INTO ADVERTISING)

COMMUNICATION STEPS—START INTERNAL BLOG, SHARE BASE PLANS WITH WHOLE ORGANIZATION

---

*ASTERISKED SECTIONS ARE PRIMARILY FOR INTERNAL MOVES

TOOL A6.1c

100-Day Checklist—Sample: Promoted from Within from Comptroller to CFO*

STAKEHOLDERS

UP: ZBIGNY (BOSS: CEO), PETER (BOSS'S BOSS: LEAD DIRECTOR), HANK (AUDIT COMMITTEE)

ACROSS: ULNA (HEAD OF OPERATIONS), TERRI (HEAD OF MARKETING), SAMANTHA (HEAD OF SALES)
    QUENTON (AUDITOR), RAJ (HEAD OF BANKRUPTCY FIRM)

DOWN: NAOMI (TREASURER), MICHAEL (ASST. COMPTROLLER), FAITH (AVP OF FINANCIAL PLANNING)

(FORMER*) FAITH (ASSOCIATE VICE PRESIDENT, FINANCIAL PLANNING AND ANALYSIS), EDGAR (CORPORATE DEVELOPMENT), DANA (CREDIT AND COLLECTIONS)

MESSAGE: BE CAREFUL WHAT YOU ASK FOR (YOU MAY GET IT)

PLATFORM FOR CHANGE: COMING OUT OF STRATEGIC BANKRUPTCY

VISION: STRATEGIC SALE WITHIN 18 MONTHS AT 4X MULTIPLE

CALL TO ACTION: RATIONALIZE OPERATIONS, BUILD COMPETITIVE ADVANTAGES

FUZZY FRONT END

PERSONAL SETUP: NO CHANGE

JUMP-START LEARNING: ESPECIALLY TREASURY

*Copyright © PrimeGenesis® LLC. To customize this document, download Tool A6.1c from www.onboardingtools.com. The document can then be opened, edited, and printed.

TOOL A6.1c   (continued)

MEET LIVE IN ADVANCE: NAOMI, MICHAEL

PHONE IN ADVANCE: RAJ, QUENTON

(ANNOUNCEMENT CASCADE*) (1) NAOMI, MICHAEL; (2) FAITH; (3) ANNOUNCE; (4) OLD FINANCE TEAM; (5) NEW FINANCE TEAM

DAY ONE: (JUN-1)—ORANGE JUICE WITH FULL FINANCE TEAM, NEW MANAGER ASSIMILATION, BANKRUPTCY LAWYERS

FIRST WEEK: REVIEW TREASURY AND CONTROL PLANS, 1:1S WITH ALL NEW DIRECT REPORTS AS CFO

TACTICAL CAPACITY BUILDING BLOCKS

BURNING IMPERATIVE (BY DAY 30–JUN-30)—WORKSHOP FINANCE LEADERSHIP TEAM

MILESTONES (BY DAY 45–JUL 15)—SET DAY II OF WORKSHOP

EARLY WINS PLANS (BY DAY 60–JUL 31)—TBD (LIKELY INVESTMENT PLAN FOR NEW INITIATIVE)

TEAM ROLES (BY DAY 70–AUG 10)—TBD (LIKELY SHIFTING RESOURCES TO NEW INITIATIVE)

COMMUNICATION STEPS—START INTERNAL BLOG, SHARE BASE PLANS WITH WHOLE ORGANIZATION

TOOL A6.1d

100-Day Checklist—Sample: New Country Manager—France*

STAKEHOLDERS

UP: LUIGI (GROUP PRESIDENT EUROPE), SUSAN (EVP INTERNATIONAL)

ACROSS: EUROPEAN LEADERSHIP TEAM; GLOBAL OPERATIONS TEAM; BRAND TEAMS

DOWN: PIERRE (MARKETING), JACQUES (SALES), MARIE (FINANCE), GASTON (OPERATIONS), SELA (HR)

(FORMER*) SINGAPORE LEADERSHIP TEAM, ASIA MANAGEMENT TEAM

MESSAGE: ACCELERATE WHAT'S WORKING

PLATFORM FOR CHANGE: MARKET TESTS WORKED! MANAGEMENT WANTS TO EXPAND!

VISION: MARKET LEADERSHIP IN FRANCE

CALL TO ACTION: MANUFACTURE, SELL, MARKET, DISTRIBUTE, IMPROVE

FUZZY FRONT END

PERSONAL SETUP: FAMILY: HOUSING, SCHOOLS, CARS, DOCTORS, ETC.

JUMP-START LEARNING: CONSUMERS, CUSTOMERS, COMPETITORS, CAPABILITIES, REGULATIONS

MEET LIVE IN ADVANCE: PIERRE, JACQUES, MARIE, GASTON, SELA

PHONE IN ADVANCE: LUIGI, KEY EUROPEAN LEADERS, SEBASTIAN (OUTGOING COUNTRY MANAGER)

*Copyright © PrimeGenesis® LLC. To customize this document, download Tool A6.1d from www.onboardingtools.com. The document can then be opened, edited, and printed.

TOOL A6.1d (continued)

(ANNOUNCEMENT CASCADE*) SEBASTIAN TELLS FRANCE TEAM (MAY 1 AM), I TELL SINGAPORE TEAM (MAY 1 PM), THEN ANNOUNCEMENT (MAY 2). THEN CALLS TO SET UP MEETINGS.

DAY ONE: (JUN-1) CAFÉ AU LAIT WITH FULL TEAM, NEW MANAGER ASSIMILATION, CUSTOMER VISITS

FIRST WEEK: REVIEW TEST MARKET, 1:1S WITH DIRECT REPORTS, VISITS TO SUPPLIERS, CUSTOMERS, AGENCIES

TACTICAL CAPACITY BUILDING BLOCKS

BURNING IMPERATIVE (BY DAY 30–JUN-30)—WORKSHOP WITH LEADERSHIP TEAM

MILESTONES (BY DAY 45–JUL 15)—SET DAY II OF WORKSHOP

EARLY WINS PLANS (BY DAY 60–JUL 31)—TBD (LIKELY EARLY REGIONAL ROLLOUT)

TEAM ROLES (BY DAY 70–AUG 10)—TBD (LIKELY SHIFTING RESOURCES INTO SALES)

COMMUNICATION STEPS—WEEKLY COFFEES, IN-MARKET VISITS WITH LOCAL MANAGEMENT

Bradt, George, and Ed Bancroft. 2010. *The Total Onboarding Program*. San Francisco: Wiley/Pfeiffer.

Bradt, George, and Mary Vonnegut. 2009. *Onboarding: How to Get Your New Employees Up to Speed in Half the Time*. Hoboken, NJ: John Wiley & Sons.

Bradt, George. 2011. *The New Leader's Playbook*. Articles on Forbes.com.

Buckingham, Marcus, and Donald Clifton. 2001. *Now Discover Your Strengths*. New York: Free Press.

Charan, Ram, Stephen Drotter, and James Noel. 2001. *The Leadership Pipeline*. San Francisco: Jossey-Bass.

Covey, Steven. 1989. *The 7 Habits of Highly Effective People*. New York: Simon & Schuster.

Coyne, Kevin P., and Edward J. Coyne Sr. 2007. "Surviving Your New CEO." *Harvard Business Review*, May.

Dattner, Ben. 2011. *The Blame Game*. New York: Free Press.

Duck, Jeannie Daniel. 2001. *The Change Monster*. New York: Three Rivers Press.

Eliot, T. S. 1943. "Little Gidding" in *Four Quartets*. New York: Harcourt Brace Jovanovich.

Gadiesh, Orit, and James L. Gilbert. 1998. "A Fresh Look at Strategy." *Harvard Business Review*, May.

Gladwell, Malcolm. 2005. *Blink*. Boston: Little, Brown.

Guber, Peter. 2008. "The Four Truths of the Storyteller." *Harvard Business Review*, January.

Harrald, John. 2006. "Agility and Discipline: Critical Success Factors for Disaster Response." *The ANNALS of the American Academy of Political and Social Science*: 604, 256.

Hilton, Elizabeth. 2001. "Differences in Visual and Auditory Short-Term Memory." *Indiana University South Bend Journal*, 4.

Linver, Sandy. 1994. *Speak and Get Results*. New York: Simon & Schuster.

Lodish, Leonard. 1984. Professor: University of Pennsylvania, Wharton School, conference in October.

Masters, Brooke. 2009. "Rise of a Headhunter." *Financial Times*, March 30.

McDermott, Meaghan M. 2008. "Brizard takes city school district's reins today." *Rochester Democrat and Chronicle*, January 2.

Neff, Thomas, and James Citrin. 2005. *You're in Charge, Now What?* New York: Crown.

Neilson, Gary, Karla Martin, and Elizabeth Powers. 2008. "The Secrets to Successful Strategy Execution." *Harvard Business Review*, June: 60.

Schein, Edgar. 1985. *Organizational Culture and Leadership*. San Francisco: Jossey-Bass.

Senge, Peter.1990. *The Fifth Discipline*. London, UK: Century Business.

Smith, Bryan. 1994. *The Fifth Discipline Field Book*. Boston: Nicholas Brealey.

Tzu, Lao, and Jonathan Star. 2003. Translation of *Tao Te Ching*. New York: Tarcher.

Watkins, Michael. 2003. *The First 90 Days*. Watertown, MA: Harvard Business School Press.

George B. Bradt has a unique perspective on helping leaders move into complex, high-stakes new roles. After graduating from Harvard and Wharton (MBA), George spent two decades in sales, marketing, and general management around the world at companies including Unilever, Procter & Gamble, Coca-Cola, and then J.D. Power as chief executive of its Power Information Network spin-off. Now he is a principal of CEO Connection and managing director of PrimeGenesis, the executive onboarding and transition acceleration group he founded in 2002. George can be reached at gbradt@primegenesis.com.

Jayme A. Check offers a dynamic and global perspective on leadership gained from executive roles in firms ranging from start-ups to the Fortune 500. Leadership positions in sales, business development, and general management at companies including J.P. Morgan, Guidance Solutions, and Brice Manufacturing have given Jayme a unique perspective on executive acceleration and development. In addition to being a PrimeGenesis founder and author of its onboarding and transition acceleration methodology, Jayme is president of Quantum Leap Associates, a firm focused on providing executives worldwide with authentic and measurable leadership skills. Jayme earned a BS from Syracuse University and an MBA from UCLA's Anderson School. Jayme can be reached at JCheck@1QuantumLeap .com and JCheck@PrimeGenesis.com.

Jorge E. Pedraza transitioned from preparing future leaders as a professor at Williams College to being a leader helping build start-ups and reinventing established businesses at Concrete Media, Le Monde Interactive, and Unison Site Management. Jorge has a BA from Cornell and a PhD from Yale. As a founding partner of PrimeGenesis, he helped develop and evolve the PrimeGenesis onboarding and transition acceleration methodology and has since deployed it to found and build Unison Site Management, the nation's leading independent cell site acquisition and management company. Jorge can be reached at jpedraza@unisonsite.com.